"Matt Lynch is an able guide to these difficult (.... s the caricatures of these texts to make way for a faith.. with close readings of biblical texts to offer fresh....................., recommend his work!"
Carmen Joy Imes, associate professor of Old Testament at Biola University and author of *Bearing God's Name: Why Sinai Still Matters*

"*Flood and Fury* helps Christians to see what violence is doing in their Scriptures—even in the mouth of Jesus! Lynch helps us to navigate the Bible's grammar of violence as people who are thankfully estranged from systemic and brute use of force. As few scholars can, Lynch plainly maps how the New Testament authors engage the violence of the Old Testament as fruitful for the coming kingdom. Of the myriad books on violence in Scripture, Lynch marries his scholarly work with his winsome writing so that the church can properly wrestle with what the biblical texts say about human and divine violence."
Dru Johnson, associate professor of biblical studies at The King's College

"Matt Lynch writes for a popular audience without dumbing down the problem of violence or providing pat answers. He invites readers to contextualize scriptural texts within a large vision of creation's shalom, the hermeneutics of reading biblical narratives alongside historical questions, and the whole canon's revelation of God's good character. Lynch's work travels new and illuminating ground. For those troubled by these texts, Lynch models pastorally honest and attentive reading that contributes to a richer understanding of the biblical narrative, God's good design for his creation, and the ways these texts intersect with present-day realities. A recommended read!"
Lissa M. Wray Beal, professor of Old Testament at Wycliffe College

"Wow, this is *the* most helpful book on the Bible I've read in a long time. Matthew Lynch is easily among the brightest, most insightful, best read—and funniest—biblical scholars working today. In his latest book, he shows he is also among the wisest. Yes, violence in the Bible is a 'wicked problem' that admits of no easy solution (see chapter fifteen), but with Lynch lighting the way, readers will emerge wiser. Buy a copy immediately and then buy a case to share among your friends. They need a copy—*we all* do."
Brent A. Strawn, D. Moody Smith Distinguished Professor of Old Testament and professor of law at Duke University

"The Bible contains violence. This book questions various interpretations of biblical violence and its possible influence on Christian doctrine and practice. Warfare, racism, and gender discrimination have been justified using the Bible, but the Bible has also sparked significant movements for individual and collective freedom, inclusiveness, and peace. At the heart of Dr. Lynch's work is an essential question regarding the biblical conception of God and how we can think about God's love, justice, and peace in the midst of it all. The insightful proposals in this book will be helpful for both teachers and students in search of understanding."
Jules Martinez-Olivieri, theologian in residence at the Surge Network and author of *A Visible Witness: Christology, Liberation, and Participation*

"The concerns this book addresses are not new, but the perspective of its author and this cultural moment are. *Flood and Fury* addresses these age-old problems with sensitivity to the unique questions of a new generation. And most importantly, Lynch does this by inviting his readers to face these issues head-on—acknowledging the struggle—all the while considering some of Scripture's most challenging texts with care, literary sophistication, and confidence in the good God we encounter there."

Michelle Knight, assistant professor of Old Testament and Semitic languages at Trinity Evangelical Divinity School

"This book sees the flood and the conquest stories not simply as problems to be solved but instead as opportunities to deepen our faith, challenge our contemporary cultural expectations, and even seek God's blessing. It presents a biblical theology of violence rooted in a detailed study of the motif of violence in Genesis 1–11 as well as in the book of Joshua. But there is a different way of seeing these texts. The book presents a legitimate approach that enhances our understanding and presents us with new questions. It is a new adventure of learning. I recommend this provocative and well-informed book."

Yohanna Katanacho, author of *The Land of Christ: A Palestinian Cry*

"In this volume, Matthew Lynch takes the reader on a journey of discovery that involves careful and scholarly engagement with the text, helpful illustrations, and his own honest and personal perspectives. Matt takes up his own challenge: to wrestle with and go deeper into the dark and impenetrable places of Scripture. His insightful and wise readings of the texts unearth more of their place and purpose within the grand narrative of salvation while, perhaps also surprisingly, demonstrating how these stories are able to reveal more of the redemptive, relational, and merciful character of God. Readers searching for answers will be both hugely relieved and extremely grateful to find this book."

Lucy Peppiatt, principal at Westminster Theological Centre, UK

"Matthew Lynch's *Flood and Fury* is a shrewd book: modest but not timid, careful but not skittish, demanding but not onerous. From start to finish, Lynch faces, unflinchingly, the hardest, ugliest parts of the Scriptures. He sees how some of the questions these texts raise for us simply cannot be answered, at least not as we expect. But he also shows us why we can and should remain at the table, troubled as we are—because our Host, mysterious as he is, is unwaveringly good and the wisest of teachers."

Chris EW Green, professor of public theology at Southeastern University and author of *All Things Beautiful: An Aesthetic Christology*

FLOOD
AND FURY

OLD TESTAMENT VIOLENCE
AND THE SHALOM OF GOD

MATTHEW J. LYNCH

Foreword by Helen Paynter

IVP Academic
An imprint of InterVarsity Press
Downers Grove, Illinois

InterVarsity Press
P.O. Box 1400 | Downers Grove, IL 60515-1426
ivpress.com | email@ivpress.com

InterVarsity Press® is the publishing division of InterVarsity Christian Fellowship/USA®. For more information,
visit intervarsity.org.

All Scripture quotations, unless otherwise indicated, are taken from The Holy Bible, New International Version®, NIV®.
Copyright © 1973, 1978, 1984, 2011 by Biblica, Inc.™ Used by permission of Zondervan. All rights reserved worldwide.
www.zondervan.com. The "NIV" and "New International Version" are trademarks registered in the United States Patent
and Trademark Office by Biblica, Inc.™

While any stories in this book are true, some names and identifying information may have been changed to protect the
privacy of individuals.

The publisher cannot verify the accuracy or functionality of website URLs used in this book beyond the date
of publication.

Cover design and image composite: David Fassett
Interior design: Daniel van Loon

ISBN 978-1-5140-0429-6 (print) | ISBN 978-1-5140-0430-2 (digital)

Printed in the United States of America ♾

Library of Congress Cataloging-in-Publication Data
Names: Lynch, Matthew, 1979- author.
Title: Flood and fury : Old Testament violence and the Shalom of God / Matthew J. Lynch ; foreword by Helen Paynter.
Description: Downers Grove, IL : InterVarsity, [2023] | Includes bibliographical references and index.
Identifiers: LCCN 2022038615 (print) | LCCN 2022038616 (ebook) | ISBN 9781514004296 (print) |
    ISBN 9781514004302 (digital)
Subjects: LCSH: Violence in the Bible. | Bible. Old Testament–Criticism, interpretation, etc.
Classification: LCC BS1199.V56 L955 2023 (print) | LCC BS1199.V56 (ebook) | DDC 221.6--dc23/eng/20221123
LC record available at https://lccn.loc.gov/2022038615
LC ebook record available at https://lccn.loc.gov/2022038616

31 30 29 28 27 26 25 24 | 13 12 11 10 9 8 7 6 5 4 3 2

For Abi,

and for my WTC and Regent College students

CONTENTS

LIST OF FIGURES
AND TABLES

FOREWORD

Helen Paynter

It was in 2004, just another ordinary school night, and I was making dinner for my husband and our three daughters. When the phone rang, there was nothing to suggest that I was about to be confronted with one of the hardest questions of my life.

"Hi Helen, it's Clare. [*Our church youth worker.*] I wonder if you can help me. [*Subtext: it's a long shot.*] One of the young people in our youth group has been reading the Old Testament properly for the first time. [*That's great! Isn't it?*] She's finding loads of grim, violent stories there, and they're really troubling her. I think she might be in danger of losing her faith. Can you tell me how to help her?"

What do we do with the violence in the Old Testament?

There are two classic responses to a question like that. One is to say, in effect, "God says it, you've got to believe it. Don't question the Word of God." The other is to reply like this: "Tell her not to bother with the Old Testament. It's all horribly violent and out of date. Just focus on Jesus."

Honesty prevented me from giving the first answer. Sometimes we have to take things on trust, but God gave us brains for a reason, and he is never honored by us dishonestly denying that problems exist. My deep commitment to Scripture as the revealed Word of God wouldn't allow me to give the second response. So I went for a third option—my mouth flapped open and nothing came out.

I had nothing useful to say to help this young woman who was asking such important questions with real integrity, and a genuine desire to press deeper into God and his ways. Nothing that wouldn't cause her to doubt the goodness of God or the faithfulness of his Word. I was disturbed and ashamed (and, incidentally, as a result of this conversation I went on to write an MA dissertation on the subject, undertake a PhD in the Old Testament, and founded a study center to tackle hard questions like this one[1]).

Because this is one of the most pressing questions facing the church today, it is important for several reasons. First, because—as with this young woman—people are in danger of losing their faith, or failing to come to faith in the first place. We are much less content than previous generations simply to accept the word of another (even of God) without questioning it. We want to understand. We need to know that the God who commands our obedience really deserves it. We have seen war on our TV screens (or more closely), and it troubles us to encounter it in our Bibles.

Second, it is important because we need to be able to trust that God's Word is true and dependable, and that it testifies faithfully to the character of God, the nature of humanity, the dealings that God has had and will have in the world, and to the great historical claims it makes, most particularly the life, death, and resurrection of Jesus Christ. If God's Word is not reliable, what are we to believe? If we construct a picture of a benign, teddy-bear God that is derived from our imaginations, not from his Word, how reliable is our construction?

Third, the question is important because taking one of the standard approaches to it (*just ditch the Old Testament*) is not only unwise and unhelpful, but it is in danger of being antisemitic. Of course, Christians believe that God did something new in Jesus Christ, but that new thing was not wholly different from what he had done before. There is much continuity between the Testaments, as well as some discontinuity. If we read carefully, we will discover that the character of the God revealed in the New Testament is exactly the same as the God we meet in the Old Testament. The narrative of *Old Testament bad, Jesus good*, is not only based on a misreading of both Testaments, but fuels a nasty strand of antisemitic theology that has caused untold harm over the centuries.

---

[1] The Centre for the Study of Bible and Violence, www.csbvbristol.org.uk

And fourth, the question is important because we need to understand the way that God's purposes bend toward peace. If we fail to read the great narrative of Scripture properly, if we extract verses or stories from their meaning and context and drop them into the twenty-first century, we are in danger of using God's good Word in ways that harm people. No, the indigenous peoples of the Americas weren't the Canaanites to be annihilated by the new Israel of the settlers. No, you can't justify bearing arms by claiming that the bullet is the natural evolution of Old Testament stoning. No, the Bible doesn't endorse the abuse of wives by their husbands. (These are all true examples of things that have been declared by people claiming to take the Bible seriously.)

So this is an important question. And it needs a reply from someone who is thoughtful, pastorally sensitive, honest, and learned. Let me introduce you to Matt Lynch.

Matt has been grappling with these questions for years. He is a hugely respected Old Testament scholar with a love for God and his people, and a commitment to struggling faithfully with God's Word for the sake of God's people. This book has emerged from some of that struggling.

Here are some things that you won't find in this book: casuistry, easy answers, tub-thumping fundamentalism.

Here are some other things that you won't find: a carelessness toward Scripture, a prioritizing of human ideas over divine revelation, bleeding-heart liberalism.

This is what you will find: a lively, engaging, delightfully human and honest exploration of the subject, deeply rooted in prayerful study, but wearing its learning lightly. You'll even find a sprinkle of humor. (Yes, really!)

So, if you struggle with the violence that you find in the pages of the Old Testament (like the young woman whose story we started with), or if you want to be useful to others who are struggling (as Clare and I desired to be), read on. You are in safe hands. Now turn the page.

ACKNOWLEDGMENTS

THIS BOOK IS WRITTEN FOR STUDENTS and for those in the church who seek to engage Scripture in all its diverse challenges and wonders. That this book stems from my own challenges as a student and by the many questions that my students posed about God's association with violence in the Old Testament. I couldn't have written a book for those individuals without the help of many friends, colleagues, and students over the years. I mention just a few here.

First, I'm grateful to Anna Gissing, who helped steer this book through its early stages at IVP, and then to Rachel Hastings, who guided this book to completion with thoughtful feedback and keen editorial oversight. I'm also grateful to the rest of the IVP team for their collaboration, including the feedback provided by their blind peer reviewer, copyeditor, and marketing team.

I'm also grateful to my previous institution, WTC (UK), for giving me a sabbatical during which I began this book. Regent College has also been immensely generous in providing space and time to research and write.

I owe an immense amount to the following individuals for reading all or portions of earlier drafts of this book. Tanya Marrow read an early draft, and provided very helpful input. Thanks also to Abi Lynch, Lucy Peppiatt, Mark Glanville, Brad Jersak, Matt Bates, Dru Johnson, Chris McKinny, Jonathan Greer, Kyle Keimer, and Michael Rhodes for their many helpful comments. Special appreciation is also due to my research assistant Parker Arnold for his careful feedback on the entire book.

I'm grateful to Brad Jersak, Andrew Klager, and students in sessions I taught at the Institute for Religion, Peace and Justice at St. Stephen's University. Thanks also to Helen Paynter for her generous foreword, and for her leadership and scholarship at the Centre for the Study of the Bible and Violence in the UK. This book wouldn't have happened without the rich and engaging environment at WTC, where I taught from 2012–2020. Students and colleagues constantly prompted me to engage Scripture more deeply and prayerfully. Students at Regent College (Vancouver) have taught me so much over the past two years alone. I'm filled with gratitude for them, and am constantly awed by their creativity and insights. Special thanks to students in my Advanced Old Testament Exegesis course and in my Wrestling with Old Testament Wrath and Violence class.

Finally, I'm grateful to my wife, Abi Lynch, for conversations about this book, her critical and constructive feedback on the manuscript, and for filling our family and community with many joyful times as this book took shape.

PART ONE

A REAL PROBLEM

(WITH OPTIONS)

MY FAMILY HAD JUST MOVED into a new place in Cheltenham, England. It was our third move in four years. I was home alone, listening to a podcast, some boxes still packed. The podcast host lamented the fact that many Christians don't know their neighbors, sounding a timely theme for me. I made a mental note to at least learn our neighbors' names.

Not more than two minutes later I walked by our front door and saw that the postman slipped an Amazon notice through our door, letting me know that our package sat with our neighbor. Point taken!

As I went outside and turned left toward no. 18, I ran into a neighbor. I'll call him James. After some light conversation, he asked what I did for work.

"I teach the Old Testament."

"Oh! Could I come speak with you some time? I have some questions," he answered.

"Of course!" I responded.

I thought this was a divinely appointed evangelism opportunity. His conversion and education in the Old Testament were only a matter of time.

But that's not what happened. As we talked, it became evident that James was in the middle of a faith crisis. He attended a very restrictive church that rebuffed any of his searching questions or expressions of doubt. He asked his questions anyway, and they shut him down. And so we talked . . . for many hours over multiple evenings, mostly about the Bible and the fallout with his family. His problems with the Bible ranged widely but boiled down to two main things: (1) God permitted Israel to enslave foreigners (Lev 25:44-46). (2) God condoned extreme violence against innocent men, women, and children in books like Joshua. For James, the first issue was personal. He's from Ghana. Texts like Leviticus 25 were used to condone the oppression of his ancestors. The land-conquest in Joshua only magnified the extreme violence embodied in his more personal connection to a history of enslavement.

I wish I could say that the fog lifted, and James walked away with restored faith as I wheeled out different ways of looking at these problems.

It didn't go that way. James ended up leaving the faith. He said he was too far down the road to turn back. He now makes YouTube videos that confront people with the problems of violence in the Bible. We still have frank conversations, and our friendship endures.

My conversations with James left me wondering why some leave the faith over such issues while others hang on. And for those barely hanging on, what resources do they have? While there are certainly good books on violence in the Old Testament, I felt a need for something that confronts hard issues but that also gives the Old Testament a greater voice and pans out to see the beautiful images of God that also weave their way through Israel's Scripture. You can end up seriously injured if you continually bang your head against the "problem of violence in the Old Testament." But equally so, you can end up brewing a crisis if you continually delay the hard questions.

As I speak with James, here's why I hold out hope. First, everyone is on a journey, and so James's story isn't finished. But also, James told me that if he had been part of a church that talked about the Bible in the ways we had—that wrestled openly about the problem of violence—he probably never would've left. Perhaps through a different kind of conversation, sustained by the work of the Spirit, there's a way for James to inch his chair back up to the table. Sometimes those we've written off can surprise us as well. In a recent visit to his old church, a pastor surprised him by listening patiently to his concerns with Scripture.

So, this book is for (1) those in the church who have persistent concerns about violent texts, (2) people who disciple those with such concerns, (3) and those who have friends on the fringes of the faith who can't get past the problem of violence.

If you think that no one around you is dealing with vexed questions about violence in Scripture, I suggest you start asking around. There's a good chance that someone like James is in your church, workplace, or neighborhood.

This book isn't designed to help you refute the skeptic, take down the New Atheists, or win over the unbeliever. Its aims are more focused, but hopefully, more durable. I hope it leaves you saying things like, *There's far more good in these troublesome texts than I thought!* Or, *I'm not alone.* Or, *The Old Testament critiques our violence!* I hope it helps you relate to a Bible, and ultimately a world, that is rife with violence, but also full of beauty and life. Most importantly, I hope the book helps you discover a God full of tender mercy and compassion at the heart of the hardest texts.

SPINNING OUT OF CONTROL

Once James started down the road with his questions about Scripture, he felt he couldn't turn back. He'd finally given voice to his nagging concerns, and they just kept flowing. In fact, they weren't nagging anymore. They were clawing at him no matter which way he turned. He told me that they occupied his mind all day.

It reminds me of what happened to me when I was driving my car once in Vancouver, British Columbia. Vancouver doesn't get much snow in the city, but one winter we had about five inches. I was driving my '82 Volvo DL down the street. I merely tapped my brakes, and the car went into a flat spin.

I braced myself for impact. Fortunately, no other cars were around. I finally stopped spinning, only to slide backward down the street until my car came to a gentle rest against a curb. Phew! After drawing breath, I took a bow. No one was hurt, and my car wasn't damaged.

But many people don't stop spinning until they hit something solid, like a tree, another car perhaps, or even a pedestrian. They don't stop gently. They crash violently.

How do we stabilize the spin before we crash? In snow and on wet surfaces, you're supposed to act counterintuitively. Turn gently into the spin, and don't *brake* . . . or at least brake lightly (Disclaimer: This is not professional driving advice!). This requires the delicate coordination of steering and letting go. But when it comes to addressing the ethical challenge of violence in the Old Testament, some people pull a hard right. They try to justify every violent text. *God says it. That settles it.* Others pull a hard left. *Violent texts in the Old Testament are just the wishful projections of a violent and barbaric people. We must resist its teachings at all costs or re-interpret them until they look nice and clean!*

But these aren't our only options. The challenge for many is that responding to violence in Scripture is counterintuitive to both impulses. It requires turning into the spin while maintaining gentle responsiveness. Part of turning into the spin is facing the problem itself. Yet pretending that your spinning car is fine is not the same as avoiding panic. We need to look at the problem(s) of violence. But as we move forward, we'll also see that there are ways to avoid a car wreck.

1

FACING THE PROBLEM
(WITHOUT BURNING DOWN
YOUR HOUSE)

KEN ESAU TELLS THE STORY that illustrates the danger of trying to "solve" a problem like violence in the Old Testament.[1] Ken had a neighbor who wanted to remove a grease stain from his garage floor. So he doused the floor with gasoline and scrubbed it clean with a wire brush. Gasoline dissolves grease and oil, so it was the perfect solution for the problem. The combination of gasoline and scrubbing rid him of that ugly grease stain. Having eliminated the problem, he shut the garage door. Problem solved!

So it seemed.

Inside the garage burned the pilot light of his hot water heater. Once the gasoline fumes filled the garage, and kaboom! The garage blew up like a bomb, his house caught fire, and everything burned to the ground.

These rather dramatic events provide a cautionary tale. Only use gasoline in well ventilated areas, well away from any active flame. Yes. But for our purposes, we're reminded to *be wary of solutions that too easily resolve all difficulties*. We may rid ourselves of one problem only to find ourselves stuck with far more destructive consequences than we ever anticipated!

The warning from this story applies to all sorts of issues encountered in the Christian life, and none more than the problem of violence in the Old Testament. For many, divine anger, violent stories, and violent prayers,

---

[1] Ken Esau, "Disturbing Scholarly Behavior: Seibert's Solution to the Problem of the Old Testament God," review of Eric Siebert's *Disturbing Divine Behavior: Troubling Old Testament Images of God, Direction* 40, no. 2 (2011): 168-78. I've reflected on this story in an earlier blog post: https://wtctheology .org.uk/theomisc/how-to-burn-down-your-house/, accessed July 7, 2022.

look like ugly grease stains on the pages of Scripture. But before declaring, "This kind can only come out with much gasoline!" let's consider the hidden costs that might lurk in the back corner. They're not always out in the open.

But we can't ignore the grease stains in the process.

THE PROBLEMS OF VIOLENCE

At first glance, the stains will certainly arrest our attention. They may appear worthy of a gasoline dousing! For instance, God commanded Moses to do the following, which Joshua later enacted: "You must destroy them totally. Make no treaty with them, and *show them no mercy*" (Deut 7:2, italics added;[2] cf. Deut 20:16-17).

The call to "destroy them totally" (Hebrew *herem*) involved annihilating the Canaanites and then dedicating their wealth to God as a sacred offering. It sounds like a bizarre mix of violence and worship. Destroying Canaanites as an offering? Most disturbingly, God commanded them to take great care to deny these nations *mercy*. Several texts in Joshua suggest that the people dutifully obeyed down to this merciless detail (Josh 6:21; 10:40; 11:11-15). As Joshua and the people entered the land, they struck down entire peoples, "devoting them to destruction." Look at Joshua 6:21: "They *devoted* the city to the LORD and *destroyed* with the sword every living thing in it—men and women, young and old, cattle, sheep and donkeys." Killing children and animals puts to rest any argument that this was only about the moral degeneracy of the Canaanites. How could children and animals be held morally responsible? Surprisingly, Joshua doesn't mention Canaanite immorality as a justification for killing the Canaanites, as do other Old Testament passages (e.g., Gen 15:16).[3] They were simply in the land and needed to go. As if to sharpen the point, Joshua tells us the following: "For it was the LORD himself who *hardened their hearts* to wage war against Israel, so that he might *destroy them totally, exterminating them without mercy*, as the LORD had commanded Moses" (Josh 11:20).

Ouch! God ensured this merciless horror show!

---

[2]Throughout this book, all italics of italicized portions of biblical quotations have been added by the author for emphasis.
[3]The possible exception in Joshua is idolatry.

At the very least, we must concede the deep tension between these texts and what we learn of God from other places in the Bible:

The LORD, the LORD,
a God *merciful* and gracious,
slow to anger,
and abounding in steadfast love and faithfulness. (Ex 34:6, NRSV)[4]

Or consider Jesus' healing of the two blind men who cried out: "Have *mercy* on us, Son of David!" (Mt 9:27). "Grant them mercy" seems to be God's heart in other texts.

The tensions build as we look at the full range of problems in the Old Testament. Violence is not a single problem. It's like one of those old Whac-A-Mole arcade games where moles would pop up randomly from their holes and you had to whack them on the head. No sooner did you hit one mole than another appeared. The *problems* of violence in the Bible are the same way. No sooner do you address one problem than another appears.

Here are some of the big problems. As you look at this list, consider what you or your friends consider to be some of the main challenges of violence in the Old Testament.

Divinely enacted violence. Some struggle with the problem of divine violence in the flood, where God drowns 99.44 percent of the world's population (animals included) to wipe it clean from sin, only to discover that humanity hadn't really changed.

Divinely commanded violence. Others look with astonished bewilderment at the problem of violence in books like Joshua, where Yahweh commands the people to wipe out the indigenous population of Canaan.

Divinely sanctioned violence. Books like Exodus and Deuteronomy permit the people to take women in war and hold slaves. Sons who dishonor parents are to be stoned, adulterers burned, and the like. Laws like these rubber-stamp acts of violence against other Israelites.[5]

---

[4]The word translated "merciful" (Heb. noun *rahum*) here is different than the verbal root used in Deut 7:2 and Josh 11:20 (Heb. verb *hanan*). However, they appear as synonyms in Ex 34:6, where the NRSV translates the noun form of *hanan* as "gracious." They also appear as synonyms in Ps 86:15 and 103:8.

[5]See Diana Lipton, "Legal Analogy in Deuteronomy and Fratricide in the Field," in *Studies on the Text and Versions of the Hebrew Bible in Honour of Robert Gordon*, ed. Geoffrey Khan and Diana Lipton,

Gruesome stories. Not all problems of violence directly involve God, though God certainly is part of the bigger picture. In Judges, for instance, well . . . let me give you a rundown of the highlights:

- Judges 1:6-7: Israel mutilates the Canaanite king Adoni-Bezek.

- Judges 1:1–3:6: Numerous battles, three of which involve the complete destruction of a civilian population, and all done with Yahweh's help.

- Judges 3: King Eglon of Moab disemboweled; Shamgar slaughters six hundred Philistines with an ox goad.

- Judges 4–5: Jael kills Sisera by driving a tent peg through his head.

- Judges 9: Abimelech killed his seventy brothers and then one thousand people in the tower of Shechem. He was then mortally wounded when a woman dropped a millstone on his head, before asking his arms bearer to finish him off (so he wasn't killed by a woman).

- Judges 11: Jephthah burns his daughter as a sacrifice to fulfill a vow.

- Judges 13–16: Samson murders thirty men from Ashkelon for their clothes and sets fire to the tails of three hundred foxes to torch their fields. The Philistines retaliate by burning Samson's wife and father-in-law, whose death Samson avenges by killing one thousand men with a donkey's jawbone. Eventually, after his capture, Samson topples the pillars of a Philistine temple, killing three thousand men, women, and children.

- Judges 19–21: A Levite's concubine is raped and dismembered, followed by a brutal war in which the rest of the tribes perform a conquest on Benjamin, to the point where there are no women left. *Violence against women thus features as a central feature of this story.* So, the rest of Israel destroyed Jabesh-Gilead, killing all but four hundred virgins, which they traffic to the tribe of Benjamin as "wives" for the

Supplements to Vetus Testamentum 149 (Leiden: Brill, 2012), 21-38, esp. 32 for a look at how narrative complicates law. For a study on law as narrative, see Assnat Bartor, *Reading Law as Narrative: A Study in the Casuistic Laws of the Pentateuch*, Ancient Israel and Its Literature 5 (Atlanta: Society of Biblical Literature, 2010); Joshua Berman, "Law Code as Plot Template in Biblical Narrative (1 Kings 9.26-11.13; Joshua 2.9-13)," *Journal for the Study of the Old Testament* 40, no. 3 (2016): 337-49.

six hundred surviving men. Then, they steal two hundred women from Shiloh to provide wives for the rest.

These stories raise questions about the apparent silence of God in the face of such rampant violence.

Violent prayers. Imagine a prayer meeting that starts with these words:

May his [an unnamed enemy] children be orphans,
and his wife a widow.
May his children wander about and beg;
may they be driven out of the ruins they inhabit.
May the creditor seize all that he has;
may strangers plunder the fruits of his toil.
May there be no one to do him a kindness,
nor anyone to pity his orphaned children. (Ps 109:9-12, NRSV)

Amen? Should we pray such Psalms? Should they be part of the church's prayerbook or songbook?

Violent prophecies. The prophets knew divine wrath. They felt it in their bones. They prophesied the destruction of Samaria, Jerusalem, the nations, the earth, the skies, and if they had known about galaxies, I don't doubt they'd have gone there too. They were keen to make sure their listeners knew that Yahweh was behind these events. He moved the nations and acted in history. Many wrestle long and hard with this brutal and sometimes sexually violent prophetic language.[6]

End-times cataclysms. This is the world imagined in the postapocalyptic video game *Fallout*.[7] While lacking the nuclear specifics, some parts of the Old Testament include visions of destruction and violence that engulf and destroy the earth (Is 34). God is involved. Humans are involved. And even the stars and moon are involved. The precise problem here is the sheer scope of violence. While God promised not to flood the earth again, it seems from some parts of the Old Testament that God reserved rights to destroy through every other possible means.

---

[6]See, e.g., Renita J. Weems, *Battered Love: Marriage, Sex, and Violence in the Hebrew Prophets* (Philadelphia: Fortress Press, 1995).

[7]A role-playing video game. "Fallout (video game)," Wikipedia, last edited June 10, 2022, https://en.wikipedia.org/wiki/Fallout_(series).

This list is not exhaustive, but it makes the point that the problems of violence in Scripture are many and varied. The moles keep popping up.

REASONS FOR THE TURN TOWARD VIOLENT TEXTS

Increasingly, I find that Christians want to face up to the Bible's violent texts. There's a veritable cottage industry of "Is God a violent monster?" books. This uptick in attention to the Bible's violent texts has several sources.

Within the church, there is an increasing emphasis on authenticity as an ideal, or even a virtue. This applies to the way we relate to one another and our sacred texts. We desire to honestly face the Bible we have, and not the one that we'd like to have or that tradition has told us we have.

American evangelicalism has also been facing its own day of reckoning. It has been turning inward to interrogate its own history of complicity in violence and cultures of violence. From violence against women exposed in the wake of the #MeToo movement, to the downfall of major evangelical leaders because of abuse, to the problems of racial injustice and violence foregrounded in the Black Lives Matter movement, evangelicals have only just begun some much-needed soul searching. Part of that inward work includes coming to grips with ways Scripture has been used to legitimate violence against the perceived "other." For these and other reasons, there's a need to continue the work of wrestling with violence in Scripture. Not only does it help us address the problem of violence *out there*. It also provides a way of talking about the problem of violence *in here*.

In addition, many evangelicals have recognized the need to turn outward. Increasing awareness of social and economic injustice has helped us grapple with the appropriate place for wrath—divine and otherwise! Those who have privilege and status often take issue with wrath as "unseemly" or "inappropriate," especially when expressed by those on the margins. Divine wrath challenges us to ask *with whom or about what is God wrathful?* Answers to this question are not easy for those of us who don't regularly worry about injustice.[8]

---

[8]Kevin Kinghorn, *But What About God's Wrath?: The Compelling Love Story of Divine Anger* (Downers Grove, IL: IVP, 2019); David T. Lamb, *The Emotions of God: Making Sense of a God Who Hates, Weeps, and Loves* (Downers Grove, IL: IVP, forthcoming).

Also, the turn toward the problem of biblical violence arises from an awareness that biblical writers were not unbiased. Isn't it convenient, many would suggest, that Israel's claim to the land is commanded by God and morally justified by the horrific practices of Canaan's previous inhabitants? To some ears, it sounds like a setup. Readers also recognize the yawning gap between how ancient cultures thought about God and violence, and how *we* do. Whether or not this is the case, it is a perception. For example, some claim that Joshua offers a "primitive" view of Israel's deity. Ancient people were violent—so the story goes—and so *of course* they thought God was also violent.[9]

Within an increasingly post-Christian culture many feel that Scripture is "on trial," so to speak, needing to answer for its complicity in crimes against humanity. From the days of Constantine to the colonialist exploits of the sixteenth through the twentieth centuries, Christians have solicited help from Scripture to provide religious backing for violence.[10] In American, Canadian, Palestinian, and many other contexts, Christians wrestle with the church's complicity in religiously based land claims and histories of exterminating indigenous people.[11] Faced with such challenges, Christians often feel morally bound to take these accusations of criminal activity seriously. Perhaps the Bible is dangerous and needs to be stripped of its privileges. Though only a few might put things in such stark terms, some may *feel* that we'd be better off letting certain Old Testament texts lie dormant. The Old Testament offers a great deal of raw material out of which to construct a

---

[9]Discussed in Eryl W. Davies, *The Immoral Bible: Approaches to Biblical Ethics* (London: Bloomsbury T&T Clark, 2010), 22-43.

[10]On which, see Thomas B. Dozeman, *Joshua 1–12*, Anchor Yale Bible 6B (New Haven: Yale University Press, 2015), 85-94; Elsa Tamez, "The Bible and Five Hundred Years of Conquest," in *Voices from the Margin: Interpreting the Bible in the Third World. 25th Anniversary Edition*, ed. Rasiah S. Sugirtharajah (Maryknoll, NY: Orbis Books, 2016), 13-26; Daniel H. Weiss, "'And God Said': Do Biblical Commands to Conquer Land Make People More Violent, or Less?" in *Scripture and Violence*, eds. Julia Snyder and Daniel H. Weiss (New York, NY: Routledge, 2020), 32-46; Rachel Havrelock, *The Joshua Generation: Israeli Occupation and the Bible* (Princeton: Princeton University Press, 2020).

[11]John S. Milloy, "The Founding Vision of Residential School Education, 1879 to 1920," in *A National Crime: The Canadian Government and the Residential School System, 1879 to 1986*, Manitoba Studies in Native History 11 (Winnipeg: University of Manitoba Press, 2017), 23-47; Munther Isaac, *The Other Side of the Wall: A Palestinian Narrative of Lament and Hope* (Downers Grove, IL: IVP 2020); Henry Louis Gates Jr., *Stony the Road: Reconstruction, White Supremacy, and the Rise of Jim Crow* (New York: Penguin, 2019), esp. 55-123.

hateful ideology, after all, whether it be allegedly "cautious" xenophobia or decisive violence: "You must *purge* the evil from your midst" (nine times in Deuteronomy).[12]

This leads to yet another reason for the recent anxiety over Scripture's violence: Violent texts are easily misunderstood in a culture that favors sound bites and Tweets. Violent texts are easily misunderstood if taken out of context and created into a meme. Even Jesus' words are susceptible to such misunderstandings. Take his words in Matthew 10:34 as an example: "Do not suppose that I have come to bring peace to the earth. I did not come to bring peace, but a sword." These texts provide easy targets for those who want to see Christianity crumble and they provide confusion for others.

NOT BURNING DOWN YOUR HOUSE

With all these difficulties facing us as we read the Old Testament, we might be tempted to take radical measures to purge Scripture of such violent stains and residue. We might want to unhitch our faith from the Old Testament, as one prominent church leader suggested—and many imply.[13]

Before rushing toward that stain-removing solution, however, we might take a cautionary cue from early church father Tertullian (ca. 150–220 CE). He wrote a multivolume work to refute a man named Marcion (ca. 85–150 CE), who doused the problem of Old Testament violence with gasoline (or its ancient equivalent) and set it ablaze.

Marcion wanted to excise divine wrath from the Christian faith, and with it, the Old Testament. He found it unbecoming of God's goodness. He suggested that the God of the Old Testament was a different God than the God and Father of Jesus. So he sought to rid the church of the Old Testament and, consequently, most of the New! It turns out that the two are deeply connected.

In his sarcastic critique of Marcion, Tertullian writes: "A better god has been discovered, who never takes offense, is never angry, never inflicts

---

[12]Deut 13:5; 17:7, 12; 19:19; 21:21; 22:21, 22, 24; 24:7.
[13]Andy Stanley, *Irresistible: Reclaiming the New that Jesus Unleashed for the World* (Grand Rapids, MI: Zondervan, 2018).

punishment, who has prepared no fire in hell, no gnashing of teeth in the outer darkness! He is purely and simply good."[14] Sounds good, right?

Hardly. Here's Tertullian's warning. *There are always hidden costs to pictures of God that eliminate challenging tensions.* Tertullian would direct our attention to the pilot light burning in the garage corner. Specifically, Tertullian points out that Marcion eliminates God's ability to act as judge: "You allow indeed that God is a judge, but at the same time destroy those operations and dispositions by which He discharges His judicial functions."[15] For Tertullian (and many biblical texts), wrath is the emotion that animates God's active concern for justice. Criticizing his wrath was like criticizing the instruments of a doctor. Wrath, in Tertullian's formulation—and arguably in the Bible itself—is tied intimately to God's exercise of justice.

Tertullian is highlighting the danger of separating God's wrath and justice. Separating the two would be like taking the scalpel from the surgeon's hand and saying, "You're here to do healing work, and not cut people open!" But the Bible sees wrath in different terms. It's the emotion that moves God to bring justice and is ultimately animated by his compassion. In Exodus 22:21-24, for instance, God warns Israel that if anyone caused the orphan or widow to cry out, "my anger will blaze" (my translation). God's anger would blaze against Israelite oppressors like it blazed against Egypt. The point of these verses is not to be precise about the exact penalty for oppressing the weak but to express the pathos of God in the face of injustice.

For Israel, God's wrath was bound up in the idea that he was the protective father of the vulnerable—whether the oppressors be foreigners or his people Israel. Wrath—like jealousy—was a sign of concern for the weak against any who would put them at risk or threaten God's legitimate claim as parent. In this sense, God's wrath toward the nations (e.g., for their mistreatment of Israel) was a deep expression of God's love for Israel and their land.[16]

---

[14]Tertullian, "Against Marcion," 1.27 in *Latin Christianity: Its Founder, Tertullian*, ed. Philip Schaff, trans. Peter Holmes, Ante-Nicene Fathers (1885; repr. Grand Rapids, MI: Christian Classics Ethereal Library, 2000), 292.

[15]Tertullian, "Against Marcion," 2.16.

[16]Mark S. Smith, *How Human Is God? Seven Questions About God and Humanity in the Bible* (Liturgical Press, 2014), 46.

For many of us, love with wrath sounds as comforting as a warm blanket of fiberglass insulation! But the Old Testament grounds love in the idea of Israel as God's covenant people (Deut 6:4-5). Love was the relational glue between covenant partners. And if we think of covenant in terms of "family substitute,"[17] love was the trusting loyalty required for healthy family cohesion. God's wrath was the protective rage he aimed at threats to that family.

But we can't swing the pendulum away from mercy toward wrath, as if wrath is always an unmitigated good. Many women, for example, experience the language of protective divine wrath against the backdrop of male wrath and violence in the church or in toxic relationships. They have been encouraged to stay in abusive relationships or churches and to shun those who challenge the party line or expose abuse.[18]

Abraham and Moses certainly recognized the problem of divine wrath—and even pleaded with God to exercise mercy! In another part of his critique of Marcion, Tertullian urges us to weigh God's "severity" against his gentleness and observe the imbalance.[19] God's character is wildly imbalanced. The coexistence of wrath and mercy is not that of equals. If we take the language of mercy versus wrath in Exodus 34:6-7 in strictly mathematical terms (love to thousands of generations versus three to four generations of judgment),[20] God's mercy outweighs by at least five hundred to one! We'll discuss this in chapter fourteen.

For important reasons, these verses—which are central to an Old Testament portrait of God—hold God's mercy and judgment together, even if they are imbalanced. Perhaps we lose something important when we avoid God's judgment and wrath; and perhaps we lose out by tossing aside violent texts. Maybe there is an understanding of God's character that only comes by exploring the revelatory value of the most troublesome texts and by teasing out the rich picture of God that the Old Testament offers.

---

[17] Smith, *How Human Is God*, 48.
[18] Thanks to Rachel Hastings for this observation.
[19] Tertullian, "Against Marcion," 2.17.
[20] "Three to four generations" is a shorthand way of saying "one household," since a typical Israelite house held three to four generations, but note the modification of this in Deut 5:9-10, which declares judgment for three to four generations "of those who hate me." Deuteronomy makes clear that God holds each generation accountable. Each can turn from the sins of the past.

The subjects of wrath and violence are uncomfortable and shouldn't be taken lightly. But I suggest that *how* we handle them, and not just the topics themselves, poses the greatest danger and opportunity. We will not all land in the same place on these matters, but let's at least stop and count the cost of doing business with easy resolutions. Let's keep the roof over our heads.

But how do we address the problems of violence in the Old Testament without burning down our house? What options are available to us? The next chapter will suggest some strategies that will help us avoid a fatal combustion.

2

FINDING OUR WAY

WHEN I TURNED TEN, my parents' friend showed up uninvited to my birthday party. Wrapped in her jacket was an eight-week-old puppy. It was a gift for me. The black and brown furball was so cute and cuddly I could barely contain my warm affection.

There's more to the story of Brownie, as she came to be named. First, our friend didn't tell my parents she was coming *or* that she was giving me a puppy. I don't know why my parents let the puppy stay, but stay she did. Second, it was a Doberman Shepherd. The furball would one day become large and powerful.

I guess Brownie's puppy eyes stole my parents' heart, or they didn't want to disappoint me. In any case, Brownie became part of our family. *How bad could she be?*

Well . . . we had no idea what lay ahead! Once she got a twelve-inch stick accidentally stuck in her esophagus and just about died. She bit nearly every dog she met (sending one neighbor's dog to counseling—seriously!). The police would often bring her home in the squad car after her neighborhood wanderings. She once jumped through a closed window; she always chewed rocks—ruining all of her teeth; she frequently climbed out of her pen; she tore the chain from her doghouse and ran away; she was hit by a car and survived; she barked incessantly, ate neighbors' trash, chased and was *chased by* a very large buck, fell through ice in a river, pulled my grandfather over when he walked her; she needed hip surgery, and tore apart a wall during a thunderstorm. I accidentally hit her in the head with a baseball bat and she needed stitches. And somehow, she lived fourteen years. Suffice it to say that our first impressions at my tenth birthday were wildly off and certainly naive.

Many Christians look back on life with God in a similar way. First meeting Jesus included all the joy, thrill, and infatuation of a new puppy owner. But years later they feel like someone stuck with a God who is defined exclusively by his violent power and unpredictability. It's easy to feel foolish, naive, or duped, especially as we watch Christians carelessly wield violent biblical texts. If we sample some of the "toxic texts" in the Bible, they seem to make Brownie look tame by comparison. What do we do?

Throughout the centuries, Christians and Jews have wrestled with the challenges of Scripture's violence in various ways. If we're going to avoid a fatal combustion, we need to know what options lie before us. In this section, we'll explore some of the big ones. I encourage you to think through which options you gravitate toward. Perhaps you're squarely in one camp, or perhaps your view is represented by a few of the options that follow. Wherever you are *now*, it's worth asking why. What factors contribute to your current views on biblical violence? Perhaps you don't know. If that's the case, read through the following list of options and try to gauge which views resonate or make you cringe.

THE OPTIONS ON THE TABLE

Evangelical theologian Roger Olson once wrote a blog post called "Every Known Theistic Approach to Old Testament 'Texts of Terror.'"[1] I've often used his list of approaches to help my students recognize the range of options Christians have considered through the ages as they work through violent texts. While it doesn't cover every option, Olson's list offers a helpful starting point. I've reproduced it here in modified form with his permission. As you read it, ask, *How do I approach the problem of violence in the Old Testament? What are the benefits and pitfalls of each approach below? Which approaches do I favor? Which had I never considered?*

1. **Reject it.** Marcion from Sinope (AD 85–160), about whom we read in the previous chapter, was so affronted by the wrath and judgement of God in the Old Testament that he proposed rejecting it entirely.

---

[1] Roger E. Olson, "Every Known Theistic Approach to Old Testament 'Texts of Terror,'" Roger E. Olson (blog), July 15, 2013, www.patheos.com/blogs/rogereolson/2013/07/every-known-theistic-approach-to-old-testament-texts-of-terror/.

Marcion believed that the God of the Old Testament was real but was a lesser deity than the high God and father of Jesus. Jesus came to save us from the evil god of the Old Testament. The main slogan of Marcionites could be, *The Old Testament is infected. Get rid of it all!*

Problems: This view is wholly unorthodox and ultimately undermines the New Testament's claims about Jesus, which are rooted in the Old Testament. Not surprisingly, Marcion's Old Testament amputation cost him a good deal of the New Testament as well. His "Bible" was little more than a few letters of Paul and an abbreviated Gospel of Luke. Marcionism was roundly condemned by the early Church, by theologians like Irenaeus, Tertullian, and Athanasius. Marcionism can also lead toward anti-Semitism. The church shares Scripture with Israel, but Marcion wanted to sever that unifying bond. Also, you lose the unified tradition with which Jesus and the apostles identified.

2. **Spiritualize it.** The slogan for this approach would be that *things are not what they seem.* Spiritualizing approaches date back to the early church as well. Theological giants like Origen, John Cassian, and much later, Anselm of Laon, believed that the stories of violence in books like Joshua are really about our need to do battle with the vices that wage war in our souls. Take this example from Origen:

> Within us are the Canaanites, within us are the Perizzites; here are the Jebusites. In what way must we exert ourselves, how vigilant must we be or for how long must we persevere, so that when all these breeds of vices have been forced to flee, 'our land may rest from war' at last?[2]

While not all of these writers were responding directly to the *violence* in the text, it seems that Origen was.

Problems: This approach depends on substituting one thing for another based on what is "worthy of God." This can lead to a loss of the Old Testament's plain sense, which is a critical part of the Old

---

[2]Origin, *Hom Josh*, i.7, Quoted in Christian Hofreiter, *Making Sense of Old Testament Genocide: Christian Interpretations of Herem Passages* (Oxford: Oxford University Press, 2018), 67.

Testament's ability to challenge (often prophetically) the church.[3] It risks creating Scripture into our own image. Also, Christians like Origen never denied the historicity of the conquest, or that God was involved. They just disputed the idea that it should be literally *applied* today. Many would argue that we don't need a spiritualizing approach to make that same point. We can get there by other means.[4] As Michael Rhodes once said to me, "It's the OT's 'earthiness' that makes it so challenging to our hyper-'spiritualized'" forms of Christianity.[5]

3. **Divine command theory.** The foremost proponent of "divine command theory"—summarized here in the slogan *God Commanded it, that settles it!*—was St. Augustine. Before he was a Christian, Augustine was offended by the violence, wrath, and "crass literalism" of the Old Testament. After converting, he taught that God's actions don't have to play by our standards of justice. Instead, God's acts become moral when God commands them. So, if God commanded the destruction of the Canaanites, it must be moral.[6]

Augustine also believed that God could inflict punishment with love, and sometimes as an act of mercy. He noted that Paul handed a man over to Satan for the destruction of the flesh (1 Cor 5:5).[7] He also argued that God worked differently at different times. While he waged war through violence in the Old Testament, the martyrs show a better victory. In the end, Augustine (and others after him, like Thomas Aquinas and John Calvin) ask us to trust God's judgements, which often appear mysterious to us but are always just.

Problems: Divine Command Theory can sever the connection between God's justice and human perceptions of justice. That makes it difficult to follow the prophetic call to act justly *like God*. If the justice of God bears little or no connection to human justice—albeit shaped

---

[3]For a tour de force treatment of the literal (not literalistic!) sense of Scripture, see Iain W. Provan, *The Reformation and the Right Reading of Scripture* (Waco, TX: Baylor University Press, 2017).

[4]For an early Christian critique of Origen's approach to interpretation, see Theodore of Mopsuestia's (AD 350–428) 5-volume work *Concerning Allegory and History Against Origen*.

[5]Michael Rhodes, personal correspondence with the author, August 2, 2021.

[6]Hofreiter, *Making Sense*, 110.

[7]Discussed in Hofreiter, *Making Sense*, 124-29.

by the guidance of Scripture—then God's ways become impossible to imitate. While God's ways are often mysterious, examples like Abraham show us that his justice and righteousness are examples to be followed. We're to learn God's ways. Moreover, Scripture also invites us to raise questions before God, even about his justice (Gen 18:19, 23-25).[8]

4. **Times change.** This view, also known as "Progressive Revelation," has a hard and soft version. The main slogan here is, *God works differently over time.*

The hard version. Augustine also anticipates this view. God did command the people of God to slaughter men, women, children, and animals in the past, but later changed his approach. God changes his ways of dealing with sin throughout salvation history. He shifts from acting like a warrior God to a God who loves peace, but will, in the future, enact violent judgement once again. Essentially, God works in different ways at different times.

Problems: This view raises serious challenges to the doctrine of divine immutability (the idea that God does not change) even regarding God's moral and ethical will.

The soft version. "Inspiration" does not mean word-for-word dictation or that every story in the Bible is to be taken at "face value." God accommodated his revelation to our ability to understand him, and people came to understand God's revelation more clearly over time. As God incarnate, Jesus is the clearest revelation of God's character and will. God's revelation of his own character and will became clearer throughout Scripture with the later (clearer) parts relativizing the earlier (less clear) parts.

Problems: It is very difficult to chart a clear trajectory from less clear to clear when tracing the theme of violence through Scripture. Some of the strongest condemnations of violence come from the

---

[8]On which see J. Richard Middleton, "God's Loyal Opposition: Psalmic and Prophetic Protest as a Paradigm for Faithfulness in the Hebrew Bible," *The Canadian-American Theological Review* 5, no. 1 (2016): 51-65 and Middleton, *Abraham's Silence: The Binding of Isaac, the Suffering of Job, and How to Talk Back to God* (Grand Rapids, MI: Baker Academic, 2021), 17-63.

Old Testament (Is 1:10-17; Prov 21:7) and some of the greatest violence appears in the New Testament (e.g., hell, future judgement).
This view is also subject to accusations of implicit Marcionism
(see option 1).

5. **Old ways of speaking.** We tend to misread ancient literature because
   we think they wrote like us. But we know from other ancient war accounts that when they said, "We left nothing alive that breathes," they
   really meant, "We won!" Of course plenty of people survived.[9] This
   approach focuses on ancient ways of writing about wars of conquest
   and asks us to avoid literalistic interpretations. If you heard a bas-
   ketball player claim, "We *destroyed* the opposition!" you know it
   simply means that they won. Put another way, this approach calls for
   literary and cultural awareness. That means paying attention to different kinds of writing, or genres (warfare rhetoric, poetic prayers,
   prophetic literature, etc.), and how they worked in the ancient world.
   Ancient stories exaggerate the extent of their victories.[10]

   Problems: While this approach helps us grapple with ancient warfare
   rhetoric, ancient warfare was still horrific. Does it really help us if the
   Israelites invaded the land of Canaan and spoke about it like the
   Assyrians? Isn't violent speech also wrong?

6. **Cultural projection.** Portions of the Old Testament (and perhaps
   also of the New) reflect the violent fantasies and practices of ancient
   (violent) people, but do not reflect God's actual desires. At times
   God's people may have misunderstood his commands and recorded
   their own beliefs about God as revelation from God. The people of
   God may have slaughtered men, women, children, and animals, but
   God did not command it. This approach's slogan would be, *Ancient
   people project their violent tendencies onto God.*

   Problems: This approach is the highwater mark of cultural imperialism. It assumes that ancient people were simply more violent than

---

[9]Lawson K. Younger, *Ancient Conquest Accounts: A Study in Ancient Near Eastern and Biblical History Writing,* Journal for the Study of the Old Testament Supplement Series 98 (Sheffield: JSOT Press, 1990).
[10]I address this approach in chap. 10.

us, and implicitly asks us to turn a blind eye to our own violence. It can also undermine the revelatory value of the Old Testament, as there is just no limit to the number of other claims about which the ancients were "obviously" wrong (e.g., that God speaks to humans, that God relates to his people via covenants).

7. **Mysterious ways.** *Embrace the mystery of it all* is the slogan here. No attempt at harmonization should be exercised; we ought simply to accept at face value the texts of terror *and* Jesus' teachings about God's love and will (e.g., for peace). We shouldn't try to diminish or reconcile either of them. The interpreter defers to the mystery of God, recognizing that "we see only a reflection as in a mirror . . . [and] know in part" (1 Cor 13:12, NIV modified).

Problems: This view can lead to belief that the ways of God are fundamentally opaque. It can also lead to the idea that behind Jesus lies a "hidden God" (Luther) who willed (and possibly still wills) extreme violence such as genocidal conquest. It can also create profound tensions between the Old and New Testaments, especially if the sense in which we're using the term "mystery" isn't clarified. The problems for Divine Command Theory (approach number 3) also apply here.

8. **Cross-centered.** *The cross trumps earlier (violent) revelations of God in the Old Testament.* This approach takes the cross as the final and definitive revelation of God's character, response to violence, and treatment of enemies. All other biblical texts must be reinterpreted in its light.

Problems: I've written at length about this elsewhere.[11] To summarize, this approach can flatten the very biblical story that gives the cross its meaning. It risks relativizing the rest of the biblical witness about God. Some proponents of this approach assume that

---

[11]See my four-part review of Gregory Boyd's *The Crucifixion of the Warrior God*, 2 vols. (Minneapolis: Fortress Press, 2017) on WTC's "Theological Miscellany" blog. Matt Lynch, review of *The Crucifixion of the Warrior God*, by Gregory A. Boyd, Theological Miscellany (blog), WTC Theology, https://wtctheology.org.uk/theomisc/crucifixion-warrior-god-gregory-boyd-review-part-4-joshua/. This link includes links to parts 1–3 as well.

the cross is the exclusive revelation of God, and so any other portrait of God (e.g., in judgement) must be reread until it looks exactly
like the cross.

WAYS FORWARD

The options I've outlined above (following Olson) offer ways of ap-
proaching violent parts of the Old Testament. We might mix and match
approaches. I do. I tend to favor a mix of numbers 4 (Times change), 5 (Old
ways of speaking), and 7 (Mysterious ways), with a touch of 8 (Cross-
centered), as you'll see throughout this book. But an "approach" only gets
you so far. It gets you to the base of the mountain and hopefully on the right
route, but you still need keen orienteering skills on the mountain. Those
skills are often developed from experience, which in turn, shapes intuitions
about which routes to take. Then those intuitions lead to greater discov-
eries. I find that Christians really need to walk through hard passages and
develop field-specific conclusions. We need to learn our ethical route-
finding skills in the wilds of actual biblical texts.

But to name what I consider the *best* approach to interpreting violent
texts it would be this: *Read it slow. Read the biblical text slowly and carefully.
Prepare to be surprised.* Ellen Davis recommends "slowing down over violent texts to consider what kind of critical and specifically theological response is appropriate."[12] My hope is that we see violent texts not simply as
problems to be solved or avoided, but instead, as opportunities to deepen
our faith in the company of other Christians now and through the ages.
Without the slow walk through specific texts, we end up trying to "solve"
problems that aren't there. That's why we need to first hear the texts that
trouble us. It's a form of loving our neighbor. Even if they infuriate, they're
still our neighbors.

In his poem "Warning to the Reader," Robert Bly describes the inside of
a wooden farm granary. We see rays of light shining through the cracks
between the granary's boardwood walls. Many birds end up trapped in
these granaries, Bly tells us. Assuming they'll find an exit by following the

---

[12]Ellen F. Davis, *Opening Israel's Scriptures* (Oxford: Oxford University Press, 2019), 95.

light, the birds fly repeatedly at the small gaps between the boards. But they can't fit. The way out, Bly tells us, "is where the rats enter and leave; but the rat's hole is low to the floor."[13] Failing to recognize this, many birds end up starved to death in the granary.

Bly's poem is an important warning for Bible readers. We're to consider the costs of flying at little bits of "sunlight" in the text while refusing the darkness. We might be tempted to fly straight toward "great is your faithfulness" (Lam 3:23) without entering the circles of pain and suffering that surround that passage (Lam 1–5). We might fly toward stories of resurrection and hope without tracing the stories of cross and suffering. Flying directly at the happy texts can leave us diminished, a pile of lifeless feathers in the corner. We think stories of light offer a quick solution for our disorientation, but they only disappoint us and those with whom we might unwittingly share our "toxic positivity."[14]

As we consider the Bible's violent texts, it's important to remember Bly's warning. The way out is so often "where the rats enter and leave; but the rat's hole is low to the floor."[15] As we consider approaches to violent texts, let's duck our heads low and peer into the darkness, and at least let our eyes adjust.

Let's consider the process of peering into the darkness before we consider how the early stories from Genesis provide us with a basic orientation to violence in the Old Testament.

Be shocked. Sometimes the best starting point is to let yourself be shocked, horrified, or frustrated with the Bible. Too often we suppress such responses to Scripture because they seem . . . unbiblical or unchristian. But if Abraham, Moses, Gideon, David felt free to respond in their frustration

---

[13]See Robert Bly, "Warning to the Reader" (poem), in *Stealing Sugar from the Castle: Selected and New Poems, 1950-2013* (New York: W. W. Norton, 2013), 72, https://books.google.com/books?id=qfG wAAAAQBAJ&lpg=PP1&pg=PA72#v.

[14]A term from Dra. Itzel Reyes' essay "Believe Me When I Say It Hurts," World Outspoken, August 23, 2021, www.worldoutspoken.com/articles-blog/believe-me-when-i-say-it-hurts#_ftn3. "Toxic positivity" is "the overgeneralization of a happy, optimistic state that results in the denial, minimization and invalidation of the authentic human emotional experience." Samara Quintero and Jamie Long, "Toxic Positivity: The Dark Side of Positive Vibes," The Blog, The Psychology Group, 2019, https://thepsychologygroup.com/toxic-positivity/.

[15]Bly, "Warning to the Reader." 72. I thank Brent Strawn for introducing me to this poem at Emory University, ca. 2008.

to God (without censure), surely we can respond honestly to Scripture without fearing loss of faith.

Hear it out. We also need to make sure we've understood the problem correctly. That means looking carefully at the biblical text, including the hard-to-look-at passages. I can't overstate how important this is, and how often readers skim quickly over the text but speak with confidence about what exactly the text is stating. Every time I've done this the Bible surprises me. It defies stereotypes. Prepare to be surprised when you give the Bible a fair hearing!

Let the whole Old Testament focus our attention. If you're like me, you get up in the morning and reach for your glasses. I can't think without them (strangely, even if it's pitch dark). The glasses bring the amorphous shapes of the room into focus and help me interpret and understand what is in front of me. Is that black object on the ground a giant spider or my sock? Is that my daughter standing in the doorway or is it my backpack? (It's that bad.) The two lenses I wear change the image my eyes perceive—and they do so in a way that helps me see what is really happening. The reality of what I'm seeing doesn't change—so it's not like the glasses rearrange the room magically. Scripture works this way, but we need to learn which texts have that focusing role.

When facing hard passages of Scripture, I've often heard it said that we need to interpret the unclear texts in the light of the clear—so we let Scripture interpret Scripture. But instead of that, I prefer to speak of Scripture *focusing* Scripture.

Here are some of the lenses Scripture offers.

- First, Genesis 1 focuses our reading of Genesis 1–11, and really of the whole Bible. The Old Testament offers this challenge: "Read the whole thrust of Scripture *this* way, by looking through the lens of Genesis 1, which sits first in the canon because it anticipates the whole." When we do this, we recognize that violence has no pride of place; that humanity reflects a God who delegates and distributes power; that humanity's role in creation is decidedly life-promoting; and that creation's rhythm is oriented toward restoration and not destruction. In sum, it offers a compelling vision of shalom—creational and right-relating wholeness—as the ideal.[16]

- Second, sometimes you need eye protection in the blazing light of violent texts. The unfiltered and UV-producing command to exterminate the Canaanites in Deuteronomy 7 must be read in conjunction with the inclusion of Rahab the Canaanite prostitute (who on the surface embodies all the "snares" of Canaan) in Joshua 2 and 6. You need the Joshua 2 and 6 "UV filters" to understand Deuteronomy 7.

  Similarly, the *exclusion* of Moabites to the tenth generation in Deuteronomy 23 must be read with the story of Ruth the Moabitess' *inclusion* in Israel. Ruth tells us that King David is a third generation Moabite! The alternative is to take off the storied-world sunglasses and stare exclusively at violent texts. But I don't think biblical writers recommend that. That's not how Scripture works. The Bible frequently introduces an idea and then circles back around to it from another angle, adding something important and asking us to think with a whole network of Scriptures that interpret Deuteronomy 23. Noting how the Bible circles back to key themes helps us see in the midday blaze.[17]

- Third, some claims about God's character—what he's really like—are more central than others. I'll explain more in chapter fourteen, but to anticipate my argument, Exodus 34:6-7 is key here:

  > And [the LORD] passed in front of Moses, proclaiming, "The LORD, the LORD, the compassionate and gracious God, slow to anger, abounding in love and faithfulness, maintaining love to thousands, and forgiving wickedness, rebellion and sin. Yet he does not leave the guilty unpunished; he punishes the children and their children for the sin of the parents to the third and fourth generation."

  Notice the tension here—God forgives, shows mercy, *and* judges. This specific list of character qualities echoes throughout the pages of

---

[16]I discuss *shalom* further in part two.

[17]On Deut 23, see Gary Edward Schnittjer, *Old Testament Use of Old Testament: A Book-by-Book Guide* (Grand Rapids, MI: Zondervan, 2021), 138-39 and related text discussions that he notes. Schnittjer discusses the Deut 23 network on p. 876.

Scripture. It's a *really* big deal! We're meant to hold this tension, but not in a balanced way. The scale is tipped toward mercy. His mercy dominates his character.

In sum, let's let the Bible do its work of placing violent texts in relation to core claims about creation (that it's meant to be nonviolent), the stories of Scripture (which give us multiple angles on difficult topics), and God (who is fundamentally merciful).

Read toward Jesus . . . as a trinitarian. Genesis 1–11 orients us to the biblical story. But that story testifies throughout to the person of Jesus. *How* the Old Testament leads toward Jesus might not be straightforward. We must avoid taking the easy "this-predicts-Jesus" road. Sometimes the pathways of Scripture take unexpected turns, where that Jesus-destination seems unclear. But at the same time, it's important to understand the many ways that the Old Testament signposts the God who became incarnate in Jesus of Nazareth.

Not only that, but Jesus himself was deeply shaped by Scripture. He grew up in a Scripture-immersed environment. For him, Scripture equaled our Old Testament (Israel's Scriptures). He believed that *not one* of its words would fail to be accomplished (Mt 5:18). He would have heard Scripture from a very young age, and would likely have memorized large portions of it.[18] So we have to ask: If (a) Jesus was deeply nourished by the OT, including books like Deuteronomy, where the command to destroy the Canaanites first takes shape; and if (b) he understood himself to be the fulfillment of the Old Testament narrative; then is there *anything* in those troubling texts that would foster a life and teachings like *his*?

I'm inclined to think so.

A Christian approach to violence in the Old Testament relates the stories of Israel and the story of Jesus. Jesus is the logical climax of Israel's stories. It might be "logical" only in retrospect, after meeting Christ. Nonetheless, the story of Jesus of Nazareth grows from the roots

---

[18]See Craig S. Keener, *Christobiography: Memory, History, and the Reliability of the Gospels* (Grand Rapids, MI: Eerdmans, 2019). On the Gospel writers' use of Old Testament texts, see Richard B. Hays, *Echoes of Scripture in the Gospels* (Waco, TX: Baylor University Press, 2018).

of the Old Testament story of God and Israel. Jesus is the destination toward which the various branches of the whole Old Testament are already reaching.[19] Jesus *is* the incarnate God of the Old Testament, after all. He is the revelation of the God already revealed in the Old Testament. This approach requires attention to the Jesus-like moves in the Old Testament.

But lest we think that the Old Testament only *eventually* leads to Jesus in the New Testament, we already see him throughout the Old Testament. Anywhere God acts, the Son acts. Many Christians think that the Old Testament portrays God the Father, and except for a few glimpses, the Son and Spirit aren't too active until the New Testament. But the New Testament insists otherwise. For instance, Jude 5 tells us that *Jesus* delivered Israel from Egypt, even though in the Old Testament we read that it was God's Spirit (Is 63:11).[20] It is the trinitarian God who acts throughout the Old Testament. The Old Testament shows us the Father, Son, and Spirit throughout.[21] So to say that the Old Testament leads to Jesus is also to say that the Old Testament already reveals Jesus at every point where Yahweh is present. The New Testament insists that there is no division in the revelation of God in the Old Testament and the revelation of God in Christ. *How* that's so requires careful reflection.[22]

Check our social location. It's easy to align ourselves with the Israelites as we read the Bible. They're the people of God. We're the people of God. Simple as that. But things aren't that simple.

When you bring yourself to the task of reading the Bible, you bring your cultural background, gender, economic background, ethnicity, race,

---

[19]This is different from some "Christocentric" ways of reading the Old Testament that essentially undermine the Old Testament's distinctive voice because of a felt incompatibility between Jesus and "the God of the Old Testament." Jesus is the God-of-the-Old-Testament-made-manifest. Instead, I prefer the term "Christo-telic," which Peter Enns uses in his article "Apostolic Hermeneutics and an Evangelical Doctrine of Scripture: Moving Beyond a Modernist Impasse," *Westminster Theological Journal* 65 (2003): 263-87.

[20]The textual variants in Jude 5 seem inclined to "resolve" the discomfort of attributing the exodus to Jesus. Yet according to Lk 9:31, Jesus even discusses the (new) "departure" (Gk. *exodon* = exodus) he was about to accomplish in Jerusalem.

[21]For a helpful discussion, see Brent A. Strawn, *Lies My Preacher Told Me: An Honest Look at the Old Testament* (Louisville, KY: Westminster John Knox, 2021), 93-103.

[22]Brent A. Strawn, "And These Three are One: A Trinitarian Critique of Christological Approaches to the Old Testament," *Perspectives in Religious Studies* 31, no. 2 (2004): 191-210.

religious background, and so much more. It's hard *not* to do this, since we've been told in Scripture itself that it's *for us* (1 Cor 10:11; 1 Pet 1:10-12).

It's true! The Bible is *for us*. However, in our efforts to read Scripture for us we can easily miss how it assumes very different audiences living in very different conditions. The Old Testament was written *to* ancient Israelites by ancient Israelites. They lived as subsistence farmers in a minor kingdom between major superpowers, and often as displaced people.

This reminds us that some contemporary social locations might illuminate Scripture's violent texts in ways that we'd otherwise miss.

Living in the wake of twenty-plus years of war in the Democratic Republic of Congo led Jacob Onyumbe Wenyi to revisit the violent rhetoric of Nahum in new ways. Nahum casts its readers into a "whirlwind of violence" that resonates with victims of war trauma. It provides an opportunity to revisit memories of Assyrian violence against Judah and discern Yahweh's abiding presence.[23] While it's easy from the comfort of our living rooms to resist the violent imagery in Nahum as the product of misguided bloodlust, Wenyi's study highlights the ways that even the most violent texts can provide "comfort" (Heb. *nahum*) for victims of violence.

In his book on the blues, Jon Michael Spencer points out that for many enslaved and oppressed African Americans, the story of Jericho's destruction held great hope:

> Up to the wall of Jericho
> He marched with spear in hand.
> "God blow them ram horns," Joshua cried
> 'Cause the battle am in my hand.[24]

To openly celebrate their slaveholders defeat would've been "perilous," Spencer points out. "Sure 'slave talk' wears a mask . . . but it 'wears it freely,' allowing liberation to be more than merely whispered."[25] Such lyrical celebration of violence sounds very different on the lips of the oppressed than on the lips of the privileged.

---

[23]Jacob Onyumbe Wenyi, *Piles of Slain, Heaps of Corpses: Reading Prophetic Poetry and Violence in African Context* (Eugene, OR: Cascade Books, 2021).

[24]Jon Michael Spencer, *Protest & Praise: Sacred Music of Black Religion* (Minneapolis: Fortress Press, 1991), 5.

[25]Spencer, *Protest & Praise*, 6.

Joshua fit de battle ob
Jericho, Jericho, Jericho,
Joshua fit de battle ob Jericho,
An' de walls come tumblin' down.[26]

While speaking directly about the collapse of the Canaanite city, it provided an allusive way for slaves to sing about the collapse of *slavery* and the political system that sustained it. Similarly, James Cone talks about participants in the Montgomery Bus Boycott (1965–1966) walking the stress "with pride until the walls of segregation, like the Jericho walls, 'come tumblin' down.'"[27]

What happens when we read Joshua, or other troubling texts of the Old Testament, from the perspective of those lacking privilege? The old Canaanite kings of Joshua's day were representatives of Egyptian colonial powers, after all. What would it be like to watch—perhaps with slight bemusement—as a band of former Hebrew slaves-turned-immigrants circles our fortress with trumpets in hand? They might trouble us, and not because of *their* violence, but because they expose *our* violence and the weakness of the seemingly impregnable walls we build.

Let the Bible bite back. Violent passages can unsettle us. But that might not be so bad if we are to be a people who remain open to reformation and critique. Theologian John Webster puts it well: "Scripture is as much a destabilizing feature of the church as it is a factor in its cohesion and continuity. . . . Through Scripture the church is constantly exposed to interruption."[28] Scripture should and does make us uncomfortable if we allow it. Walter Brueggemann's reflections also help us here. He notes that among the Protestant Reformation's primary insights was that

> Scripture [ought to] have its own voice, . . . [and be] heard in its own liberated radicality. This "voice of the Bible" speaks its truth and makes its

---

[26]Lyrics drawn from Richard A. Long and Eugenia W. Collier, eds., *Afro-American Writing: An Anthology of Prose and Poetry*, 2nd ed. (University Park: The Pennsylvania State University Press, 2010), 111.

[27]James Cone, *The Cross and the Lynching Tree* (Maryknoll, NY: Orbis, 2011), 69. Ellen Davis discusses the immediacy of reading Judges with women in Malakal, South Sudan, who lived the reality of the violence of Judges on a daily basis. Ellen F. Davis, *Opening Israel's Scriptures* (New York: Oxford University Press, 2019), 149.

[28]John Webster, *Holy Scripture: A Dogmatic Sketch* (Cambridge: Cambridge University Press, 2003), 46-47.

claim in its own categories, categories that are recurrently odd and unaccommodating. . . . Scripture study is an attempt to receive, understand, and explicate this revelation [of God]—hopefully to receive, understand, and explicate this revelation in all its oddity, without reductionism, domestication, or encumbrance.[29]

To summarize Webster and Brueggemann, perhaps the Old Testament has its own critique to level against us! Perhaps our view of the problem of violence is too diminished and stands in need of expansion. Let's not domesticate it.

A crucial part of Scripture's ability to critique us involves submitting ourselves, as readers, to the Bible's own scrutiny. One of the claims I make in this book is that Scripture often has a more expansive understanding of the *problem* of violence than we do. If we assume that the Bible is only a problem to be solved, we might miss its challenge to those of us who live in powerful and affluent societies.[30]

Orient to mystery. Any attempt to wrestle with violence in the Old Testament will prove unendingly frustrating and inadequate without a robust doctrine of divine mystery. Embracing mystery doesn't mean that we abandon hard thinking, throw our hands in the air, or suppress our horror over some of the actions attributed to God in the Bible. Rather, embracing mystery celebrates our capacity to explore the ways of God, while acknowledging our inability to fully comprehend the ways of God.[31] Our limited knowledge is not an unfortunate byproduct of being human. Our limits remind us that we sit in the hands of a God whose capacities and wisdom categorically exceed our own. Embracing the challenge of violence as a *mystery* rather than a *riddle-to-be-solved* opens new possibilities. Mystery

---

[29]Walter Brueggemann, *Old Testament Theology: Testimony, Dispute, Advocacy* (Minneapolis: Fortress Press, 1997), 3.

[30]See Rob Nixon, *Slow Violence and the Environmentalism of the Poor* (Cambridge, MA: Harvard University Press, 2011); Jeffry Odell Korgan and Vincent A Gallagher, *The True Cost of Low Prices: The Violence of Globalization* (Maryknoll, NY: Orbis Books, 2013); Gary A. Haugen and Victor Boutros, *The Locust Effect: Why the End of Poverty Requires the End of Violence* (New York: Oxford University Press, 2015); Michelle Alexander, *The New Jim Crow: Mass Incarceration in the Age of Colorblindness* (New York: The New Press, 2020); Danielle Sered, *Until We Reckon: Violence, Mass Incarceration, and a Road to Repair* (New York: The New Press, 2019).

[31]For a nuanced theological reflection on mystery, see Steven D. Boyer and Christopher A. Hall, *The Mystery of God: Theology for Knowing the Unknowable* (Grand Rapids, MI: Baker Academic, 2012); Steven D. Boyer, "The Logic of Mystery," *Religious Studies* 43 (2007): 89-102.

acknowledges that God's ways are indeed greater than our ways, but also that in his mysterious goodness God revealed his ways to us so that we could know and become like him. We live in the tension of a *revealed* mystery—something disclosed to us that can be known in part—and the *concealed* mystery of a God who also transcends our rational comprehension.

Wrestle for blessing. What I've listed above are just preliminary ways that we can begin to think through actual texts, but of course we will need to wrestle with some rough texts. The metaphor of wrestling comes from the story in Genesis 32, where Jacob is about to meet up with his brother Esau, from whom he'd been estranged for about twenty years. He goes to a river alone and at night. Without explanation, he encounters a man who wrestled him until daybreak. In that all-night wrestling match, Jacob overpowers the man, who then puts Jacob's hip out of joint and asks to be let go. But Jacob refused to release his wrestling partner until he blessed him. Jacob refused to let this man go, it seems, because he began to recognize that this was no ordinary man, but God himself.

In an act of blessing, the man changes Jacob's name to *Israel*, which means, "God-striver" or "God wrestler." Being Israel involves God-wrestling. God-wrestling involves not shying away from hard challenges, pushing through the hard stuff. But it also means that encounters with God, though they may leave us lacking the power we once thought we had, may also leave us blessed.

That's been my experience of wrestling with violence in the Bible. It strips me of my naive conceptions of the Bible and moves me deeper into the mystery of my faith. It brings unexpected blessings. As Phyllis Trible says:

> We struggle mightily, only to be wounded. But yet we hold on, seeking a blessing: the healing of wounds and the restoration of health. If the blessing comes—and we dare not claim assurance—it does not come on our terms. Indeed, as we leave the land of terror, we limp.[32]

For Christians who journey with Jesus, we find ourselves in familiar-yet-mysterious territory. The theological lessons at play in the Jacob/Israel

[32]Phyllis Trible, *Texts of Terror: Literary-Feminist Readings of Biblical Narratives*, Overtures to Biblical Theology 13 (Philadelphia: Fortress Press, 1984), 4-5.

story sit at the center of discipleship. James and John learned this lesson . . . eventually. They longed to understand their (presumably exalted) status in the coming kingdom. They hoped to share in Jesus' glory by sitting on his right and left. But they hadn't counted the cost of their request or the need to share in Jesus' suffering (Mk 10:35-45). Brueggemann writes,

> They want thrones, an equivalent to asking the name. Jesus counters by asking them about cups, baptisms, and crosses. Like Jacob, they are invited to be persons of faith who prevail, but to do so with a limp.[33]

Personal Wrestling

I'm often asked why I've taken an interest in Old Testament violence. Many stories come to mind, but two stand out and impact my decision to focus on the Genesis flood and the "fury" of Joshua's conquest.

In 1999 I spent a semester in Israel at Jerusalem University College, where I met Abi, whom I eventually married. During that semester, Abi invited me to visit Hebron. Hebron is a city in the West Bank that lies *mostly* under control of the Palestinian Authority. Part of the city is occupied by Israel and is home to some Israeli settlers and Palestinians. We went with the Christian Peacemaking Team, which monitored life in the shared zone, where life was often fraught with conflict. It was the first time I'd heard firsthand from Palestinians about life under the occupation. A thirty-foot-high chain-link fence with countless rocks lodged between its wires bore witness to the mounting frustrations of living a caged existence. Of the violent outbursts against Israeli soldiers that often-occupied Western media, one man said, "When you corner a cat, it scratches." Another man kept his teeth in his pocket to remember the soldier whose gun had knocked them out. "How can we teach our kids not to hate? How?!" another man asked. Parents worried for their children's safety because of rampant violence. I don't mean to minimize the complexities of the Palestinian-Israeli conflict here, but it was an important event in my life. For the first time I was forced to think concretely about injustice, and the way that certain claims to land—some of which find their rooting in the Bible—carry real-world implications.

---

[33]Walter Brueggemann, *Genesis*, Interpretation (Louisville, KY: Westminster John Knox, 1982), 271.

Another formative event started on my first day of graduate studies at Regent College. It was September 11, 2001. I first heard about the Twin Tower attack in my Hebrew class with Phil Long. The reports were too unreal to absorb. After class we filed into the chapel where we exchanged what news we knew and wondered what was next. Chapel turned into a raw lament service where students and faculty gave voice to their distress and grief over what took place that morning. The events that morning shaped my entire graduate school experience. I studied theology and biblical studies against the backdrop of the emerging War on Terror, the Axis of Evil, and the Afghanistan and Iraq invasions. I wrote papers on just war and pacifism, violence in Joshua, and regularly discussed with classmates the ways that books from Genesis to the Gospels articulate a compelling vision of peace.

Two biblical stories began to occupy my attention on this subject: Genesis and Joshua. Genesis posed the problem of divine violence on an incomprehensible scale in the flood, yet it did so after offering a striking vision of creational peace. Joshua posed the problem of divinely authorized violence in startling terms. *You* are to show them no mercy! As I began teaching at Westminster Theological Centre in the UK, students and faculty colleagues frequently wondered about these stories, prompting me to dig further into the Old Testament's portrait of God and God's relationship to violence. What follows is my attempt to wrestle these stories for a blessing. As I do so, I hope that I—we—can remain open to *their* challenge as well. They have their questions for us, about our violence, and about our willful silence in the face of bloodshed that continues to cry out for justice.

PART TWO

SHALOM AND
ITS SHATTERING

CHILDREN'S BIBLE STORIES have a way of forming us. The characters we meet become our own friends or foes. The places they live become
our own playgrounds and adventure lands. We re-enact, imagining ourselves in their shoes. I can remember my son reading the story of David and
Goliath and immediately swinging round a pillow and flinging it across our
dining room. The story begs for the reader to identify with David. Kids
usually take the bait. And for good reason! The Bible seems designed to pull
readers into its storied world.

But those children's Bible stories also have a way of shaping how we read
them. This is so for two stories in particular—the Great Flood and the
Conquest of Canaan. Most children's Bibles refer instead to "Noah's Ark"—
emphasizing the life-saving vessel—and "Joshua and the Walls of Jericho"—
emphasizing the walls' miraculous collapse. Framed in these ways, children's stories mute Scripture's violence to highlight God's gracious
deliverance. I haven't yet seen kids' story Bibles with titles like "Noah and
the Drowned Animals" or "Joshua and the Slain Children"![1]

As adults, many of us return to those stories with new questions. What
about those who weren't in the ark? What about the 99.9 percent who
didn't make it? And what about the little children in Jericho who were put
to the sword alongside their parents, grandparents, and family's animals?
Where's the justice in all of this?

We can end up caught between versions of the story that feel sanitized
on the one hand and horrific on the other. The children's versions can feel
fake and the adult versions, too awful to contemplate.

We'll explore these two stories in parts two and three. I want us to press our
ears up to these stories, hold them up to the light, turn them over, and let them
speak.[2] I guarantee that they hold good news. But the good news doesn't
always leap off the page. "Global Flood Ruins All But The Righteous Few!"
hardly cheers the downcast. To hear good news, we'll have to read them with
patience and empathy, and ruminate on the tensions and paradoxes they hold.

---

[1] This may be a more recent trend, however, since the massively popular 1965 *The Children's Bible* (New
York: The Golden Press, 1965), 178, 182, talks about the "Invasion of Canaan" and even details how
Israel "put all its inhabitants to the sword."

[2] I intentionally invoke Billy Collins's poem "Introduction to Poetry," Poetry Foundation (website),
1996, www.poetryfoundation.org/poems/46712/introduction-to-poetry.

To orient ourselves to this task, we must start where the Bible starts. This will help set the stage for understanding the Great Flood and conquest stories. That sequence is intentional, since Creation helps us read the flood and conquest accounts with the right lenses.

VIOLENCE AS AN ANTI-CREATION PROBLEM IN THE BEGINNING

The Old Testament confronts us with the problem of violence from its earliest pages. I'm not talking about the flood yet, or even Cain's murder of Abel. The first reference to violence appears earlier in the story. After Adam and Eve eat from the forbidden tree, God spells out the consequences of their decision to trust the serpent's voice, "I will put enmity between you and the woman, and between your offspring and hers; he will *strike* your head, and you will *strike* his heel" (Gen 3:15, NIV modified).[3]

Notice that word "enmity." Sounds pretty Bible-ish, right? The rare Hebrew term translated "enmity" (Heb. *'evah*) refers to the malice accompanying violent deeds. It appears next in the Bible's homicide laws:

> Or if out of *enmity* (*'evah*) one person hits another with their fist so that the other dies, that person is to be put to death; that person is a murderer. The avenger of blood shall put the murderer to death when they meet. But if without *enmity* (*'evah*) someone suddenly pushes another or throws something at them unintentionally . . . (Num 35:21-22)

The presence of "enmity" is what moves a crime from unintentional to intentional. It's like intent-to-kill-with-malice. Each of the five uses of the term "enmity" in the Old Testament are violent in nature.[4]

Genesis 3 describes the serpent's and woman's offspring "striking" each other (Gen 3:15). To point out the obvious, that's violent language! Genesis 3:15 is not (only) about a spiritual conflict between the woman's offspring and evil enemy forces. It depicts real-world flesh-and-blood violence. Violent enmity would characterize the struggle between Eve's offspring and the serpent's offspring, who represent forces opposed to God.

---

[3] NIV has been modified to reflect the fact that "strike" is the same exact verb in Hebrew.
[4] The two other occurrences of *'evah* are in Ezek 25:15; 35:5.

Jesus knows this. He refers to those who descend from "your father, the devil . . . [who] was a murderer *from the beginning,* not holding to the truth, for there is no truth in him" (Jn 8:44). He also refers to some of the leaders as a "brood of vipers" who would beat, crucify, and kill God's prophets (Mt 23:33; cf. 12:34). Jesus recognizes that the devil was bent on violence from the earliest days. He also picks up on the link between violence and deceit. Cunning violence is precisely the way the story of Genesis unfolds. In Genesis 4 we read that sin lies crouching at Cain's doorway and overtakes him, leading to murder (Gen 4:7). Just like the sneaky serpent who strikes at the heel, violence would weasel its way into Cain's heart. Then he'd lure his brother into the field for the kill.

For Genesis, humanity's very first rebellion planted the seeds of violence. I can't emphasize enough that Genesis puts violence at the heart of all that opposes creation after the first act of rebellion. Violence threatened to tear creation apart. After killing Abel, the ground refused to produce crops for Cain (Gen 4:12; cf. 2 Sam 21:14; Job 31:38-40; Hos 4:1-3). This is an important part of understanding what eventually happens in the Great Flood. Specifically, violence opposes God's good creation. It's ecocidal. We'll see why this is important in the next few chapters.

But these chapters aren't all about violence. In fact, the first word Scripture breathes is of peace and goodness. Genesis begins with a vision of shalom, or right-relating wholeness, flourishing, and peace. By describing shalom and the shattering of it, the Old Testament gives us an education in how to think about the problem of violence.

3

SHALOM IN CREATION'S DNA

IT'S EASY TO WALTZ through the first creation story (Gen 1) and miss
the elephant in the room. Ancient stories often started explaining the
world's beginnings through sensational tales of violent struggle and destruction. Stories of violence among gods spilled over into bloody stories
of creation and then the ongoing violence between humans.

But flip open the Bible to page one and there's no violent conflict. If you
were an ancient reader, you might do a double take and then fall off your
chair . . . or rock. *Where's the story of divine conflict, the slaying of enemies, and
the destruction of divine foes?*[1]

Genesis 1 denies violence a place at the cosmic table. It doesn't even get
an invite. Violence isn't woven into the fabric of creation like it is in other
creation accounts. To see how and why this is so remarkable, and what it
means for our thinking about violence and the Great Flood, let's look at the
earliest portion of Genesis 1.

A GLARING OMISSION

Where you start a story tells you a lot about where it's going. It's easy to
think that the Bible *had* to start with the story of earth's creation. It didn't.
Ancient stories from Israel's neighbors often began with stories of the *gods'*
creation (*theogony*). That wasn't an option for Israel, whose God always was.
But it could've begun differently. It could've told us about happenings in

---

[1]Other parts of the Old Testament *do* envision such beginnings, but likely refer to the more conflic-
tual exodus from Egypt, which Scripture portrays as a new-creation event. For instance, Ps 74 describes God breaking the heads of water monsters and crushing Leviathan's head while establishing
day and night and forming the earth. But not Gen 1. Gen 1 offers a different picture to help orient
readers. See Terence Fretheim, "Creation and the Foundation Narratives of Israel," chap. 4 in *God
and the World in the Old Testament: A Relational Theology of Creation* (Nashville: Abingdon, 2005).

the angelic realm. But it didn't. Genesis chose instead to tell us about the world's condition before God gave it shape and form. It tells us that the world was "formless and empty," with the breath (or, Spirit) of God fluttering over the watery depths (Gen 1:2). The story wants us to long for the formed and filled world we inhabit.

Hebrew has a fun way of saying "formless and empty"—*tohu wabohu.* Say it with me now! This fun phrase has a serious point, depending on how you interpret it. Some scholars think it describes chaos that God had to violently subdue. Israel's prophets use *tohu,* or the whole phrase, *tohu wabohu,* to describe the desolation of the earth due to divine judgment (Is 34:11; Jer 4:23-27). Noting such parallels, some suggest that there was a hostile force that needed to be brought into line.[2] Yet those texts use the terms to talk about the *inversion* of creation. If creation becomes *tohu wabohu* after its completion, it is indeed a tragedy! But an initial state of formlessness is not an inherently bad thing.

In addition to prophetic parallels, some scholars point to the faint echoes of a Babylonian creation story called the *Enuma Elish* in Genesis 1:2. In the *Enuma Elish* creation emerged out of a violent struggle with the watery forces of chaos. The deity Marduk made the heavens and earth from the split carcass of the chaotic ocean god-monster named Tiamat. Then he formed humans from the blood of a slain god named Kingu. In two fell swoops this story says that violence is part of creation's DNA. Violence is part of the necessary order of things.[3]

Yet Genesis 1 lacks any such violent struggle between God and the forces of chaos or evil. The Spirit (or breath) of God is simply *present* over the waters, and without any more hostility than a mother eagle over her young.[4]

---

[2]Robert S. Kawashima refers to the precreation waters as a "menacing condition" in "The Jubilee Year and the Return of Cosmic Purity," *Catholic Biblical Quarterly* 65, no. 3 (2003): 373. Some also imagine a war in heaven that preceded creation. See, e.g., Gregory A. Boyd, *God at War: The Bible and Spiritual Conflict* (Downers Grove, IL: InterVarsity Press, 1997). However, there is no evidence that Gen 1 imagines such a war as its backdrop.

[3]John Walton points out that *theomachy,* or violent conflict between the gods, is not an ingredient to all ancient Near Eastern creation accounts. After a survey of the relevant literature, Walton argues that only the Babylonian *Enuma Elish* and the Egyptian Instruction of Merikare link *theomachy* and *cosmogony.* John Walton, "Creation in Genesis 1:1–2:3 and the Ancient Near East: Order out of Disorder After *Chaoskampf,*" *Calvin Theological Journal* 43 (2008): 50-51. However, *Enuma Elish* is an enormously influential and important creation myth, so it's significance cannot be overstated.

[4]The verb **rahaf,* which describes the Spirit's action over the water, occurs only elsewhere in the Old Testament to describe the mother eagle over her young (Deut 32:11), and in only one other place to describe the 'trembling' of the prophet's bones (Jer 23:9).

David Tsumura develops this point in a several-hundred pages' study of Genesis 1:2.[5] It's an important verse, so I'll try to summarize his insights here. Tsumura shows that Genesis 1:2 sets the stage for the creation drama that follows. In Genesis 1, God transforms the *unproductive and uninhabited* waters of Genesis 1:2 to a *productive and inhabited* world. The phrase *tohu wabohu* simply refers to earth's "not yet" condition, rather than to any primeval chaos or violence. The watery sea is unformed, not yet ready to sustain life. But it isn't threatening God. Think of it like playdough waiting to be shaped, rather than an enemy to be subdued.

The writer of Genesis could have said that waters were *surging*—a common way of expressing liquid hostility in Scripture (Ps 46:3; 93:3-4; Jer 5:22). But instead, we're told that the waters were simply in their "not yet formed" state. These waters anticipated and even yearned for form and inhabitants by virtue of the Spirit's presence "sweeping down" on them. They weren't yet the "seas" as we know them, but they were about to be. The following translation of Genesis 1:2, adapted from Tsumura, reflects these ideas:

> Now the earth was unproductive and uninhabited;
> darkness upon the face of the deep;
> and the breath (or Spirit) of God swept down over the face of the water.[6]

The world was *not yet*.

Genesis 2 makes a similar conceptual point. It describes the land's *not yet* state:

> When no plant of the field was *yet* in the earth and no herb of the field had *yet* sprung up—for the LORD God had not caused it to rain

---

[5]David Toshio Tsumura, *Creation and Destruction: A Reappraisal of the* Chaoskampf *Theory in the Old Testament* (Winona Lake, IN: Eisenbrauns, 2005); cf. David T. Tsumura, *The Earth and the Waters in Genesis 1 and 2: A Linguistic Investigation,* Journal for the Study of the Old Testament Supplements 83 (Sheffield: Sheffield Academic Press, 1989).

[6]Tsumura, *Earth and the Waters,* 42. Translation of the Hebrew verb *merahephet* is difficult, as it occurs just once elsewhere in the Hebrew Bible (Deut 32:11). Based on this text and uses of the cognate verb r-ḥ-p in Ugaritic, the verb is associated with the flight movements of birds when they are preparing for an action. For instance, in the Aqhat myth, we read the following of birds sent from Anat to strike Aqhat: "The birds will circle [r-ḥ-p] [above him],/ [The flock of h]awks will hover(?)" (CAT 1.18 IV 21, cf. 31-32). Simon B. Parker, trans., "Aqhat," in *Ugaritic Narrative Poetry,* ed. Simon B. Parker (SBLWAW 9; Atlanta, GA: Scholars Press, 1997), 49-80 [66].

upon the earth, and there was no one to till the ground; but a stream would rise from the earth, and water the whole face of the ground (Gen 2:5-6, NRSV).

Genesis 1 and 2 contain no hint of rebellion or opposition to God. Notably, the "breath" (*ruah*) of God (Gen 1:2; 2:7, my translation) begins to transform creation from potential to actual. God uses his power to pour life into a world awaiting its first breath.

Here's why this all matters. If there's no opposition to God in these early creation accounts, and if these introductory stories are trying to teach us to see the world as it ought to be, then *violence has no essential place in God's creation*. It doesn't belong. It's not a necessary evil to help maintain cosmic balance. It's not a tough love principle that undergirds everything. No, these creation stories lack violence. It's a glaring omission for its time!

FURTHER OMISSIONS

Once we note this omission, others stand out.

We notice that the water poses not one (fluid) ounce of hostility throughout Genesis 1. This is a big deal for ancient people who lived primarily in the central highlands of Israel and Judah. I once heard an Israeli man say that the ancient Israelites never did like water: when they crossed it, they always went on dry land. His tongue-in-cheek comment helped me understand the remarkable qualities of Genesis 1. There, the water was benign—even *good*. Proof of its goodness comes in the royal invitation that creation—even the waters—join in the creative process: "Let the water under the sky be gathered to one place, and let dry ground appear" (Gen 1:9). *It was so.* "Let the water teem with living creatures" (Gen 1:20). *It was so.* The waters are obedient, not hostile. They're invited to the party, and they join with malice toward none.

As if to make the point with a megaphone, Genesis then talks about the creation of "great sea monsters" (Gen 1:21, NRSV). Like the sea itself, sea monsters usually represented hostile enemies in the Old Testament. Sea monsters are not friendly pets throughout Scripture. One psalm portrays

Yahweh's martial victory over the "monster in the waters" (Ps 74:13). Isaiah says that Yahweh would eventually draw his sword and "Leviathan the gliding serpent, / Leviathan the coiling serpent; / he will slay the monster of the sea" (Is 27:1).[7]

But in Genesis 1, sea dragons are delightfully nonhostile. They're among the good creatures that God made for the sea. God so welcomed them into creation that he "blessed them and said, 'Be fruitful and increase in number and fill the water in the seas'" (Gen 1:22). *And it was so.* These beautiful beasts aren't simply neutralized or domesticated by God. They're blessed, called good, and set among the other wonderful creatures of God's good earth, as if to say, "Let there be more sea monsters!"

Can I get an Amen?

NONVIOLENT RULE

Okay, so the waters aren't violent. God has no hostile opponent. He didn't need to use violence to create the world. But what about humans? You might object to this nonviolent interpretation of Genesis 1 by noting God's command for humans to "rule" and "subdue" the earth in Genesis 1:28. Those acts sound domineering, if not violent. Were humans called to exercise violence if necessary? Was there an enemy lurking in the shadows requiring humans to patrol with a nightstick? Some think so.

When I was in college, John Eldredge published a book called *Wild at Heart.*[8] His book eventually became a New York Times bestseller. Eldredge argued that men and women are essentially different in their passions and desires, and that those differences are hardwired. Men *are* warriors. Women *are* princesses. Men were summoned to embrace their warrior self and to foster a church culture that allows for warrior men.

Eldredge's book appealed to men who felt trapped by the monotony of office life and longed for adventure. But the adventure Eldredge offered reinforced cultural assumptions about innate masculine violence and female passivity that just needed to be channeled in the right direction.

---

[7] The same Hebrew word appears in Gen 1:21, Ps 74:13, and Is 27:1.

[8] John Eldredge, *Wild at Heart: Discovering the Secret of a Man's Soul* (Nashville: Thomas Nelson, 2001). John Eldredge and Stasi Eldredge cowrote *Captivating: Unveiling the Mystery of a Woman's Soul* (Nashville: Thomas Nelson, 2005), which does include a chapter called "Warrior Princess."

How do we know that men *are* warriors? Scripture says so, Eldredge claims. He would direct our eyes to Genesis 1 and Exodus 15:

> Every boy knows he is made for battle, and he longs to be the mighty hero. Give him a cape, a sword, a light saber and he comes alive in a world of Jedi knights, superheroes, snowball fights, and "what can we blow up next?" *But of course*—man is made in the image [Genesis 1] of a Warrior God: "The Lord is a warrior, the Lord is his name" (Exodus 15:3). God himself is a warrior. And we are made to be like him. Thus every man needs a battle to fight.[9]

Notice that his inferences about creation are imported from Exodus 15. Eldredge wants us to know that boys and men are specifically designed to fight and conquer. They're *made for fighting*. Violence is part of the male DNA.

Many Christian boys hear this message from a young age. They're told that they're wild. They're fighters. They're hardwired that way. Girls, by contrast, are hardwired to await rescue.[10] (An aside: And as I write this, my daughter is begging me to have a snowball fight![11] . . . Okay, back from the fight [I lost].)

Eldredge loses sight of the context in Exodus 15. The point of Exodus 15 is that God is a warrior and Israel is to stand and await rescue. Men included. God's warrior status nullified Israel's. Israelite men *didn't* need their swords. That's the whole point of the story. God isn't telling Israelite men to stand their ground and fight the pursuing Egyptians to protect their Israelite women. Moses instructs *all the people* to stand and watch, "The LORD will fight for you; you need only to be still" (Ex 14:14).

Eldredge also bypasses the context of Genesis 1, which gives us a fuller picture of what it means to rule and subdue as image bearers. Instead, he places hefty stock in the idea that men are created and designed for war.

---

[9]Wildatheart.org, "Your Core Passions," Tribe: Real Men (blog), accessed June 17, 2022, https://wildatheart.org/story/real-men/your-core-passions.

[10]Wildatheart,org, "Your Core Desires," Tribe: Captivating Women (blog), accessed June 17, 2022, https://wildatheart.org/story/captivating-women/your-core-desires. In the brief description of women's "core desires," the *Wild at Heart* website uses the phrase "to be" thirteen times for women, compared with three times for men, highlighting female passivity.

[11]Feb 14, 2021, Vancouver, BC.

But if we want to understand human design, shouldn't we start with a passage that speaks more directly to that design?

> Then God said, "Let us make humankind in our image, in our likeness, so that they may rule over the fish in the sea and the birds in the sky, over the livestock and all the wild animals, and over all the creatures that move along the ground."
>
> So God created humankind in his own image,
> in the image of God he created them;
> male and female he created them.
>
> God blessed them and said to them, "Be fruitful and increase in number; fill the earth and subdue it. Rule over the fish in the sea and the birds in the sky and over every living creature that moves on the ground." (Gen 1:26-28, NIV modified)

According to Genesis 1, all humans are made in God's image. As God's "image," humans occupy a unique place in creation. The Hebrew term for image (*tselem*) usually refers to forbidden idols in the Old Testament (e.g., Num 33:52; 2 Kings 11:18). But here it has a positive sense. Humans are God's "icons," pointing the way to the Creator God. Men and women are designed as co-images that reflect God's rule.

But what kind of rule is this? If you skim the surface of Genesis 1, you might absorb a domineering picture of human power. Humans are rulers who can impose their will on the earth by ruling, subduing, and multiplying. The *Earth Bible Project*, a book collaboration by scholars who read the Bible ecologically, would say so. They claim that "rule" is an unacceptable way of portraying humanity's role in the earth. Instead, we should talk about "mutual custodianship." Instead of ruling *over*, "custodians can function as partners, rather than rulers, to sustain a balanced and diverse Earth community."[12] Rule promotes violence against the earth, according to these scholars.

I like the idea of mutual custodianship, but must ask: Is ruling always bad? Reading Genesis 1 with the *Earth Bible Project* suggests that

[12]Norman C. Habel and Shirley Wurst, eds., *Earth Story in Wisdom Traditions*, The Earth Bible 3 (Sheffield: Sheffield Academic Press, 2001), 22.

antagonism is stitched into the fabric of creation because of God's command "subdue" and "rule."[13] But is that what Genesis 1 teaches?

Hardly. Although the words subdue and rule can be used to describe violent acts, they don't necessarily in this context. Genesis 1:26 and 28 seem to envision cultivation of some variety. Humans weren't meant to just "let nature be." The physical world would be shaped and cultivated by humans to unlock its life-giving potential.[14] Sometimes cultivation requires pulling up weeds, pruning, and the like. But those acts are hardly violent. This sounds like the mutual custodianship that the *Earth Bible Project* envisioned.

It's mistaken to read violence into this text, especially since creation was deemed "good" seven times in Genesis 1. God delighted in this creation, so why would he command humans to treat it violently? It was the food source for humans, and it was also commanded to put forth multiplying vegetation. The most obvious sense of *subdue* is thus agricultural development *that preserves and unlocks the earth's goodness.*

Subduing also involved sharing. Genesis 1:29-30 reminds us that humans share food sources with animals who were created on the same day. Subduing the land was not to be done at the expense of animal multiplication or food sources. All actions in Genesis 1 are toward life: life-enabling rule, multiplication, earth-filling, and ultimately, goodness.

What It Means to Rule. Back in the day when things went viral on email, I received a list of "Children's Books You'll Never See Written." There were some real zingers there: *Curious George and the High Voltage Fence, Some Kittens Can Fly!* and so on. A few of them highlighted the politics of elementary school, where kids often first learn the dark side of human rule. There was *Controlling the Playground: Respect Through Fear* and *How to Become the Dominant Military Power in Your Elementary School.*[15]

---

[13] As many have noted, the Hebrew terms for "subdue" (*kabash*) and "rule" (*radah*) are powerful images. *Kabash* connotes forceful conquest (cf. Josh 18:1) and *radah* royal dominion (Num 24:19).

[14] A point noted by contemporary ecologists, e.g., Robin Wall Kimmerer, *Braiding Sweetgrass: Indigenous Wisdom, Scientific Knowledge, and the Teachings of Plants* (Minneapolis: Milkweed Editions, 2013); cf. Charles C. Mann, *1491: New Revelations of the Americas Before Columbus*, 2nd ed. (New York: Vintage Books, 2011) on the importance of forest management and controlled burns throughout the Americas before the arrival of Europeans.

[15] These have been reproduced here: "Children's Books You'll Never See," Laugh Break (website), accessed June 17, 2022, https://laughbreak.com/lists/childrens-books-youll-never-see/.

Thankfully, these books aren't part of our kids' school curriculum (to my knowledge). But in the church, the Bible is part of our curriculum, or at least it should be. So, when the Bible calls humans to rule, is it advocating a kind of respect through fear? Some would argue that it is, simply because the concept of rule (*radah* in Hebrew) or dominion is so often tied to domination. In our cynical society, it's hard to imagine a form of authority that doesn't depend on some or other form of violence, coercion, and control.

Does Genesis address this? Yes. I think so.

First, God grants humanity "rule" over realms of creation that they can't directly control—especially before modern technology. Humans rule over the "fish in the sea" and "birds in the sky." These two realms lie outside the possibility of total human control; good luck exercising control over the birds in the sky!

Later Israelite law certainly places humans in a position of power over some members of these domains for the purpose of sacrifice and food. For example, Leviticus 20:25 shares an emphasis with Genesis 1 on "animals" "birds" and the creature that "moves along the ground": "You must therefore make a distinction between clean and unclean *animals* and between unclean and clean *birds*. Do not defile yourselves by any animal or bird or anything that *moves along the ground*—those which I have set apart as unclean for you" (Lev 20:25). Yet even here, certain creatures within these domains are explicitly forbidden to humans. Moreover, Genesis 1:29-30 makes clear that these creatures aren't yet given to humanity for food. Humans are given a vegetarian diet of veggies, fruit, and grains. The only realm for their implicit use is seed-bearing and fruit-bearing plants. Here again, God gives humans permission to use these goods in a way that reflects the fundamental goodness of creation and the God who created them. And some animals remained outside of Israel's hands.

RULING THE BEASTS AND ANCIENT KINGS

Because they considered themselves the unique images of their gods, ancient Near Eastern kings would set up images of themselves in their conquered territory. It gave them a way of declaring their dominion after victorious military campaigns. Some scholars, detecting hints of violence in

Genesis 1:28-30, claim that humans were God's victory icons, set up to broadcast God's "dominion in a conquered region."[16] Yet if Genesis 1:2 leaves no room for divine violence or warfare, what are we to make of this idea that God placed his image in this newly created territory?

In his study of animal images in the ancient world, Brent Strawn observes that ancient Assyrian and Egyptian kings frequently dramatized their military victories over humans through hunting expeditions.[17] Ancient Assyrian kings would often boast of all the animals they destroyed in these hunts. "Not only are descriptions of hunts found before or after descriptions of battles," Strawn adds, "the inscriptions . . . often depict the king's enemies as animals to be vanquished." Assyrian warfare rhetoric (and Egyptian royal images) was flush with violent speech against animals. Even more, as the unique image of the god(s), the king's action was an expression of the divine will and character. Kings were violent like the gods.

Figure 3.1. Assurbanipal hunting the lion, from the North Palace in Nineveh (ca. 645–635 BC)

[16]Edward M. Curtis, "Image of God (OT)," *Anchor Bible Dictionary*, ed. David Noel Fredman (New York: Doubleday, 1992), 3:389-91; Claus Westermann, *Genesis 1–11*, trans. John J. Scullion, Continental Commentaries (Minneapolis: Augsburg, 1984), 147-61.

[17]Brent A. Strawn, "Comparative Approaches: History, Theory, and the Image of God," in *Method Matters: Essays on the Interpretation of the Hebrew Bible in Honor of David L. Petersen*, eds. Joel M. LeMon and Kent Harold Richards, SBL Resources for Biblical Study 56 (Atlanta: SBL, 2009), 117-42.

The differences with Genesis 1 are startling, and they relate specifically to violence.[18] God gives humanity a strictly vegetarian diet immediately after announcing their creation in his image. This speaks volumes about the God humanity represents—he cares for his creation—and the kind of imaging in which humanity is to engage—a life-promoting kind. Strawn observes that the image of God in Genesis is royal, but not in the violent manner of Assyrian kings "who kill in battle and the hunt with the approval and power of the gods."[19] Humanity is royal like the God of Israel. This God is a God who creates a good world, a world in which violence has no necessary place. Violence isn't part of how things are supposed to be. Placing image bearers in creation is broadcasting the kind of rule God desires, not the territory God conquered.

CONCLUSION

Genesis 1 is the gateway to the Bible. It shows us a world of right-relating wholeness that involves peace between God, humans, and creation. Genesis 1 undermines attempts to see any violence lurking in creation. God didn't need to wield his sword to create the world. Had he done so, you could easily make the case that wielding the sword is just what it takes for God—and us!—to keep the world going. As J. Richard Middleton notes, "Creation-by-combat . . . ontologizes evil, and assumes it is equally primordial with God and goodness."[20] But according to Genesis, violence isn't part of creation's DNA. Only goodness is. The traditional ancient combatants (primordial oceans, chaotic waters, sea monsters, animals) are simply part of God's good creation.[21]

We also saw that human rule and subjugation are life-promoting. Dysfunctional rule only emerges in Genesis 3–4, where men began to hold dominion over women and violence begins to take shape.[22] At that point, the objects of human rule and subjugation shifted. No longer did humans use their power exclusively to cultivate the land and enable God's good animals to flourish. Instead, they turned against one another and against

---

[18]Strawn, "Comparative Approaches," 134.

[19]Strawn, "Comparative Approaches," 134.

[20]J. Richard Middleton, "Created in the Image of a Violent God? The Ethical Problem of the Conquest of Chaos in Biblical Creation Texts," *Interpretation* 58, no. 4 (2004): 350.

[21]Middleton, "Created in the Image of a Violent God?," 353.

[22]At this point God first wields the sword to guard access to the Tree of Life (Gen 3:24).

creation itself. By the time of Noah, God looks at creation, and instead of declaring it "very good" (Gen 1:31), he declares it "ruined" (see Gen 6:12).

But in Genesis 1, human rule is decidedly life-promoting. Genesis 2 then clarifies the nature of that rule. Humans are placed in God's Garden to "serve and care" for *the ground* (see Gen 2:15).

That's a humbling task, and an important reminder. As one of my friends and colleagues once put it, when we feel like dirt it's important to read Genesis 1 and remember that we're made in God's image. But when we think we're the best thing that ever hit the planet, it's important to read Genesis 2 and remember that we're made from and for the dirt. Royal rule finds its purpose in the service and care of creation.[23]

Jon Levenson writes that the Genesis 1 creation story serves as an "overture to the entire Bible, dramatically relativizing other cosmogonies [creation stories]."[24] Genesis 1 "constitutes a normative framework by which we may judge all the violence that pervades the rest of the Bible."[25] On the topic of violence, the Bible asks us to look through a nonviolent lens. Let *this* story shape your perspective on any violence that later emerges. Let it shape your perspective on any other ways that humans wield power and exercise rule. By looking through that lens we see the ways things are *supposed* to be, and thus where things *will be* (Rev 21–22).

---

[23]Not everyone thinks Genesis 1–2 promote a peaceful vision. In his influential book *The Temple and the Church's Mission*, Gregory K. Beale argues that the command to "rule and subdue" from Gen 1:26-28 should suggest to us that Adam's task "was to widen the boundaries of the Garden in ever increasing circles by extending the order of the garden sanctuary into the inhospitable outer spaces." For Beale, the Edenic task involved guarding from threats of chaos (because it was a sanctuary of God's presence) and conquering new realms to spread the "glorious presence of God." Beale isn't saying that the picture in Gen 1–2 is violent. Yet it's hard to avoid the conclusion that Gen 1–2 pave the way for "necessary" violence in the name of "widening" the Garden's boundaries "into inhospitable outer spaces." While other portions of Scripture certainly envision violent conquest, nothing in the Garden of Eden suggests that the first humans were to extend its borders or subjugate hostile forces. Quite the opposite, they were to tend the Garden, which implies *it* as the object of their keeping and care, with nary a word about what might lie outside Eden's borders. Moreover, the idea that guardianship involves protection against lurking threats runs contrary to the vision of an entirely good creation. *The Temple and the Church's Mission: A Biblical Theology of the Dwelling Place of God*, New Studies in Biblical Theology 17 (Downers Grove, IL: InterVarsity Press, 2004), 81-85, cf. 163.

[24]Jon D. Levenson, *Creation and the Persistence of Evil: The Jewish Drama of Divine Omnipotence* (San Francisco: Harper & Row, 1988), 100.

[25]Middleton, "Created in the Image of a Violent God?," 355.

4

VIOLENCE AGAINST WOMEN
IN THE BIBLE'S PROLOGUE

WHEN I FIRST STARTED PENNING thoughts on violence against women in Genesis 1–11, two mass shootings had just taken place: one in El Paso, Texas and one in Dayton, Ohio. These shootings ended thirty-one lives and injured many more. As usual, analysts struggled to explain the prevalence of such mass shootings in the United States. Obviously, the widespread availability of guns is a factor, but motivations for these shootings seem to run deeper.

A 2019 *New York Times* article identified "hatred of women" as the common denominator among mass shooters. Increased access to misogynistic forums and websites now accompanies increased access to guns.[1] A study cited in the article also indicates that nearly half of all mass shooters have a history of domestic violence, particularly against women. Another in-depth study analyzed twenty-two mass shootings since 2011 found that 86 percent of the shooters had a history of domestic violence. Thirty-two percent of the shooters had a history of stalking and harassment, and 50 percent specifically targeted women.[2] Domestic violence feeds public terrorism.[3]

Another version of this chapter appears as Matthew J. Lynch, "The Roots of Violence: Male Violence Against Women in Genesis," in *The Biblical World of Gender: The Daily Lives of Ancient Women and Men*, ed. Celina Durgin and Dru Johnson (Eugene, OR: Cascade Books, 2022), 61-70. Used with permission.

[1] Julie Bosman, Kate Taylor, and Tim Arango, "A Common Trait Among Mass Killings: Hatred of Women," *New York Times*, August 10, 2019, www.nytimes.com/2019/08/10/us/mass-shootings -misogyny-dayton.html.

[2] Mark Follman, "Armed and Misogynist: How Toxic Masculinity Fuels Mass Shootings," *Mother Jones*, May/June 2019, www.motherjones.com/crime-justice/2019/06/domestic-violence-misogyny -incels-mass-shootings/.

[3] A 2015 Lancet study on intimate partner violence compiled data from 66 surveys in 44 countries and included the experiences of nearly half a million women. It found that the "greatest predictor

WHERE SCRIPTURE STARTS

The link between male (domestic) control of women and public violence raises questions for Christians about how Scripture feeds or resists such trends. Unfortunately, many Christians begin their thinking about men and women with texts that seem to support male control. They start with the headship or submission verses and proceed from there. This approach not only ignores where the Bible itself begins (Genesis 1–2), but it also divorces such passages from the strong critiques of male-centered control and violence that weave their way through the biblical story.

If we start where the Bible starts, our picture of male authority and violence shifts. By placing these chapters first, the writer of Genesis says, "Look through *these* lenses to understand the biblical story." Genesis 1–2 begins with a compelling vision of male-female equality.[4] Women and men are made in God's image, called to rule in creation (Gen 1), and they share in the sacred task of keeping the Garden (Gen 2). But once humanity rebels, male dominance enters the picture. As an awful consequence of sin, men would now "rule over" women (Gen 3:16). Male dominance and rule represented a distortion of God's intention for men and women.

Recognizing the tragic emergence of male dominion in Genesis 3 helps us see its connection to three brief (but often ignored) mini stories that appear in Genesis 1–11. Genesis 1–11 is known as the Primeval History, because it gives us important background to the biblical story that follows. Each mini story in Genesis 1–11 foregrounds the link between the new forms of male dominance and violence. Together they show the rise of societal violence from its domestic breeding grounds. They tell us that a

---

of partner violence was social 'environments that support male control,' especially 'norms related to male authority over female behaviour.'" Julia Baird with Hayley Gleeson, "'Submit to Your Husbands': Women Told to Endure Domestic Violence in the Name of God," ABC News (Australia), July 17, 2017, www.abc.net.au/news/2017-07-18/domestic-violence-church-submit-to -husbands/8652028. For the study, see Lori L. Heise and Andreas Kotsadam, "Cross-national and Multilevel Correlates of Partner Violence: An Analysis of Data from Population-based Surveys," *Lancet Global Health* 3 (2015): 332-40, www.thelancet.com/journals/langlo/article/PIIS2214 -109X(15)00013-3/fulltext.

[4]See Richard Hess, "Evidence for Equality in Genesis 1–3," *Equality* 7, no. 3 (Autumn 2008), www .cbeinternational.org/sites/default/files/Hess.pdf. And recently, Lucy Peppiatt, *Rediscovering Scripture's Vision for Women: Fresh Perspectives on Disputed Texts* (Downers Grove, IL: InterVarsity Press, 2019).

distorted masculinity isn't just one of many contributing factors in the origins of violence. It is a leading cause.

Boasting about violence. Our first mini story involves a man named Lamech (Gen 4:19-24). It offers us the first clear link between patriarchy and violence.[5] Lamech is Cain's descendant and the seventh generation from Adam. We're clearly meant to see Lamech as a fatal consequence of Adam's now-distorted dominance in creation, and of Cain's violence. Cain's great-great-great grandson Lamech is the first polygamist in the Bible. This detail, mentioned in passing during the recitation of Cain's genealogy, is deliberate (Gen 4:19). He stands in contrast to the seventh-generation Lamech in Seth's line (Gen 5:25), who fathered Noah and prophesied *rest* in the land and *relief* from the ground's curse (Gen 5:29).

We're told that Lamech "took" wives for himself (Gen 4:19), an act that occasionally suggests forced marriage.[6] As he increases his matrimonial dominion, he utters this victory taunt over his wives:

> Adah and Zillah, listen to me,
> wives of Lamech, hear my words.
> I have killed a man for wounding me,
> a young man for injuring me.
> If Cain is avenged seven times,
> then Lamech seventy-seven times. (Gen 4:23-24)

We don't know why Lamech killed this young man. Perhaps he was Adah or Zillah's former husband. Or perhaps Lamech was jealous and got injured in a fight. In any case, Lamech felt the need to sing his victory song *to his wives*. It has the feel of a veiled threat, especially with implied divine backing. Just as *God* would avenge Cain's killer sevenfold, Lamech threatens to avenge *himself* seventy-seven-fold if anyone should avenge his already-excessive violence. Apparently, his wives "needed" to hear about his deeds and the Godlike vengeance he'd exact.

Claus Westermann calls Lamech's poem a "sword song," observing its narrative position after the note about Tubal Cain's invention of bronze and iron (Gen 4:22). Demons lurked among humanity's technological advances.

---

[5] It might be implied already in the man's *ruling* over his wife (Gen 3:16).
[6] Cf. Gen 6:2, where the "sons of God" *took* wives.

Lamech's song sounds eerily similar to the taunt song of Samson, another violent polygamist. The mighty Samson married a Philistine woman from Timnah, only to promptly abandon her (Judg 14). When he later took a sudden interest in her, he learned that her father had given her to another man. Incensed, Samson did the natural thing. He tied 150 pairs of foxes to flaming torches and set them among the Philistine grain fields and olive groves, scorching everything in sight (Judg 15:1-5). The Philistines retaliated by torching his wife and father-in-law's home, killing both. Samson vowed to avenge this act (Judg 15:7), so he let himself be captured and bound to get behind enemy lines (anticipating his final act in Judg 16). Seizing the opportunity, he burst his captor's bonds and drew the closest weapon—a donkey's jawbone! With it, he slaughtered a thousand Philistines, uttering this taunt song:

> With a donkey's jawbone
> I have made donkeys of them.
> With a donkey's jawbone,
> I have killed a thousand men. (Judg 15:16)

Samson named the corpse heap Ramath Lehi, or Jawbone Hill, to warn any Philistine who might attempt avenging him.

Lamech's song takes a similar delight in outsized vengeance. And he wasn't just bragging. His song issued a warning shot for anyone who might retaliate. Its purpose, as Westermann puts it, was to "strike terror."[7] William Brown makes a similar point: "For Lamech to direct his terror-inspiring taunt to his wives is curious and suggests an additional dynamic at work, one that threatens to tear the fabric of his household at its seams."[8] In short, Lamech boasts—to the two women he had taken for himself—of violence done and violence to come.

Lamech merges menfolk's newfound dominance (Gen 3:16) with the murderous impulses of Cain (Gen 4:1-12). Violence and misogyny grow like twins east of Eden.[9]

[7] Claus Westermann, *Genesis 1–11*, trans. John J. Scullion, Continental Commentaries (Minneapolis: Augsburg, 1984), 337.
[8] William P. Brown, *The Ethos of the Cosmos: The Genesis of Moral Imagination in the Bible* (Grand Rapids, MI: Eerdmans, 1999), 173.
[9] Eric Peels, "The World's First Murder: Violence and Justice in Genesis 4:1-16," in *Animosity, the Bible, and Us: Some European, North American, and South African Perspectives*, ed. John T. Fitzgerald, Fika Van

Taking wives and becoming warriors. Genesis 6:1-4 tells us a bizarre little story. It reads like a paper scrap torn from a fantasy novel. Divine beings called "the sons of God" have sex with human women and produce a race of powerful warriors:[10]

> When humans began to increase in number on the earth and daughters were born to them, the sons of God saw (**ra'ah*) that the daughters of humans were pleasing (**tov*). So they took (**laqah*) as wives from (*min*) any whom they wanted. Then the LORD said, "My spirit will not abide in mortals forever, for they are flesh; their days shall be one hundred twenty years."
>
> The Nephilim were on the earth in those days—and also afterward—when the sons of God went in to the daughters of humans, who bore children to them. These were the heroes that were of old, warriors of renown. (Gen 6:1-4, my translation)[11]

In Genesis, this story about *warriors* precedes the account of the earth filling with *violence* before the Great Flood. This connection is hardly accidental. The warriors contributed to all the violence that eventually ruined the earth.[12]

Rensburg, and Herrie F. van Rooy, Society of Biblical Literature Global Perspectives on Biblical Scholarship 12 (Atlanta: Society of Biblical Literature, 2009), 19-39.

[10]Identifying these "sons of god(s)" (*bene ha'elohim*) is tricky. The most straightforward reading suggests that these are divine beings, known only elsewhere in the Old Testament from the books of Job, Deuteronomy, and Psalms (Deut 32:8; Job 1:6; 2:1; 38:7; Ps 29:1; 89:7). Others have insisted that the phrase rendered "sons of god" refers to dynastic rulers, the despots of the ancient world. Yet as Clines points out, a purely human interpretation of the phrase "sons of god" is unlikely. While they are certainly portrayed as tyrants, the phrase "sons of god" rarely if ever refers to kings in general in the ancient world, much less so in the Bible. More likely these are despotic divine beings. For a discussion on the identity of the sons of God, see William A. Van Gemeren, "The Sons of God in Genesis 6:1-4: An Example of Evangelical Demythologization?," *Westminster Theological Journal* 43, no. 2 (1981): 330-43.

[11]The mysterious nature of this passage has been cause for endless speculation and embellishment in Jewish and Christian traditions. Second only to the equally enigmatic Enoch fragment of Gen 5:24, Gen 6:1-4 has fueled the apocalyptic imagination in works like the third-century BC "Book of Watchers" (*1 Enoch 1–36*), which fills in many of the gaps left by Genesis 6:1-4. See Archie T. Wright, *The Origins of Evil Spirits: The Reception of Genesis 6:1-4 in Early Jewish Literature*, 2nd rev. ed., Wissenschaftliche Untersuchungen zum Neuen Testament II/198 (Tübingen: Mohr Siebeck, 2003).

[12]Notice the coordinated references to humanity's "increasing" (Gen 6:1) and its "increased" (Gen 6:5) wickedness. Ronald S. Hendel, "Of Demigods and Deluge: Toward an Interpretation of Genesis 6:1-4," *Journal of Biblical Literature* 106, no. 1 (1987): 23; Kenneth A. Matthews, *Genesis 1:1–11:26*, New American Commentary (Nashville: Broadman & Holman, 1996), 322. The early Jewish *Book of Watchers* also makes this connection. It explains how the offspring of the divine-human

In this respect, Genesis parts company with its ancient neighbors. Israel's neighbors from Greece to Egypt and from Assyria to Babylon all celebrated divine-human union to explain the great warriors and kings. For instance, two of the most famous stories from the ancient world (The Gilgamesh Epic and Heracles) both include king-like hero figures with a divine parent. Genesis takes this common demigod theme and turns it on its head.[13]

The storyteller also wants us to see that these divine beings replicate the first sin, but in a new key.[14] Note the shared language (I've put the Hebrew in parentheses):

> the sons of God saw (*ra'ah) that the daughters of humans were pleasing (*tov). So they took (*laqah) as wives from (min) any whom they wanted. (Gen 6:2, NIV modified)

> When the woman saw (*ra'ah) that the tree was pleasing (*tov) for eating . . . she took (*laqah) from (min) its fruit and ate. (Gen 3:6, NIV modified)

As in the beginning, the divine beings saw and took what was good to them. This casts decidedly negative light on their actions. And like the original transgression, it ushers in a new era of male domination (as in Gen 3:16) and violence (as in Gen 4). This new era was defined by violent, women-taking rulers (Gen 6:4).

The next one to "see" and "take" is Pharaoh. Pharaoh "saw" (*ra'ah) Abraham's "beautiful" wife Sarah and "took" (*laqah) her (Gen 12:14-15, 19). The examples multiply.[15] Shechem, "prince of the land . . . saw" (*ra'ah) Jacob's daughter Dinah, "took" (*laqah) her, and raped her (Gen 34:2). His

---

unions turn on humanity and fill the earth with violence (1 Enoch 7–9). In other words, the story wants us to draw a connection between the women-grabbing demigods (Gen 6:1-4) and the eruption of violence on earth (Gen 6:5-13).

[13] Thanks to Chris McKinny for this observation. I am not suggesting here that Genesis was directly aware of Heracles, but that the similarities are striking. The belief in the demigod status of kings and heroes is well known in the ancient world, with kings like Gilgamesh of Uruk and Theseus of Athens prominent among them.

[14] These divine beings set their sights on human daughters and had to have 'em. They took whomever they wanted. Some scholars contest the idea that the story reflects negatively on the daughters' actions, for instance, Gordon Wenham, Genesis 1–15, Word Biblical Commentary (Grand Rapids, MI: Zondervan, 1987), 141. Wenham argues strangely that the daughters consented and that their fathers gave approval (just as Adam consented to Eve's transgression). This view lacks any support and misses the primary critique of the gods' actions as a prelude to the "great" heroes of old.

[15] These kings also sound like the vengeful act of Lamech who "took [for himself] . . . wives" (Gen 4:19, NRSV) and boasted of killing a boy who had wounded him.

violence prompted Levi and Simeon to butcher an entire city in retaliation. Later, Samson "saw" (**ra'ah*) a Philistine woman (Judg 14:1) and sent his parents to "take" (**laqah*) her (Judg 14:2) because she was pleasing to his "eyes" (Judg 14:3, 7, ESV).[16] Later, King David "saw" (**ra'ah*) the "pleasing" (**tov*) Bathsheba and sent officials to "take" (**laqah*) her (cf. Gen 26:7; Esther 1:11; 2:3). To underwrite his theft, David then acted violently by having Bathsheba's husband Uriah killed (2 Sam 11). Notice a pattern? *Martial and marital domination went hand-in-hand for kings and other men of power.*

Genesis 6:4 tells us that the offspring of the divine beings were "warriors [*gibborim*] of old" and "men of renown." These are super warriors, those with exceptional strength, as their descent from the divine beings tells us.[17] Genesis even associates them with a mysterious group known as the Nephilim (Gen 6:4), the ancestors of the giant Anakim who later terrorized the land of Canaan as warrior-kings (Num 13:28, 33). We'll revisit these giants in chapter twelve.

Instead of recognizing that all humans image God, now a select group of warriors positioned themselves as gods on earth. David Clines puts it well: "We now have the presence of the divine on earth in a form that utterly misrepresents God through its exercise of royal violence and despotic authority over other humans."[18] With this short mini story, Genesis 6:1-4 offers a mocking-yet-sober "founding story" of the so-called "great"

---

[16]The negative evaluation of Samson's actions is suggested not only from Samson's violations of his parents' vow, but from the similarity between Samson's words in Judg 14:3 and 7 and the refrain that in Israel "everyone did as they saw fit" (lit. what was right in their own eyes; Judg 17:6; 21:25; and related, Judg 18:1; 19:1).

[17]As Mark Smith notes, the range of applications for "divine beings" (*'elohim*) in the Old Testament suggests that the term basically denotes "power" that is "extraordinary," though possessed in varying degrees by divinities. Mark S. Smith, *God in Translation: Deities in Cross-cultural Discourse in the Biblical World* (Grand Rapids, MI: Eerdmans, 2010), 11-15. On *gibbor* see Robin Wakely, "גִּבֹּר," in *New International Dictionary of Old Testament Theology and Exegesis*, ed. Willem A. VanGemeren, 5 vols. (Grand Rapids: Zondervan, 1997), ad loc., Westermann, *Genesis 1–11*, 363-83. On giants in the Old Testament and Ancient Near East, see Brian R. Doak, "The Giant in a Thousand Years: Tracing Narratives of Gigantism in the Hebrew Bible and Beyond," *Ancient Tales of Giants from Qumran and Turfan: Contexts, Traditions, and Influences*, eds., Matthew Goff, Loren T. Stuckenbruck, and Enrico Morano (Tübingen: Mohr Siebeck, 2016), 13-32.

[18]David J. A. Clines, "The Significance of the 'Sons of God' Episode (Genesis 6:1-4) in the Context of the 'Primeval History' (Genesis 1–11)," *Journal for the Study of the Old Testament* 4, no. 13 (1979): 37; Carol M. Kaminski, "Beautiful Women or 'False Judgment'? Interpreting Genesis 6.2 in the Context of the Primaeval History," *Journal for the Study of the Old Testament* 32, no. 4 (2008): 457-73.

warrior-kings. Like many great cultures of the ancient world, Genesis 6 grants kings a founding story. But it does so by telling a tragic story about humanity's embrace of violent male domination. Once again, domestic violence (taking women) accompanies public violence (warrior-kings).

Nimrod, the man's man. Genesis 1–11 offers a third mini story to tell us what these warrior-kings are all about. The storyteller slips this fragment of a story between names in a genealogy:

> Cush was the father of Nimrod,
> who became a mighty *warrior* (*gibbor*) on the earth.
> He was a hunter-*warrior* (*gibbor*) before the LORD;
> that is why it is said, "Like Nimrod, a mighty hunter before the LORD."
> (Gen 10:8-9, NIV modified)

Nimrod was also the post-flood equivalent of Cain. He was violent and he founded cities (Gen 4:17). A brief genealogical aside tells us that he founded the great imperial centers of the ancient world, including Babylon and Nineveh (Gen 10:10-12). While his story doesn't focus on violence against women, he's a warrior (*gibbor*) cut from the same cloth as the warriors (*gibborim*) in Genesis 6.[19]

Nimrod's name is a little joke. It means "let us rebel" or "we rebel." It is usually *against* the powerful and oppressive ruler that the oppressed rebel. For instance, just a few chapters after this story we learn about several kings from the Jordan Valley who rebelled against an Elamite king who had oppressed them for twelve years (Gen 14:4).

But Nimrod is the mighty warrior. He's the oppressor. So, the joke's on him. Nimrod's name includes his own downfall.

As a hunter (Gen 10:9), Nimrod takes his place among the great kings of Mesopotamia, but especially among the Assyrians. The prophet Micah even refers to Assyria as "the land of Nimrod" (Mic 5:6). For the Assyrians, mighty rulers were mighty hunters. They went together. One Assyrian poet celebrates the king's brutal slaughter of wild animals, mighty men, women, and babies:

---

[19]Genesis uses the same term (*gibbor*) to make the link (Gen 6:4; 10:8-9 [3x]), and the Greek Septuagint translation even calls them "giants" (*gigantes*) in Gen 6:4.

Let us go and bring massacre upon the mountain beasts,
With our sharpened . . . weapons we will shed their blood. . . .
A journey of three days he marched [in one].
Even without sunshine a fiery heat was among them,
He slashed the wombs of the pregnant, blinded the babies,
He cut the throats of the strong ones among them.[20]

Human enemies—whether pregnant women, babies, or strong opponents—were slaughtered because of their association with all that is "wild" in nature. The king subdued the earth through violent domination.

So, when we hear that Nimrod was a mighty hunter, we're probably not meant to imagine a bearded man donning his camos and orange for an early morning out with his buddies. The claim that Nimrod was a mighty hunter was linked clearly to his role as founder (and ruler) of empires, including the all-too-violent Assyrian Empire. These warrior-rulers ruled by conquering nature and exerting dominion over their fellow humans.

CONCLUSION

These short stories warrant our attention because they're about beginnings. Beginnings in the Bible aren't just providing FYI detail about when and where or even how things began. Stories of origin are about the essential nature of things, about fundamental questions. As John Goldingay puts it, modern "Western movies project questions into the future and ask whether there will be a future. Middle Eastern stories project them into the past and ask about the security of the created world."[21] They're about diagnosing the core problems that plague humanity everywhere, and not just in its darkest corners. The mini stories we explored tell us about three beginnings:

1. The beginning of polygamy (domestic violence): Lamech, the first polygamist tried to outdo God by promising seventy-seven-fold vengeance and taunting his wives.

---

[20]From "The Hunter," translated by Benjamin R. Foster in *Before the Muses: An Anthology of Akkadian Literature*, 3rd. ed. (Bethesda, MD: CDL Press, 2005), 336-37.
[21]John Goldingay, *Genesis*, Baker Commentary on the Old Testament: Pentateuch (Grand Rapids, MI: Baker Academic, 2020), 153.

2. The beginning of the warrior-kings (military violence): Divine beings seized women and, surprise, surprise, their sons became warriors.

3. The beginning of "great" cities (political and civic violence): One warrior named Nimrod was the first warrior-hunter, an ideal (royal) male in the ancient world. He founded the great Mesopotamian cities.

Each of these stories sits within the story of humanity's "falling out" with God and each other. They help explain why the earth was filled with violence, and why it's still filled with violence.

These stories also set the stage for a pattern of bravado and violence that weaves its way through Genesis and the rest of Scripture. Remember, we're supposed to see the rest of the biblical story through the Genesis 1–11 lens.

Abraham's nephew Lot was willing to offer his violent male neighbors his two daughters' bodies for a night's peace (Gen 19). Shechem raped Leah's daughter Dinah, which led to further violence when Simeon and Levi slaughtered all the inhabitants of Shechem's city (Gen 34).

The important point for our study is that these stories of male dominance and violence against women belong within the broader narrative portrait of humanity's *rebellion against God*. From the beginning, Genesis draws a direct line of connection between male domination and violence. The two are inextricably bound as byproducts of the falling out between God, humanity, and creation.

The striking link between male domination and violence in these stories challenges us to consider the threads connecting male dominion to violence against women. It forces us to consider the domestic, cultural, spiritual, and political forms misogynistic violence takes. The fact that these challenges of male domination occur so prominently in Genesis 1–11 suggests that they have a kind of priority for us as readers and citizens in a world where 603 million women still live in a country where domestic violence isn't criminalized.[22] Challenges remain. The Old Testament offers some troubling depictions of women.[23] However, if Genesis 1–11 is our lens

---

[22]According to the 2013 "Commission on the Status of Women," https://www.unwomen.org/en/news/in-focus/csw57-stop-violence-against-women. Accessed July 6, 2022.

[23]For resources on this subject, see Alice Bach, ed. *Women in the Hebrew Bible: A Reader* (New York: Routledge, 2013); Linda Day and Carolyn Pressler, eds., *Engaging the Bible in a Gendered World: An*

for reading the rest, its stories should lead us to become deeply suspicious of anything less than the pursuit of male-female equality envisioned in Genesis 1–2.[24] To that extent, Genesis 1–11 is also good news for men. There's no *essential* link between maleness and violence woven into the fabric of creation or programmed into the male DNA.[25] The vision of male-female shalom can be pursued east of Eden.

Introduction to Feminist Biblical Interpretation in Honor of Katharine Doob Sakenfeld (Louisville, KY: Westminster John Knox, 2006).

[24]For a compelling overview of the Bible's egalitarian ideals, see Lucy Peppiatt, *Rediscovering Scripture's Vision for Women: Fresh Perspectives on Disputed Texts* (Downers Grove, IL: InterVarsity Press, 2019). For recent critiques of female subordination within American Evangelicalism, see Kristin Kobes Du Mez, *Jesus and John Wayne: How White Evangelicals Corrupted a Faith and Fractured a Nation* (New York: Liveright Publishing, 2020). For historic perspective on female subordination, see Beth Allison Barr, *The Making of Biblical Womanhood: How the Subjugation of Women Became Gospel Truth* (Grand Rapids, MI: Baker Books, 2021). A helpful study is Nancy Murphy's article, "If I Were an Abuser What Church Would I Want to Attend?" Andrew J Bauman (website), March 9, 2020, https://andrewjbauman.com/abuserchurch/.

[25]Discussed in Dennis T. Olson, "Untying the Knot? Masculinity, Violence, and the Creation-Fall Story of Genesis 2–4," in *Engaging the Bible in a Gendered World: An Introduction to Feminist Biblical Interpretation in Honor of Katharine Doob Sakenfeld*, eds. Linda Day and Carolyn Pressler (Louisville, KY: Westminster John Knox, 2006), 73-86.

5

CREATION'S COLLAPSE

WHEN I LIVED IN CHICAGO, the church I attended offered a free pottery class. We only had to pay for the clay. Someone had donated a kiln and two pottery wheels to the church to help foster the arts. My then-girlfriend (now my spouse) and I took the class and loved it. It was a steep learning curve, but worth the effort. I still have the mug I made twenty years ago, #thankyouverymuch.

When throwing clay and shaping it on a potter's wheel, you learn quickly to do so with the kiln in mind. If your clay has air bubbles, it will explode in the hot kiln. If the clay has thin sections, they'll likely break. At 1,800 to 2,400 degrees Fahrenheit, air bubbles and thin spots can't withstand the heat. So, if you're spinning clay and you notice air bubbles or thin spots, you can't just hope for the best or try to patch things up. It'll never work. Your only option is to turn the clay back into a formless ball and start over.

This is what happens in the Great Flood of Genesis 6–8. God takes an already ruined creation and turns it back into *useful formlessness* so that he can begin to form it again. This point is crucial, and I don't want us to miss it. *Creation was already ruined before the Great Flood.*

Unfortunately, popular interpretations of the Great Flood often go like this:

(a) Things got bad.

(b) God got mad.

(c) God ruined everything.

It's a simple story. The problem is that (b) and (c) are wrong. Let's look closely.

VIOLENCE RUINS CREATION

Genesis 1–2 wants us to envision the world in terms of a deep ecology— an ecology in which our moral and physical worlds are entwined. The land senses the moral health of its inhabitants. It's especially attuned to human- on-human violence (both personal and structural) since it threatens cre- ation. The land then reflects the health of its inhabitants, breaks into a fever, and even vomits when humans are morally ill (Lev 18:28; 20:22; cf. Deut 11:8-17).

Creation is bound together by a web of life-sustaining relationships that are physical, moral, and theological. The lines connecting these relation- ships run not only between animals, plants, and the land, but between God, creation, and the world. The Hebrew word for that is *tov*—or, "good." Goodness, according to Genesis 1–2, is about rightly ordered, properly functioning, life-giving, and aesthetically pleasing relationships. The climax of the first creation account in Genesis 1 affirms creation's fundamental goodness in crystal clear terms: "God saw all that he had made, and behold, it was supremely good."[1] God's creation is deemed fit for purpose, for life, and for enjoyment.

Tragically, violence tears at the goodness of creation, bringing it to a point of collapse and destruction. Violence threatened the life-sustaining web of relationships that bound it together. When Cain killed his brother Abel, for instance, the *ground* refused to yield crops for him (Gen 4:11-12). Why should the ground get involved? Because humanity (Heb. *'adam*) is from the ground (Heb. *'adamah*). Violence ruined what was *very tov*!

Notice God's assessment of the earth's condition after we read that the *whole* earth filled with violence: "And God looked at the earth, and behold, it was ruined!" (Gen 6:11, my translation). This inverts our picture of the goodness affirmed in Genesis 1:31. Brown's assessment is apt: "Violence and its accompanying effects make up the antithesis of creation's 'goodness.'"[2] The earth's ecology edged toward the brink of collapse.

---

[1] I draw the phrase "supremely good" from the CEB translation of Gen 1:31.

[2] William P. Brown, *The Ethos of the Cosmos: The Genesis of Moral Imagination in the Bible* (Grand Rapids, MI: Eerdmans, 1999), 54.

CREATION-CONSUMING VIOLENCE

When my family lived in Atlanta, we had to get a termite bond for our house. Home insurance didn't protect against termite damage because termites were very common. Homeowners needed specific coverage for termites by subscribing to a pest control service that checked their home and its perimeter for evidence of termites. To the untrained eye, an Atlanta home might look strong and secure. But if looking closely, they might notice little piles of sawdust, wood tunnels, or they may even hear the "munch, munch" of termites in the walls. If a termite infestation went unchecked, a house might be deemed structurally unstable.

In Genesis 6, God deems his good creation ruined. It was a teardown. What leads to this assessment?

First, the extent of human evil and violence was total. Genesis 6:5 says that "every" human plan was "only" evil "all" the time.

Second, violence was creation-wide and extended well beyond humans. Participants in violence even included *animals*. Genesis 6:12 (ESV) tells us that "all *flesh*" ruined itself because of violence—a phrase used throughout the flood narrative (Gen 6–9) to describe all creatures. In other words, everything breathing the "breath of life" was somehow implicated in a system of total and creation-destroying violence—animals included. Genesis 6:13 reports that the earth was "filled" with violence. So, God resolved to ruin "all flesh" that had the "breath of life" (Gen 6:17, ESV).

It may sound strange that land creatures and birds corrupted their ways. How can this be? We need to recall here that at this point in the story, creation and humanity were locked in a mutually antagonistic struggle. The earth produced thorns and thistles *in direct response to humans*. The serpent was subjugated beneath the other creatures (Gen 3:14), not to mention the violence between the serpent's offspring and the woman's (Gen 3:15). The violent struggle increased when Cain murdered Abel, such that now the ground would no longer yield any of its strength to Cain (Gen 4:12). In other words, creation turned violently against itself.

An analogy to this animal-including violence is found in the book of Jonah, where in an ironic and humorous turn of events the king of

Nineveh issues the following decree: "But let *people and animals* be covered with sackcloth. Let everyone call urgently on God. Let them give up their *evil ways* and their *violence*" (Jon 3:8, NIV modified).

This story maintains the possibility that humans and animals should lament before God and turn from violence. James Limburg says, "This is one of the many biblical illustrations of the solidarity between humans and animals."[3] The idea of animals in sackcloth sounds comical. And it is! But it also gives the writer a way of depicting a culture that Israel considered rife with total violence.[4] That seems to be the point here. Violence touched every aspect of their world.

Another clue pointing toward the participation of *all* creatures in this circle of violence emerges after the Great Flood. God speaks directly to the problem of total violence with this warning: "And for your lifeblood I will surely demand an accounting. *I will demand an accounting from every animal.* And from each human being, too, I will demand an accounting for the life of another human being" (Gen 9:5, NIV modified).

God requires the life of an *animal* for taking a human life.[5] God not only needed to deal with human violence, but also with animal violence, because the problem of violence was creation-wide.

The idea of holding animals responsible for their violence seems bizarre for modern readers. Also, many of us don't live our lives near any animals except household pets or pests. However, we need go no further than Israel's law to see how animal violence touched Israelite lives. Israelite law held that if an ox "gores a man or a woman to death, the bull must be stoned to death, and its meat must not be eaten" (Ex 21:28). Animals were held liable for bloodshed.

So, after the flood God introduced limits on the extent to which violence could run amok. The pre-flood picture, by contrast, is designed to portray a situation of creation-consuming violence. Violence was everywhere.

---

[3]James Limburg, *Jonah*, Old Testament Library (Louisville, KY: Westminster John Knox, 1993), 82.
[4]The reference to the Ninevites' "evil way" (*ra'* + **derek*) and "violence" (*hamas*) brings together the two offenses highlighted in the pre-flood account (Gen 6:5; 6:11-13).
[5]The Hebrew reads literally, "I will require *from the hand* of every beast." This connects conceptually to the scene in Jonah, where the king asks humans and animals to turn from the evil and violence "that is in their hands" (Jon 3:8, NRSV).

Total violence led to total collapse. The termites had destroyed creation's framing. The creational home may have appeared solid from the outside, but the divine inspector declared the house a teardown. To adopt Luther's well-known phrase, creation was "curved in upon itself."[6] The scope of creation's ruin cannot be overstated. According to Genesis, the reach and impact of violence is far wider than a human-centered approach will allow. Violence destroys the network of relationships that sustain creation. It shreds the fabric of creation. Violence is an ecological crisis. In this way Scripture is way ahead of its time in recognizing the ecological impact of violence. Conversely, the persistence of creation in the face of violence testifies to the sustaining grace of God—his unrelenting commitment to creation's preservation in the face of creation-disintegrating violence. Therein lies the struggle that comes to a head in Genesis 6. Will God find a way to preserve creation from total ruin?

God's Pain

You might get the impression that God sat in the comfort of heaven while violence tore the earth to shreds. But according to Genesis, God didn't just witness this earth-destroying violence. God felt humanity's violence. God was "pained to his heart" (Gen 6:6, my translation).

The Hebrew term for pained ('atsav) here recalls its earlier use to describe the effects of sin on the woman's childbearing (Gen 3:16) and the man's labor (Gen 3:17).[7] But this is the first emotion ascribed to God in the Bible.[8] Yahweh felt the painful effects of creation's violent collapse in himself. Walter Brueggemann writes:

> The evil *heart of humankind* (v. 5) troubles the *heart of God* (v. 6). This is indeed "heart to heart" between humankind and God. How it is between humankind and God touches both parties. As Ernst Würthwein suggests, it is God who must say, "I am undone."[9]

---

[6] Martin Luther, *Lectures on Romans*, trans. and ed. Wilhelm Pauck (Louisville, KY: Westminster John Knox, 1961), 159.

[7] Observed by Mark G. Brett, *Genesis: Procreation and the Politics of Identity* (New York: Routledge, 2000), 39. Gen 3:16 (NRSV) states that the woman's pain in childbearing would be "increased" such that she would now give birth "in pain." Likewise, the man would now work the ground "in [painful] toil."

[8] Noted by John Goldingay, *Genesis*, Baker Commentary on the Old Testament: Pentateuch (Grand Rapids, MI: Baker Academic, 2020), 126.

[9] Walter Brueggemann, *Genesis*, Interpretation (Louisville, KY: Westminster John Knox, 1982), 77.

Violence hurt God. God's commitment to involvement in creation came at a price—a very high price. Genesis uses the verb *'atsav* to describe the pain and distress Dinah's brothers felt after she was raped (Gen 34:7). Their horror-filled pain at this outrageously violent act mirrors God's earlier response to the violence that ripped through creation.[10]

According to the author of Genesis, God was not dispassionately removed from creation in a detached "governance" capacity. Nor was he merely annoyed by the boisterous noise of humans who dared to rob him of sleep, as in the Mesopotamian flood account in the *Enuma Elish*. No, God so bound himself to creation that its state affected God's self. He had resolved from the beginning to become present in the world's formlessness; he shared his power with humanity; he revealed himself through his image-bearers. So it is without surprise that he felt the pain of creation's collapse. God's response is akin to his pained grief over Israel's waywardness.

> "Is not Ephraim my dear son,
>   the child in whom I delight?
> Though I often speak against him,
>   I still remember him.
> Therefore my heart yearns for him;
>   I have great compassion for him,"
>   declares the Lord. (Jer 31:20)

The phrase "my heart yearns for him" can be translated "my heart moans for him." As Brueggemann notes, "God's heart is profoundly torn."[11]

The pain of God's heart may also be tied to his decision to *ruin* creation in Genesis 6:7. According to the logic of the story, God's decision to ruin creation was unavoidable. Violence had rotted creation's core. Demolition was the only option if creation was to have a future. God didn't come to this decision out of anger.[12] In fact, the flood story never mentions divine anger. Instead, God's grief takes center stage. The picture accords with the words of Lamentations, that God does not willingly afflict or grieve anyone

---

[10]Credit to Michael Rhodes for pointing out the link with Gen 34:7.

[11]Walter Brueggemann, *A Commentary on Jeremiah: Exile and Homecoming* (Grand Rapids, MI: Eerdmans, 1998), 287.

[12]It should be noted that Is 54:7-10 seems to interpret the destructive flood in terms of an act of "brief" anger that is utterly overwhelmed by God's enduring and steadfast love.

(Lam 3:33). Or as Ezekiel states, God takes "no pleasure in the death of the wicked" (Ezek 33:11). Turning creation back to formlessness may have been part of God's consequent will—which follows from certain conditions—but it was certainly not part of his antecedent will (God's original plan).[13]

God *witnesses* creation's collapse and *facilitates* its collapse. Talk about a paradox! The *Creator* God ruins *creation*. Genesis 6:13 records God's resolve:

> And God said to Noah,
> "The end of all flesh has come before me,
> for violence has filled the earth because of them.
> So, behold I am about to ruin them with the earth." (my translation)

God decides to ruin what he already declared "ruined."

Is God off the hook for his actions because he feels grief?

As I suggested above, the kind of ruining that God does is qualitatively different from the kind of ruin brought about by violence. Violence ruined a good creation, contrary to God's purposes. By contrast, the Great Flood facilitates the possibility of renewal. The termite-ridden house needed to be pulled down *so that* rebuilding could occur.

The flood story contains hints that something else is at work. God returns creation to its pre-creation state of watery formlessness (Gen 1:2)— the kind of formlessness that's suitable for re-creation. God acts as a potter, who sits at the spinning wheel and discovers that his clay pot is full of air bubbles and thinning walls. The wet pot has begun to collapse under its thin walls, and the clay is thoroughly corrupted by air bubbles. In fact, as he looks, he sees its sides peel away and start flapping around as the pot spins on the wheel. It is useless. Utterly ruined . . . by violence.

So, what does the potter do? He stops the wheel and takes the clay into his hands. He forms a new ball of clay out of the old. He returns the clay back to a state of *useful formlessness*. The potter returns the clay to this pre-formed state *in order to remake it*.

---

[13]On God's consequent and antecedent will, see Roger E. Olson, *Arminian Theology: Myths and Realities* (Downers Grove, IL: InterVarsity Press, 2009), 123.

God's watery response reveals more than his destructive power. To see this, we will look further at God's *creative* response in the next chapter.

EXCURSUS: THE FLOOD AND HISTORY

Are we meant to read this story as a literal description of something God did in history?

I've already suggested that the story emphasizes God's creation-preserving acts, and not *his* violence. Violence is what destroyed creation. I recognize that this interpretation leaves some questions unresolved. One of which is whether such a flood ever happened. It matters a great deal if the flood happened as it is described in the book of Genesis. Let me offer several comments on this matter:

- Flood stories much older than Israel's "floated" around among Israel's neighbors from as early as 2700 BCE. We can detect distinct echoes of flood stories like those found throughout Mesopotamia (Sumerian King List, Eridu Genesis, Atrahasis, Gilgamesh, or Enuma Elish) in Israel's flood story.[14] These other stories may suggest the shared memories of localized cataclysmic events, like the periodic flooding of the Tigris river region, that storytellers draw from when speaking about watery new beginnings.[15] Israel participates in this world by drawing from the flood story's basic structure but then engaging it critically and creatively, asking us to look at the story *this* way.[16] For instance, Yahweh is the only God in the Great Flood. There's no distinction between the divine antagonist sending the flood and the protagonist who saves the hero and animals in a boat.

- The story itself suggests a nonliteral (or at least noncosmic) event. For instance, Cain's descendants are allegedly the progenitors of all

---

[14]Christopher B. Hays, *Hidden Riches: A Sourcebook for the Comparative Study of the Hebrew Bible and Ancient Near East* (Louisville, KY: Westminster John Knox, 2014), 75-96.

[15]Alan Dundes, ed., *The Flood Myth* (Berkeley, CA: University of California Press, 1988); Y. S. Chen, *The Primeval Flood Catastrophe: Origins and Early Development in Mesopotamian Traditions* (Oxford: Oxford University Press, 2013); Irving Finkel, *The Ark Before Noah: Decoding the Story of the Flood* (London: Hodder & Stoughton, 2014).

[16]As argued by Walter Moberly, "On Interpreting the Mind of God," in *The Word Leaps the Gap: Essays on Scripture and Theology in Honor of Richard B. Hays*, ed. J. Ross Wagner, C. Kavin Rowe, and A. Katherine Grieb (Grand Rapids, MI: Eerdmans, 2008), 48.

nomads and musicians, but they would've been cut off in the flood (Gen 4:20-21). The Nephilim and warriors described in Genesis 6:1-4 exist before and after the flood (Num 13:33).

- There are serious scientific problems with the idea of a global flood that covered the earth's highest mountains, as well as the water pressure that it would have required, and so on. The backdrop to this story may include the memory of local (yet major) floods that often inundated the land between the Tigris and Euphrates rivers.[17]

- The story was written before humans knew that there are approximately 6.5 million land species in the world. The idea that they all fit into a 107,000-square-foot ark stretches credulity. That would've required about 0.2 square inches per species, or 0.1 square inches per animal, before even considering their food needs or offspring![18]

Does this all mean that the story isn't true? By no means! Instead, we take seriously what the authors of this story are trying to communicate. Jesus refers to a man who went down to Jericho and was robbed and left for dead. He was passed by a Levite, priest, until a Samaritan showed him pity. Asking, "But is it true? Did it *really happen*?" misses the point. It may not be literal. But it's still *true* if understood in terms of its literary genre.

In a similar way, the Genesis flood story uses a popular cultural story of a great flood (employing the genre of founding or primordial stories) that usually featured violence between gods to tell the story of one God whose purposes for creation could not ultimately be thwarted. The Great Flood story may have roots in the accounts of regional floods that occurred in ancient Mesopotamia. But the story's message and truthfulness doesn't depend on us pinning down those details with certainty. Genesis wants us to know that it's *violence*, and not *God*, that ruins creation. God persists in preserving the creation he loves. Helen Paynter highlights the rhetorical

---

[17]For a brief, helpful discussion, see Eric H. Cline, *Biblical Archaeology: A Very Short Introduction* (New York: Oxford University Press, 2009), 73-75.

[18]Those who argue for a literal ark and global flood are quick to point out that the text only claims that two of every "kind" entered the ark, and not two of every species. But this distinction is faulty since the Hebrew *min* refers to every type or species of animal. Biblical writers were not being scientifically precise, and they certainly didn't mean anything akin to biological designations like "phylum," "class," "order," "family," or "genus."

purposes of this story: "God appears, for a time, to lose the battle with the forces [of violence] that oppose him. But out of the carnage emerges a man—the one blameless man—into a new-created world, to be the progenitor of a new humanity [and creation]." Paynter fills in the theological point: "God works in patterns, and this is an imperfect rendering of the pattern that is wholly realised in the cross and resurrection of Jesus Christ."[19] The story can still communicate these powerful theological truths by reworking a known cultural story.

In sum, the writer of Genesis transposes a familiar flood story into a new key to tell us something important about God's ultimate triumph over creation-destroying violence in a time when it seems that violent chaos had the upper hand.

---

[19]Helen Paynter, *God of Violence Yesterday, God of Love Today? Wrestling Honestly with the Old Testament* (Eugene, OR: Wipf & Stock, 2019), 95.

6

SHALOM REDUX

In that day I will make a covenant for them
with the beasts of the field, the birds in the sky
and the creatures that move along the ground.
Bow and sword and battle
I will abolish from the land,
so that all may lie down in safety.

HOSEA 2:18, NIV MODIFIED

IN EARLIER CHAPTERS, we noted that Genesis 1–2 portray shalom as God's purpose and ideal for the world from the beginning. The story from Genesis 3–8 details the rapid unraveling of God's peace-engendering purposes. It seemed that violence had the upper hand. Darkness was over the watery deep. We're back in a world that looked much like the time *before* God separated the waters above from the waters below (Gen 1:6-7): "In the six hundredth year of Noah's life, on the seventeenth day of the second month—on that day *all the springs of the great deep* burst forth, and the *floodgates of the heavens* were opened" (Gen 7:11).

The waters above and the waters below let loose, blotting out all life upon the earth. Once God secures Noah & Co. in the ark (Gen 7:9), we don't hear from God until he begins restoring creation. Genesis 7:11 doesn't attribute this watery chaos to God. We know from Genesis 6 that the flood was God's decision (Gen 6:7, 13, 17), but Genesis 7 mutes that point. God's resolution is simply to let creation run its course:

"Everything on dry land that had the breath of life in its nostrils died" (Gen 7:22).

God withdraws the divine life-support system that kept creation going in its ruined state. He stops propping up the already ruined walls of his pottery. If God is involved, it is only to facilitate the consequences of creation's violence.[1] He allows violence to destroy itself while preserving the seeds of a new creation in the ark.

The first explicit reference to divine action during the flood event itself highlights God's re-creative, and not his destructive, work.[2] Echoing Genesis 1:2, we read, "But *God remembered Noah and all the wild animals and the livestock* that were with him in the ark, and he sent a wind (or 'Spirit,' Heb. *ruah*) over the earth, and the waters receded" (Gen 8:1).

This verse casts light back on the significance of the flood itself. God brought the flood to prepare the way for a new creation. Brown captures this moment well:

> The flood is creation's counterpart, a once perfect creation beset by a "perfect storm" at God's behest. . . . The flood has the focused aim of bringing creation back to the drawing board by means of a *controlled* cosmic meltdown, or more accurately, dissolution. Chaos, consequently, cannot be identified wholly with water.[3]

Brown's point is that water was not primarily a destructive agent. Violence was. Water was just a way of enacting a *"controlled* cosmic meltdown" to return the clay of creation back to useful formlessness.

Afterward, the potter began to re-form the world by his Spirit-breath, as in the beginning (Gen 8:1).

GOD REMEMBERS

Genesis 8:1 brings together two important ideas. First, "God remembered." This is covenant language, harkening back to when God told Noah his

---

[1] Terence E. Fretheim, *God and World in the Old Testament: A Relational Theology of Creation* (Nashville: Abingdon Press, 2010), 79-82.
[2] Gen 8:1 occurs at the structural midpoint of the flood narrative. See Gordon J. Wenham, "The Coherence of the Flood Narrative," *Vetus Testamentum* 28, no. 3 (1978): 336-48.
[3] William P. Brown, *The Ethos of the Cosmos: The Genesis of Moral Imagination in the Bible* (Grand Rapids, MI: Eerdmans, 1999), 59.

intention to flood the earth. "But with you," God had promised to make a covenant (Gen 6:18). He doesn't say what that covenant involved, except that it required Noah entering the ark with delegates from the whole animal kingdom. The point of the promised covenant seems to be that God would preserve a microcosm of creation in the ark. The seemingly innocuous phrase "God remembered Noah and all the wild animals and the livestock" (Gen 8:1) signals God's active interest in maintaining this covenant initiated in Genesis 6:18.

Further, God "made a *ruah* blow over the earth" (Gen 8:1, my translation), just as his *ruah* (wind/breath/spirit) swooped down over the deeps in Genesis 1:2 and later blew over the Reedy Sea as Israel crossed (Ex 14:21). The combined message in this verse is that the covenant God saves and re-creates. As Ellen Davis points out, covenantal re-membering is about healing the wounds of creation.

We read as much in Leviticus: "Then will I *remember* my covenant with Jacob; I will *remember* also my covenant with Isaac and also my covenant with Abraham, *and I will remember the land*" (Lev 26:42, NRSV).[4] When we hear that God *remembered* Noah and the animals, we're not to imagine that God suddenly recalled something forgotten. Instead, God is making good on something promised (Gen 6:18) and restoring something broken. Re-membering addresses violent sins of the past against the land and its creatures, and mends what was broken. God remembers Noah and his creatures in an act that leads him to care for them and prepare the earth for renewal.

After God's Spirit-breath swept over the waters, dry land appeared (Gen 8:13). A new creation had begun.

The story makes a powerful point. *God is at work healing creation from the wounds of violence through his covenant partners.* Here are three specific ways that this healing work continues after the flood.

VACCINATION

Since the coronavirus pandemic, it's ever clearer that vaccinations are essential to human flourishing. We need something to protect us from the

---

[4]Ellen F. Davis, *Scripture, Culture, and Agriculture: An Agrarian Reading of the Bible* (New York: Cambridge University Press, 2009), 84.

worst effects of the Covid-19 virus. It's no less the case for creation, according to Genesis.

If God is the potter in the flood story, he's the physician afterward. We see God promising to protect creation *despite* the persistent problem of human sin. This constitutes a kind of inoculation. Creation needs God's sustaining protection against the pathogens of violence that followed Noah and his family into the ark. Notice God's words here:

> As long as the earth's days,
> seedtime and harvest,
> cold and heat,
> summer and harvest
> day and night,
> will not cease. (Gen 8:22, my translation)

Maintaining the to and fro of days and seasons is only possible through divine intervention. Otherwise, violence would destroy the earth again.

God also determined that he would "never again curse the *ground* because of humans" (Gen 8:21).[5] This verse is radical. It suggests that the words of Noah's father Lamech would transpire:

> This one! He'll comfort us
> from our labor,
> from the anxious toil of our hands,
> *from the earth which Yahweh cursed.* (Gen 5:29, my translation)

The idea that God *removed* the curse may sounds surprising. After all, the problems that existed before the flood seem to persist long after! While this is true, God's response to persistent sin and violence was different after the flood. Rather than allowing creation to shrivel completely in response to sin and violence (and reach another tipping point), God protected creation by removing the curse. We see further evidence for the removal of the land curse by comparing Genesis 4:12 with Genesis 8:21:

---

[5]Some interpreters insist that God would not *further* curse the ground. Yet from the perspective of Gen 8:21, no such idea is in view. I discuss this in detail in my book *Portraying Violence in the Hebrew Bible: A Literary and Cultural Study* (New York: Cambridge University Press, 2020), 78-80.

When you work *the ground* it will *no longer* yield its strength to you. (Gen 4:12, my translation)

No longer will I curse *the ground* on account of humankind. (Gen 8:21, my translation)

The reversed word order of the same phrases in Genesis 8:21 reflects a principle that scholars call Seidel's Law. According to this principle, ancient authors would cite one text but reverse the word order to indicate reuse. In Genesis 4:12, God tells Cain that the ground would no longer yield produce. This spelling-out of its cursed state signals the beginning of the end for the earth. Yet after the flood, Yahweh states that he'd no longer do this. God confronts the land-related problem of violence head on. God also resolves to never again "strike down" (**nakah*) humankind (Gen 8:21, my translation). This evokes God's resolve to exact vengeance on any who would "strike down" (Heb. *nakah*) Cain (Gen 4:15, my translation).[6] The ground-destroying curse is reversed.[7]

By removing the curse and sustaining the seasons, God would ensure creation's survival no matter what viruses of violence came its way. Violence would still sting, but it would not have the last word. *Yahweh resolved to sustain creation in the face of human corruption.* As Goldingay notes, "Humanity will continue to exist on account of God's mercy, not on account of its deserving."[8]

But this raises questions, especially considering the caveats in Genesis 9:11 and 9:15 that God would never again destroy the earth *with water*. Does God keep asteroid collisions, cosmic conflagrations, super-volcanic eruptions, or a new ice age in his back pocket as possible future options for destroying the earth, and just not a great flood? Does God backpedal on his earlier claims that God would always sustain the earth (Gen 8:22)?

Certainly not! Watery formlessness—or a Great Flood—is the ancient way of expressing "un-createdness." God is saying that he'd never again

---

[6] I discuss this text in Lynch, *Portraying Violence*, 80-81.

[7] John Goldingay, *Genesis*, Baker Commentary on the Old Testament: Pentateuch (Grand Rapids, MI: Baker Academic, 2020), 150, thinks that because Gen 8:21 uses a different word for "curse" than Gen 3:17-19 (*qalal* instead of *'arar*), the text "is not referring to an abrogation of the curse." However, his analysis doesn't account for the close affinities between Gen 8:21 and Gen 4:12, and the reversal of the land's absolute hardening in response to human violence.

[8] Goldingay, *Genesis*, 151.

uncreate the world. He's fully committed to *this* creation despite the ongoing problem of violence.

FROM SEVENFOLD TO ONEFOLD

God's second response to violence addresses the need for equivalent justice.[9] After stating God's commitment to keeping creation intact despite human sin, God expresses a desire for societal justice. God would ensure like-for-like punishment for bloodshed. At this point in the story, God only says that *he* would maintain justice. But whereas earlier he promised sevenfold vengeance for anyone who killed Cain (Gen 4:15), now he'd maintain equivalent justice. Here's what God says in the first half of Genesis 9:6, in its mirror arrangement (my translation):

> A Whoever *sheds*
> > B the *blood*
> > > C of *the human*
> > > C′ in exchange for *the human*
> > B′ his *blood*
> A′ will be *shed*

This verse gives careful expression to the principle of equivalence. None should expect (or take) sevenfold vengeance for violence. Instead, *justice* would characterize God's dealings in the world.

The verse restricts the management of equivalent justice to God. God's declaration takes the form of a tightly structured proverb. Proverbs describe underlying principles that sustain the world. Nothing in this proverb suggests that God gives *humans* the power to take the life of the perpetrator. God's not yet saying what humans *should* do, but the implication of the verse is that humans *shouldn't* seek vengeance. Genesis 9:6 should be translated: "Whoever sheds the blood of a human, *in exchange for* that human shall his blood be shed," and not "*by a human* shall his blood be shed."[10]

---

[9]A version of this section was published on Scot McKnight's *Christianity Today* blog. Matthew J. Lynch, "Timing, BLM, and the Death Penalty," *Jesus Creed* (blog), June 22, 2020, www.christianity today.com/scot-mcknight/2020/june/timing-blm-and-death-penalty.html. I've reused elements of that blog post here with permission.

[10]Jacob Milgrom, *Leviticus 1–16*, Anchor Yale Bible Commentary 3 (New Haven, CT: Yale University Press, 1998), 705.

That right to avenge—as in the story of Cain—lies solely in God's hands. But unlike Cain's sevenfold vengeance, post-flood vengeance is proportionate. It's just.

While God later gives Israel the right to take life as punishment for murder (e.g., Ex 21:23; Num 35:31; Deut 19:21), these creation laws that govern the nations (Genesis 9) don't grant that right. Genesis 9 addresses *God's* right to address bloodshed in the post-flood world. The proverb doesn't hand humans or the state power over life and death.[11] A full understanding of how and why the law in Israel legitimates state violence against murderers cannot be pursued here. What we can say is that a proper understanding of Genesis needs to be the starting point from which we try to understand those later passages, and not the other way around.[12]

We also note that God will not always exercise that right. Sometimes he would choose not to exercise that right, as he did with Cain, and does later with Moses and David. It's best to see this passage within the broader biblical "vengeance-is-mine-not-yours" tradition since God is the sole actor here. Power over life and death belongs in God's hands (Lev 19:18; 1 Sam 26:9-11; Rom 12:19; 1 Thess 4:6), and we're not to take it.[13]

Other parts of the Old Testament make the same point. In the same breath that Leviticus 19:18 prohibits revenge, it commends love for neighbor, a point that Jesus clearly recognizes (Mt 22:39; Mk 12:31). This tradition seeks to limit the human propensity to take excess vengeance, seeks to promote neighborliness and protection for the vulnerable, and seeks to leave the avenging of murder in God's hands.

In another symmetrically arranged proverb that seems to draw its inspiration from Genesis 9:6, Jesus challenges us to consider what would happen if humans *did* take the divine prerogatives of Genesis 9 for themselves:

---

[11]There are other reasons to question the use of Gen 9 in support of capital punishment. See Michael L. Westmoreland-White and Glen H. Stassen, "Biblical Perspectives on the Death Penalty," in *Religion and the Death Penalty: A Call for Reckoning*, eds. Erik C. Owens, John D. Carlson, and Eric P. Elshtain (Grand Rapids, MI: Eerdmans, 2004), 123-38.

[12]Thanks to Michael Rhodes for helping me articulate this point.

[13]Rom 13:4 gives a limited exception to this general point. For a discussion of this text, see Esau McCaulley, *Reading While Black* (Downers Grove, IL: InterVarsity Press, 2020), 47-70.

A For all
  B who take a sword
  B' by a sword
A' will be destroyed. (Mt 26:52, my translation)

In short, Genesis 9 responds to violence by establishing the principle of proportionate justice and by warning the violent that their acts will be called to account by God. Human life is precious. This part of the story also informs us that sevenfold vengeance will no longer be God's way in the world. Vengeance belongs with God, and he may (or may not) choose to take it.

An Eternal Arms Reduction Treaty

I can recall with vivid clarity the fear and anxiety I felt as a young American boy at the prospect of a nuclear war with the Soviet Union. Even though I grew up in the age of *Perestroika* and *Glasnost*, the residual fear of impending nuclear war between the United States and the USSR remained. While long after the fraught Khrushchev years, it's sobering to remember that the last nuclear weapons test in the United States was in 1992 at the Nevada Test Site. Nearly every night I would pray that God would prevent a nuclear apocalypse. I even took batteries and taped them into a toilet paper roll with a fuse out the end in case I needed to fight Soviets from my treehouse.

Military strategy was not in my future.

It was with great relief, then, that in my junior high years I learned of the START treaty—the STrategic Arms Reduction Treaty between the United Stated and the Soviet Union. I read about it with great interest and even wrote a report on it for my current events class. This bilateral treaty, signed in 1991, was the largest and most ambitious arms treaty of its day.[14] To my young mind, this treaty signaled the beginning of answered prayers, the hope of a world without nuclear war (though, paradoxically, I always hoped that the United States would retain the upper hand in nuclear stockpiles). While it may come as no small comfort, it led to the reduction of the global

---

[14]START I expired in 2009, and a New START treaty was signed by Barack Obama and Dmitri Medvedev in 2010 and is still in effect. See www.state.gov/new-start/, accessed June 7, 2022.

nuclear warhead stockpile from about seventy thousand in 1985 to around fifteen thousand today, around an 80-percent reduction.

The ongoing threat of nuclear war looms as I edit this chapter. Russian President Vladimir Putin has put his nuclear deterrence forces on notice.[15] European and North American allies fear the risk of escalating the Ukraine war into an international nuclear war. The need for *full* disarmament is ever urgent.

So, when I read the post-flood stories in Genesis 8–9, I see a disarmament process. If in Genesis 9:3-6, God asks humans to lay down their arms against their fellow image bearers, in Genesis 9:8-17 God makes a covenant with all creation to lay down *his* weapons. While God's *covenant* was irrevocable, it follows on the heels of a call for humans to forsake violence. God initiates a kind of START treaty with all creation in Genesis 9:8-17. Since Genesis 1–11 provides us with a pair of lenses for viewing the problem of violence in *all Scripture*, then these verses are crucial. They tell us about God's ongoing efforts to establish peace in the wake of the Great Flood.

Let's look at this treaty's key features.

First, God vows never again to ruin creation with a flood. As noted earlier, a cosmic flood does not just symbolize one type of natural disaster. The Great Flood (with a capital 'F') was a shorthand way of referring to the undoing of creation. God would *never again* destroy creation.

God's promise recalls his earlier promise: "*Never again* will I curse the ground because of humans. . . . And *never again* will I destroy all living creatures, as I have done" (Gen 8:21, NIV modified). God commits himself eternally to the well-being of creation. What a promise!

A second resolve of Yahweh's START initiative is to make a covenant with all creation for all generations. This is no humans-only covenant. God commits himself forever to Noah and his descendants, and to "every living creature of all flesh . . . for all generations to come" (Gen 9:12, my translation). Put simply, God makes a permanent covenant with the earth and

---

[15]Al Jazeera and Other News Agencies, "Putin Puts Russia's Nuclear Deterrent Forces on Alert," Al Jazeera, February 2, 2022, www.aljazeera.com/news/2022/2/27/putin-puts-russias-nuclear -deterrent-forces-on-alert.

its creatures (Gen 9:15). This casts doubt on any end-times scenario that would see the world destroyed.[16]

But what does this covenant include? Is it just a commitment to never destroy? Not if we keep Genesis 9:1-7 in view. God had just commanded Noah to "be fruitful and multiply, abound on the earth and multiply in it." God commissions Noah as a second Adam to live in a way that reflects the life-promoting rule of God. God then promises to create the conditions for humanity, and therefore all creation, to become what it was supposed to be (Gen 9:8-18). Violence would never again destroy the earth.

Third, God lays down his bow in the clouds as a "sign" of the covenant. It's like a visual guarantee. The Hebrew term that is translated rainbow in many English translations (Gen 9:13, 14, 16) blunts the force of the image here. The Hebrew term is "bow," a weapon. This is the same word used throughout the Old Testament for the arrow-shooting weapon of war and hunt.[17] And this bow points upward toward God. When God says, "I have set my bow in the clouds" God is essentially saying: "I swear on my own life."

This "sign of the covenant" was thus a poignant reminder that even when rain clouds gather (Gen 9:14), God would never again destroy creation with a flood. God disarmed. And God will protect. In fact, he embedded the sign of his disarmament and protection within the very clouds that would sometimes threaten destruction. *As in his covenant with Cain, this is a covenant of protection from the ruinous effects of violence. The sign* of the covenant tells us something about the nature of this covenant. With Cain, God put a "sign" on him to show that he was ending the cycle of vengeance that threatened to spiral out of control (Gen 4:15). Here God gives another, more enduring sign. He laid down his bow and transformed it into a colorful sign of peace and hope—the two predominant

---

[16]For a fuller treatment, see J. Richard Middleton, *A New Heaven and A New Earth: Reclaiming Biblical Eschatology* (Grand Rapids, MI: Baker Academic, 2014).

[17]See Ellen van Wolde, "One Bow or Another? A Study of the Bow in Genesis 9:17-26," *Vetus Testamentum* 63 (2013): 124-49. Van Wolde's study rightly draws attention to the consistent use of *qeshet* to describe the warrior's bow. Less convincing is her argument that in this scene God is handing over his bow of dominion and power to humanity. On the bow in the sky in light of *Enuma Elish*, see B. F. Batto, "Creation Theology in Genesis," in *Creation in the Biblical Traditions*, ed. Richard J. Clifford and John J. Collins (Washington, DC: Catholic Biblical Association of America, 1992), 33-34. Assyrian reliefs would sometimes include a bow to signal peace or hostility between the king and someone in his presence.

characteristics of his covenant with creation. He would protect creation from ever again collapsing.

CONCLUSIONS

The Bible's early narratives give us lenses for viewing the rest of the story. The rest of the Bible has its fair share of violence. It's easy to become disoriented in that fog of violence and lose sight of the Bible's original vision for shalom. But when we do, it helps to recall Jesus' words about another matter, "It was not this way from the beginning" (Mt 19:8). The *beginning* of the story provides us with Scripture's vision for where things *ought* to be headed.

Genesis 1 portrays a world where violence isn't necessary for the world's flourishing. In fact, violence is anti-creation. Violence is Enemy No. 1, which becomes clear as the story of Genesis 1–11 unfolds. That story tells of a violent struggle to come (Gen 3:15), of sibling violence (Gen 4:1-16), of gratuitous violence (Gen 4:23-24), of violence against women (Gen 6:1-4), and of creation-consuming violence (Gen 6:11). Genesis wants us to understand that violence is diametrically opposed to God's good purposes in creation.

The Great Flood represents the tragic climax of violence that ultimately ruined creation. And lest we think that God fell victim to the processes of violence, Genesis maintains, paradoxically, that *God* also brought the floodwaters of destruction. In the words of Terence Fretheim, God "mediates [and directs] the consequences of sin that are already present in the situation" through the destructive force of the Great Flood.[18] The flood was the end and natural result of violence.

But God's purposes were ultimately against violence.

God decided to let the floodwaters burst forth and rain down to return the earth to a state of *useful formlessness.* Then, brooding over those wild waters God "remembered" his covenant with the earth and began to recreate (Gen 8:1).

God's post-flood responses address the problem of violence at its roots. Violence is a creation-consuming problem, as it is throughout the Old Testament. So, God's responses were creation-wide. He promised to inoculate

---

[18]Terence E. Fretheim, "God and Violence in the Old Testament," *Word & World* 24, no. 1 (2004): 24.

creation from the worst effects of violence. He'd uphold the cycles of creation to ensure that human evil would never again cause its ruin. God established the legal principle of proportionate justice to govern human and animal worlds. God made a covenant to ensure that all creation would be able to fulfill its purpose, leading ultimately toward a community of shalom. As a sign of this covenant, God laid down his weapon to mark his commitment to creation's well-being.

Seeing God give up his fighting weapon gives us a chance to pause in wonder. The Creator God is so committed to his creation that he'd sooner point the bow at his own heart than see his creation overturned again. God's dedication to creation—even to God's own hurt—ripples through the pages of Scripture. Hosea gives us an analogous picture when speaking about God's dedication to his wayward son Israel. Though he had every right to turn in hostile judgment toward his rebellious son, God turns from wrath, he says, "for I am God, and not man" (Hos 11:9). His divine character leads him toward compassion. He decides against the path of judgment. He *cannot* treat his people like Admah and Zeboyim—two cities God had "overturned" in judgment (Deut 29:23). God tells his rebellious son that he would sooner be "overturned" than see Israel "overturned" (Hos 11:8). This is a God who takes wrath on himself to move in compassion toward his people. God's turn toward his people is costly. God says, "I am overturned" as he extends mercy toward his beloved son. This is a God who pursues his children and when faced with the prospect of seeing them overturned, allows himself to be overturned instead. This is the God of Noah and the God of the cross, who instead of seeing creation overturned takes the arrow in his own heart. This God eventually enters the floodwaters of baptism and death to fulfill all righteousness with his own life (Lk 3:21-22; Rom 6:4).

AND MORE: THE OLD TESTAMENT GOSPEL OF PEACE

We've seen that the beginning of the biblical story (Gen 1–11) promotes peace and sees violence as a major threat to God's purposes for creation. Genesis puts violence at the heart of all that opposes creation after the first act of rebellion. To that end, violence is one of *the* major problems that God works to address in his subsequent dealings with humanity and creation. Not surprisingly, the beginning and end of the biblical story foreground shalom. We could also talk about the *end* of the story as the Old Testament sees it. The long arc of history bends toward peace, according to the Old Testament.[19] Isaiah envisions a day when the wolf would dwell with the lamb (Is 11:6; 65:25), and no one would injure or destroy on Mount Zion (Is 65:25). The nations would stream to Jerusalem to learn how *not* to have war as they turn their weapons into garden tools (Is 2:4). When it seemed that all was lost, God would once again enact a Noah-like covenant with Israel. "I have sworn not to be angry with you," God says, and "never to rebuke you again." God would enact his covenant of peace and never remove his steadfast love (Is 54:10). And that's just Isaiah![20]

This prophetic vision of shalom is gospel. In fact, the phrase "good news" comes from Isaiah:

> How beautiful on the mountains
> are the feet of those who bring good news,
> *who proclaim peace,*
> who bring good tidings,
> who proclaim salvation,
> who say to Zion,
> "Your God reigns!" (Is 52:7)[21]

Jesus' announcement of "the good news of the kingdom" (Mt 4:23) aligns him with the likes of Isaiah, who announced the arrival of God's reign and his dominion of peace. The gospel of peace (Acts 10:36; Eph 6:15) has deep Old Testament roots.

As Strawn notes, "This arc of nonviolence indicates that something 'in-between' the peaceful bookends has gone terribly wrong; the 'in-between'

---

[19]Discussed in Brent A. Strawn, *Lies My Preacher Told Me: An Honest Look at the Old Testament* (Louisville, KY: Westminster John Knox, 2021), 43.

[20]Bernard F. Batto, "The Covenant of Peace: A Neglected Ancient Near Eastern Motif," *Catholic Biblical Quarterly* 49, no. 2 (1987): 187-211.

[21]The phrase "good news" appears first in Is 40:9-11 and also appears in Is 41:27; 60:6). Frederick J. Gaiser, "The Gospel According to Isaiah," *Word & World* 38, no. 3 (2018): 239-51; Steve Moyise and Maarten J. J. Menken. *Isaiah in the New Testament: The New Testament and the Scriptures of Israel* (New York: T&T Clark, 2005); John F. A. Sawyer, "The Gospel According to Isaiah," *Expository Times* 113, no. 2 (2001): 39-43; Matthew Seufert, "Isaiah's Herald," *Westminster Theological Journal* 77 (2015): 219-35.

is marked by violence, but it was not originally so, neither is it to be so, again, in the end."[22] The violence in between—as much as it may be to confront— is not how things *ought to be* from a biblical perspective.

Moreover, the prophetic vision is that God's response to violence is not just to enact justice for wrongs done, or to return creation back to its original state. The prophetic vision of a peaceful end *exceeds* the glory of God's original creation. God would one day restore double for the sufferings his people endured. Once again, Isaiah: "Instead of your [exilic] shame *you will have a* double *portion* [of blessing]" (Is 61:7, NASB italics original; cf. Joel 2:25-26). A superabundance of shalom marks the surprising restoration of Israel's, and ultimately creation's, fortunes.

Our task now is to consider one of those "in between" stories: the conquest. There are hard realities to confront here, but my plea is that we read it as a story "in between" the shalom of creation's beginning and the surpassing shalom that the prophets foretold.

---

[22]Strawn, *Lies*, 43.

PART THREE

READING JOSHUA

WITH YESHUA

I ONCE WENT THROUGH THE ONLINE HELL of applying for a work visa so that my family could move to England. I was about to start my previous job at Westminster Theological Centre. I'm convinced that the UK put three fortress walls and two large moats between me and any human being, leaving me to "choose your own adventure" by navigating sometimes-contradictory web pages. But soldier on I did, eventually reaching a live human being (via phone) at the British Consulate in Philadelphia.

The consulate officer asked me why I was moving to England, to which I replied that I'd be teaching the Old Testament at a theological college. "Ahhh!" he began his tirade, "Violence! Bloodshed! Anger! Judgement! Hail-stones!" On and on he went. I laughed (a coping mechanism) in response and mumbled something about it being more complicated than that. And while his tirade may sound excessive, his stereotype is common. He had already settled the question of the Old Testament's preeminent qualities.

I often begin my Old Testament courses with a question like, *What are your immediate reactions when you think about "The God of the Old Testament"?* Christian students will frequently use terms like the British Consulate officer. I'm used to that. One student put it this way: "I often turn to Jesus to get away from the God of the Old Testament." This student was aware of the theological contradiction but didn't know a way out that didn't involve leaving the Old Testament behind. It's why many people avoid the Old Testament. Better to let it rest unopened than face some potentially faith-destroying truths. We're followers of *Jesus*, and not the Bible, strictly speaking. Such Christians don't want anyone, and certainly not the author of Leviticus, Joshua, or Jeremiah to mess with the beauty of God that they experience in Jesus. I get that.

But cracks soon form.

For those who feel that their image of God is cracking because of violent texts, I hope that our journey through Joshua will prove helpful.

We'll do so with our christological hats firmly in place. As my colleague Bob Ekblad says, "We need to read the Old Testament with Jesus as our Rabbi." How should we do so with this book about Jesus' namesake? The Greek name for Jesus and Joshua is the same (*Iēsous*) after all.

The following chapters move us from flood to fury in pursuit of that question. Whereas the Great Flood raises questions about God's general violence toward all creation, the conquest fury of Joshua presents the problem of specific violence toward Canaanite men, women, children, and animals. The problems of violence seem to intensify, since God commands Israel to carry out acts of merciless violence. It all feels very close to the ground. You can still visit Jericho, touch its rocks, envision the scenes of horror from the book.

However, I'm convinced that Joshua holds good news . . . and not that the Canaanites are now gone! There's so much to see.

7

WIELDING THE SWORD

JOSHUA'S VIOLENCE IS DISMAYING for many adults. But it's a delight for many kids, especially for those who don't experience much real-world violence. My son once told me Joshua was his favorite book. The ambush of Ai in Joshua 8 sealed the deal. Somehow, when he was five or six, he managed to convince our vicar to let him stand before the church and narrate the story of how Israel defeated the people of Ai. The story is gripping, full of military intrigue. Joshua and the Israelite army lured the people of Ai away from their town, pretending to run in defeat. Then, as Joshua lifted his weapon toward the city, an Israelite ambush leapt out to attack the unarmed city and slaughter its inhabitants. Through it all, Joshua "did not draw back the hand that held out his sword until he had destroyed all who lived in Ai" (Josh 8:26, NIV modified).[1] And with a certain glee, my son then polished off his recitation with this last detail from Joshua: "He impaled the body of the king of Ai on a pole and left it there until evening" (Josh 8:29). The church laughed nervously.

The sword clearly holds symbolic power for the writer of Joshua. It's a symbol of God's assured victories and the Canaanites' assured destruction. It was with the sword, after all, that Israel was going to put to death, "men and women, young and old, cattle, sheep and donkeys" (Josh 6:21). We're going to look at how Joshua portrays weapons in this chapter before we address the killing of Canaanites more directly. We're looking at weapons because later we'll see that Joshua is doing something subversive with them. To spoil the ending here, Joshua later tells Israel that it was "not . . . with

---

[1] The Hebrew term translated "javelin" in the NIV is *kidon*, probably a curved sword or scimitar.

your own sword and bow" that Yahweh gave them the land (Josh 24:12). It was Yahweh's own action.

But we don't know that yet at the beginning. In fact, a tone of assurance pulls the reader in, and could give off an air of "command and conquer" (with weapons). Sword-wielding plus divine assurances seem like the perfect recipe for a successful conquest. God commissioned Joshua to lead the people into the land. He told him that every place he stepped would be his (Josh 1:3), and that "no one will be able to stand against you all the days of your life" (Josh 1:5). That's music to the ears of a new leader, who until now, had lived in the shadow of Moses. The reader may expect to see some Canaanite heads roll as the Israelites sharpen their weapons for war.

WOUNDED BEFORE WAR

The reader is primed for battle . . . except that Joshua doesn't even mention weapons until much later in the story. And the very first time the people use weapons (literally "flint swords") it's against themselves. Yup, it's there in the text, right after they cross the Jordan: "The LORD said to Joshua, 'Make flint knives and circumcise the Israelites again.' So Joshua made flint knives and circumcised the Israelites at Gibeath Haaraloth (a.k.a. 'Hill of the Foreskins')" (Josh 5:2-3).[2]

I want to name the obvious here for a moment. This is not good military strategy (nor is it an endearing geographical name). I can just imagine Joshua addressing his officers: "Gentlemen, tomorrow at dawn we cross the Jordan. And when the enemy least expects it, we'll attack! . . . ourselves . . . with swords, to prepare for war!"

This command follows Joshua's own commissioning in Joshua 1, where he and the people are to prepare for battle by meditating on Torah (Josh 1:8). Their future success depended on their ability to remember, recite, and keep the law. In fact, Joshua's first chapter never mentions weapons, armies, or fortifications. Only the law.

Joshua's command for the people to circumcise themselves undermined any machismo that might've otherwise propelled Israel into battle. No

---

[2]Where the text reads, "circumcise," the Hebrew is literally, "circumcise again," in reference to the second generation. The Greek Septuagint says that God commanded the people to "sit down."

taunting the enemy, scheming battle plans, or any military preparation. Instead, we find circumcision days before battle.[3]

This would have been physically painful and symbolically disempowering. As Mark Buchanan points out, "Circumcision makes a man childlike. It makes him defenseless. It incapacitates him."[4]

We know from earlier in the Bible that circumcision was a way of rendering yourself unfit for battle, vulnerable to attack. In Genesis, Jacob's sons Simeon and Levi promised to let the Canaanite Shechemites keep their captured sister Dinah, *if only they would circumcise themselves* (Gen 34:15). The Shechemites had raped Dinah and were so keen to keep her and potentially acquire other Israelite women that they complied. They walked right into a trap. When the Shechemites were "sore," Simeon and Levi rescued Dinah, massacred every male in Shechem, and plundered the city (Gen 34:25-29).

In short, circumcision renders you impotent in battle.

Circumcision in Joshua becomes a kind of anti-military-strategy. When Joshua calls the people to prepare to cross the Jordan (Josh 1:11) he never mentions preparing weapons. The preparations he mentions were more about worship than war. They ready the ark for crossing the Jordan by consecrating themselves. They ready food for Passover, not for a campaign. They ready themselves by clinging to Torah.

Circumcision plays an important role in this mix. Through the act of circumcision, God "rolled away the stigma of Egypt" (Josh 5:9, my translation).[5] The stigma likely relates to their identity as slaves of an imperial power. By taking on the sign of the covenant with Yahweh, the people said *no* to the slave-branding of Egypt and reidentified as the people of Yahweh.[6]

Accepting that new identity was still humbling, but in a different way. Israel could have repudiated its old identity by saying, "We were once slaves. Now, we're warriors!"

---

[3] The situation is akin to Gideon *reducing* his army in Judges 7.
[4] Mark Buchanan, *The Rest of God: Restoring Your Soul by Restoring Sabbath* (Nashville: Thomas Nelson, 2006), 97.
[5] The verb "rolled away" (Heb. *galal*) sounds like the word Gilgal, hence the name.
[6] Though circumcision was apparently practiced in Egypt (Jer 9:25-26), the Israelites weren't in Egypt. Moreover, the practice took on a new significance within Israel.

But that's not God's way. Instead, God raises up an army who was, from the beginning, marked by this act of self-weakening and reliance on God's deliverance.[7]

For Joshua, the best military strategy is completely nonmilitary in nature. It all relates to the Torah. This shouldn't surprise us, since Joshua begins with a call to meditate on Torah (Josh 1:8). Torah meditation is commended throughout Scripture, and most powerfully in Joshua. Joshua is a guide for later generations of Israel to take seriously the call to put the Torah at the center of their lives. That's why obedience to the law of circumcision was so important, even before battle.

But why was Israel uncircumcised in the first place? Weren't they coming to displace the *uncircumcised*? Circumcision was *the* marker of God's covenant people. It was what sociologists call a "boundary marker." It helped determine who was in and who was out, in the strongest terms. Genesis 17 tells us that any uncircumcised Israelite was to be "cut off" since they have "broken [Yahweh's] covenant" (Gen 17:14). Moreover, for Israel, the term "uncircumcised" was a kind of slur for denigrating enemies. When confronted with Goliath, David asks, "Who is this *uncircumcised* Philistine that he should defy the armies of the living God?" (1 Sam 17:26).

If the name of the game is God's people versus the Canaanites, Israel doesn't come into the land looking very godly. Like their enemy, they lacked the covenant mark. Like their parents, who worshiped the golden calf (Ex 32) and the gods at Peor (Num 25), they were covenant breakers.

Yet there was Israel, in the land and *un*circumcised! Clearly this underscored the unfaithfulness of their *parents* who perished in the wilderness. But it also raises questions about Israel's own connection to the covenant with Yahweh. Why did they wait so late in the game to identify as God's people?

IDOLATORS

The book of Joshua flags another Torah violation at the end of the book. Just as Joshua 5 depicts an uncircumcised Israel, the end of Joshua reveals

---

[7] It's worth recalling Jacob's wounding before his military encounter with his brother Esau. Jacob walks away limping from his wrestling match with God (Gen 32:31), and only then meets Esau and his four hundred men (Gen 33:1-3). Jacob meets him bowing low to the ground, humbled by his divine encounter.

an idolatrous Israel. They were hardly different from the Canaanites they came to dispossess! In his farewell speech, Joshua implores the people to "throw away the gods your ancestors worshiped beyond the Euphrates River and in Egypt, and serve the LORD" (Josh 24:14, NIV modified). To underscore the point, Joshua says it twice more in the same passage (Josh 24:15, 23). This is an astonishing accusation, with potentially far-reaching consequences! To this point, we hadn't been told that Israel worshiped any other gods after the golden calves and the gods at Peor.

But here they are, just like their parents.

The Torah stipulates death-by-stoning for idolaters within Israel (Deut 12:29–13:11). But here Joshua just says, *put them away*. In his wisdom, Joshua discerned the gracious heart of the law that emanated from a God who rarely exacted what the law permitted. Israel's success in the land depended on rooting out their own idolatry as much as it did on eliminating risks from "out there."

Perhaps the point of this story is that the problems Israel encountered were not just "out there." They were also "in here." The line separating good from evil ran through every heart.[8] Just as Israel needed to *become* the circumcised people, they needed to *become* nonidolaters. Torah meditation was greatly needed.

SWORD-WIELDING FRENEMY

Joshua's second sword encounter was equally startling, probably to him as much as to us. Not long after Israel's little stopover at the "Hill of Foreskins"—and fortunately after they'd healed up—the people advanced toward Jericho.

On the night before battle, Joshua was alone in Jericho, probably meditating on the divine assurances earlier given: "I will be with you wherever you go" (three times in Josh 1 alone!) and "Be strong and courageous" (four times in Josh 1). How Joshua landed *in Jericho* before battle is unclear, but

---

[8] I borrow here from the well-known phrase in Aleksandr I. Solzhenitsyn's *The Gulag Archipelago 1918–1956: An Experiment in Literary Investigation I–II*, trans. Thomas P. Whitney (New York: Harper & Row, 1974), 191: "If only there were evil people somewhere insidiously committing evil deeds, and it were necessary only to separate them from the rest of us and destroy them. But the line dividing good and evil cuts through the heart of every human being. And who is willing to destroy a piece of his own heart?"

the situation soon turned from unclear to bizarre. Suddenly a man appeared with his sword drawn.

Joshua responded with the natural question: "Are you for us or for our enemies?" (Josh 5:13).

This is textbook binary thinking, the sort that divides the world along the lines of good guys and bad guys, black and white, circumcised and uncircumcised, insiders and outsiders. The pressures of war or crisis often provoke binary thinking. Byron Williams points out how a post-9/11 world led many to find refuge in the same type of binary thinking that characterizes children.[9] You know, sharp rules. Clean lines. Boundaries. Good versus Evil.

But the man Joshua encountered refused Joshua's sharply divided categories: "Neither!" he replied. "But as commander of the army of the LORD I have now come." Notice the clear delineation between the LORD's army and the *Israelite* army. Had God's army been the same as Israel's, the man would've simply said, "I'm with y'all!"

This is a defining moment for Joshua, where he—like Moses—encounters God in a new and unexpected way.[10] It's time for him to ditch *Theology for Dummies* and let God reframe his categories.

Ancient battle accounts included stories of the gods visiting a hero before battle and presenting them with a sword or bow. The purpose was to assure them victory.[11] One temple image from Egypt shows the high god Amun-Re giving Ramesses III a sword and assurances before battle, and it includes these words: "Take to thee the sword, my son, my beloved, that thou mayst smite the heads of rebellious countries."[12] But instead of giving Joshua a weapon or assuring him of victory, this angelic commander *wields* the sword.

So, Joshua asks what God commands him (trying to fit himself into God's own military hierarchy), and he's instructed, "Take off your sandals, for the place where you are standing is holy" (Josh 5:15). This is a flashback

---

[9]Byron Williams, "Black and White Thinking Doesn't Work in a Grey World," *Huffington Post*, October 2, 2006, www.huffpost.com/entry/black-and-white-thinking_b_30747.

[10]Lissa M. Wray Beal, *Joshua*, Story of God Bible Commentary (Grand Rapids, MI: Zondervan Academic, 2019), 126-27, draws out the points of connection between the stories of mysterious divine encounters of Moses (Ex 3), Joshua (Josh 5), and Gideon (Judg 6).

[11]Wray Beal, *Joshua*, 129.

[12]W. F. Edgerton and J. A. Wilson, *Historical Records of Ramses III* (Chicago: University of Chicago Press, 136), 4, qtd in Wray Beal, *Joshua*, 129; also discussed in Gordon H. Matties, *Joshua*, Believers Church Bible Commentary (Kitchener, ON: Herald Press, 2012), 137.

to Exodus 3, where Moses meets God on sacred ground at the burning bush and learns God's name (Ex 3:14). Then Joshua bows down in worship before the great and mysterious God.

And here the enigmatic episode ends. But why doesn't God reaffirm his earlier promise to guarantee victory for Joshua and the people? Why doesn't the story resolve the encounter, instead of just leaving us with the image of Joshua bowing low before the nonaligned God?

Here's my hunch. *The storyteller wants to unsettle and dislodge the binary us-them categories implied by a surface reading of the book's earlier chapters.* The conquest story, left unexamined, can foster nationalistic confidence, religious certainty, and a simple story of success. But Joshua needed to un-couple his perceptions of God from the narrow confines of nationalistic thinking. He needed to learn the significance of Yahweh's name, revealed earlier to Moses in the form of a mystery: "I AM WHO I AM." (Ex 3:14). God was far less aligned and far freer than Joshua imagined.

Ellen Davis likens Joshua's encounter with the angel to the Celtic notion of "thin places." The instruction for Joshua to stand barefoot marks this place as another burning bush (cf. Ex 3:5). A "thin place" is where some-thing of the divine shows through, at this moment destabilizing the basic perception on which the notion of conquest rests, the opposition between "us" and "them."[13]

Joshua wasn't the only Israelite leader to learn this lesson. His mentor Moses had his own meeting with a divine sword-wielder. On his journey to Egypt, Moses, his wife Zipporah, and their son meet God, who was "about to kill him" (Ex 4:24).

What?!

Why would God attack the very man just commissioned to liberate the Israelites from Egypt? Plus, wouldn't this undermine Moses' confidence that God was on his side, and on the Israelites' side?

In any case, Zipporah acts fast. She pulls out a flint knife of her own . . .

Let me pause here. First, isn't it interesting that Zipporah was armed? Second, Moses must have thought, *Oh no! God's attacking me and now my wife pulls a knife on God!* But she does something else. She quickly circumcises

---

[13]Ellen F. Davis, *Opening Israel's Scriptures* (New York: Oxford University Press, 2019), 137.

their son, and then christens Moses as her "bridegroom of blood" (Ex 4:25). Scholars have long puzzled over this incident, and I don't intend to solve the puzzle here. But it is worth pondering the similarity between these events. In both stories, a divinely assured "hero" is about to embark on a major mission. In both stories, the hero meets a threatening or attacking divine figure. In both stories, circumcision is crucial. The great Jewish philosopher Martin Buber captures the spirit of these stories: "It is part of the basic character of this God that he claims the entirety of the one he has chosen; he takes complete possession of the one to whom he addresses himself."[14] The single qualification for God's leader is not military prowess, but that they belong to him entirely. Moses and Joshua had to learn this. Zipporah understood this.

When we pan out from these stories, we see a regular pattern wherein God reminds his leaders and liberators that *they are not exempt from the danger of proximity to God, or of the need to remain totally devoted to him.* Think of God asking Abraham to raise his knife over Isaac (Gen 22) or God wrestling Jacob (Gen 32). Or consider Balaam, who encountered the sword-wielding angel (Num 22:23, 31). Later, David encountered an angel with drawn sword after he wrongly initiated a census in Israel (1 Chr 21:16). We can fast-forward to Jesus who met the murderous Saul on the Damascus Road and blinded him before commissioning him to preach to the Gentiles (Acts 9).

These stories anticipate the call of Christ to take up our cross daily, and the call to recognize that we are crucified with Christ (Mt 16:24-26; Gal 2:19-20). The sword of the Lord is a terrible thing, and not just for our enemies. The sword of the Lord cuts both ways, and right through the lines that we use to delineate insiders and outsiders (cf. 1 Pet 4:17).

SWORD OR NO SWORD

Of course, we can't deny that Israel did use its sword to kill and destroy the Canaanites. Joshua tells us as much fourteen times (Josh 6:21; 8:24; 10:11, 28, 30, 32, 35, 37, 39; 11:10, 11, 12, 14; 19:47). Israel struck down their enemies "by the edge of the sword" goes the phrase.

---

[14]From Martin Buber's *Moses: The Revelation and the Covenant*, quoted in J. Gerald Janzen, *Exodus*, Westminster Bible Companion (Louisville, KY: Westminster John Knox, 1997), 44.

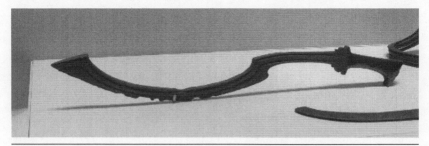

Figure 7.1. A bronze sickle sword recovered from Late Bronze layers at Aphek

However, the book places precious little stock in the sword's power. At the end of his life, Joshua asks the people to cast their minds back over the conquest: "You did not do it [i.e., take the land] with your own sword and bow" (Josh 24:12), he says. Instead, Yahweh drove out the Canaanites by his own power.[15] This is surprising news! After the command to put people to the sword (Deut 7) and the reports of this happening throughout the book, what are we to make of this claim? Is Joshua senile?

We might reconcile the seeming contradiction by saying that the strength behind their weapons was divine. As they struck people down, they did so by God's *power*. That may be, but the language in Joshua 24:12 is stronger, and is meant to *undermine* confidence in weaponry. It suggests that God *drove out* the people of the land before Israel, such that they simply didn't need to use their swords. I'll return to this theme later. It's really important. For now, notice that Joshua's summary description of the swordless victory sticks in Israel's memory.

The psalmist later says:
It was *not by their sword* that they won the land,
nor did their arm bring them victory;
it was your [i.e., Yahweh's] right hand, your arm,
and the light of your face, for you loved them. (Ps 44:3)

The psalmist then disavows his trust in weaponry: "I do not trust in my bow, / my sword does not bring me victory" (Ps 44:6). His point isn't that

---

[15]The text states that God drove out the Canaanites by sending *tsirah* ahead of the people. Scholars debate whether this should be translated as "hornet," "terror," or "panic." In any case, the force used to drive out the Canaanites is divinely appointed and contrasted with Israel's own weaponry.

he never fights (see Ps 44:5), but that his weapons are of little consequence, and are *never* a reliable object of trust.

This conviction led Israel to even reject certain weapons. For instance, Israel couldn't use horses. As Matthew Schlimm notes, this would be like "the US Congress outlawing the army from having tanks."[16] Yet the Israelites sang, "A horse is a vain hope for deliverance; / despite all its great strength it cannot save" (Ps 33:17) and "Some trust in chariots and some in horses, / but we trust in the name of the LORD our God" (Ps 20:7).

Without Joshua 24:12, we might think that swordsmanship was crucial to Israel's success in the conquest. Or we might think that bronze weaponry mattered, that bows and spears were important. But they weren't essential. The essential power at work in the conquest was the power of Yahweh. Joshua wants us to see the continuity between God's actions in the past and the conquest. When the Egyptians chased Israel with chariots and horsemen, it was Yahweh who defended them and routed the Egyptians (Josh 24:6-7). When the Amorite kings in the Transjordan came out to fight Israel, "I [Yahweh] destroyed them from before you" (Josh 24:8). Noticing the emphasis on Yahweh's exclusive military prowess doesn't rid us of the difficulties with Israel's sword-wielding elsewhere in the book. However, it does keep our attention on the point (pun intended!) that Israel's swords didn't make much difference.

THE SWORD AND VIOLENCE IN JOSHUA

I don't think it's by accident that the first two times we see the brandished sword in the book of Joshua, the unexpected happens. The sword is not laid first on the necks of the Canaanites. In the first case, the Israelites use the sword to render themselves—the *un*circumcised (!)—vulnerable and submissive to the demands of the covenant. This is symbolic disarmament before battle. Israel's conquest would be about trust, not the power of the sword.[17]

---

[16]Matthew Schlimm, "'Dad, Why Does Deuteronomy 20 Talk About Killing the Boys and Girls?'" *Christian Century*, June 21, 2021, www.christiancentury.org/article/critical-essay/dad-why -does-deuteronomy-20-talk-about-killing-boys-and-girls.

[17]Cf. Buchanan, *Rest of God*, 97.

The second time, Yahweh's own army commander raises his sword in a profoundly mysterious expression of nonalignment. He will not be paraded in to provide unqualified support for Israel's army.

Further, the critique of weaponry in Joshua 24:12 (and Ps 44) raises questions about the value of military strength for Israel. Their weaponry and strength mattered little. As Joshua 1 reminds us, their obedience to Torah was far more important. This obedience theme becomes important throughout the book.

There's one more weapon that Joshua brandishes at the beginning of the book. But it's not a sword. In Joshua 1:8 Yahweh tells Joshua that his success depended on *Torah*, the book of the law. By meditating on it day and night, Joshua would succeed. The word *succeed* refers here to military success but is linked to the act of Scripture meditation. With this command, Yahweh bursts any militaristic bubble that might have buoyed Joshua's ego. Rather than sword or spear, Joshua would need to be a man of the book. Bookworms unite!

As it turns out, that book of the law includes a heavy dose of kindness toward foreigners, strangers, and outsiders. How then would Joshua carry out a command against the Canaanites while meditating on a book that in many cases commended their inclusion?

In the next chapter, we'll address that question. We'll look at Israel's very first incursion into enemy territory (Josh 2), where they encounter the archetypal Canaanite—Rahab. This story takes another jab at settled perceptions of who's *in* and who's *out*. Like these "brandished sword" episodes in Joshua 5, the Rahab story signals that there's far more at work in Joshua than an attempt to provide Israel with an unambiguous founding story of destructive victory over the idolatrous and uncircumcised infidels.

JESUS AND THE SWORD

We've seen so far that Joshua is ambivalent about the power of the sword, especially against the enemy. As Christians, it's easy to assume that swords had *no* place at all in the ministry of Jesus. He told Peter to put away his sword, after all, with a rebuke that "all who draw the sword will die by the sword" (Mt 26:52).

But other passages ask us to consider the sword's role. Simeon tells Mary that a sword would "pierce" her own soul, which may refer to the pain she would experience at Jesus' death or the divisions caused by Jesus' ministry (Lk 2:35). Jesus would bring about the "falling and rising of many" (Lk 2:34). Like the Angel of the Lord in Joshua, Jesus refused existing lines of division. He exposed the idolatry of insiders and found faith among outsiders. He forged new alliances and divided old ones.

Later, Jesus suggests as much. He tells his twelve disciples that he didn't come "to bring peace to the earth . . . but a sword" (Mt 10:34). Jesus' sword would set "a man against his father, / a daughter against her mother, / a daughter-in-law against her mother-in-law" (Mt 10:35). These verses raise the bar of discipleship, showing that Jesus-loyalty can even divide us from what we previously considered our highest priorities.

We'll find that the sword does similar work in Israel. It will set Israelite against Israelite and Canaanite against Canaanite. Mark and Luke Glanville's words about Joshua are apt: "These texts [in Joshua] were shaking up the identity of the people of Israel, re-forming the family of Yahweh as a community that heeds the Torah."[18] So too in Jesus' ministry. While the literal swordsmanship of Joshua is missing in Jesus' ministry, the effect is no less costly or dangerous.[19] That's why Jesus warns his followers to count the cost. Walking in Jesus' way might be like a sword through the soul, or through the family.

Joshua's Torah-meditating military strategy anticipates another kind of sword-wielding in the New Testament. The book of Hebrews observes that the anticipated rest that Israel was supposed to achieve in Canaan was only ever partial (Heb 3–4).[20] Israel never fully settled the land. But a future day of rest awaits God's people (Heb 4:9).

Like God's people in Joshua's day, we Christians must "make every effort to enter that rest" (Heb 4:11) so that we don't end up falling like the

---

[18]Mark R. Glanville and Luke Glanville, *Refuge Reimagined: Biblical Kinship in Global Politics* (Downers Grove, IL: IVP Academic, 2021), 56; Caryn A. Reeder, *The Enemy in the Household: Family Violence in Deuteronomy and Beyond* (Grand Rapids, MI: Baker Books, 2012).

[19]Yet see Lk 22:36-38.

[20]The Old Testament also recognizes this point already. The ideal of "everyone under their own vine and under their own fig tree" was only "during Solomon's lifetime" (1 Kgs 4:25, NIV modified).

wilderness generation. Hebrews then unveils its conquest strategy. Taking a page from Joshua, Hebrews then reminds those of us at the edge of that Promised Land that "the word of God is alive and active. Sharper than any double-edged sword, it penetrates even to dividing soul and spirit, joints and marrow; it judges the thoughts and attitudes of the heart" (Heb 4:12, NIV modified). Hebrews understands the heart of Joshua. Joshua insists from beginning (Josh 1:7-8) to end (Josh 22:5; 23:11) that Israel's entrance into the land depended on the "sword" of God's Word. That would be Israel's greatest weapon.[21]

---

[21]Revelation also picks up on the theme of the "sword" of the Word (Rev 1:16; 2:16; 19:15, 21; cf. Eph 6:17; 2 Cor 10:4-5).

8

NEGOTIATING
WITH THE ENEMY

WHEN JESUS GATHERED with his disciples in the upper room on the night before his arrest, he knew that one of his mortal enemies was there. He shared bread with him: "The hand of him who is going to betray me is with mine on the table" (Lk 22:21). Sitting down to eat a meal with Judas was not a departure from Jesus' normal "policy," however. He frequently ate and associated with those who opposed him, or with those who were supposed to be his opposition. For Jesus, those thought to be "insiders" were often "outsiders," and vice versa.

Sitting down with the enemy is often seen as a weakness by staunch militarists, those for whom insiders and outsiders are clearly delineated. Back in 2015, the Obama Administration endured intense criticism for brokering a nuclear deal with Iran. Negotiating with an avowed enemy was ruled out of bounds as a matter of principle, but also as a matter of security. Some claimed that the deal would "embolden" the Iranians and provide them with funds to support terrorist networks throughout the Middle East and beyond.[1] In the wake of the various terrorist acts, the desire for ever stronger barriers between "us" and dangerous outsiders is understandable.

The Trump administration's later "America First" policy might seem to provide an apt comparison for Joshua's policy. Israel was promised the land. So, they'd take it. *Israelites First.* And they didn't come in to negotiate treaties and "work together." Moses' words to the conquest generation seem to reflect a hardline foreign policy: "Make no treaty with them" (Deut 7:2).

---

[1]BBC, "Iran Nuclear Deal: US Conservatives Condemn Agreement," BBC News, July 14, 2015, www .bbc.co.uk/news/world-middle-east-33527844.

These words lead immediately into the command to show the Canaanites no mercy.[2] Moses referred not only to the conquest, but more generally to the way they should relate to any Canaanites once they settled in the land. Treaty-making with known enemies could only ever lead to disaster.

But the people do make treaties with the enemy. Three times, in fact: twice in Joshua, with Rahab's family (Josh 2) and the Gibeonites (Josh 9), and then once in Judges with a family from Bethel (Judg 1). Are we to view these as violations of Moses' command? Should Israel have *ideally* rejected all discussion with the enemy to avoid contamination?

To address these questions, let's look at the first treaty.

TREATING WITH RAHAB, THE ARCH CANAANITE

Israel stumbled into its first deal with the Canaanites. Here's how it unfolded.

After his divine commissioning service (Josh 1), Joshua deploys two *spies* from Shittim to go "view the land." For readers of the story, this should raise a red flag. Israel's last spy mission was a total disaster. Twelve spies went on a reconnaissance mission from Kadesh-Barnea. They spied out the land and then ten of them reported that it was unassailable. That effectively killed any optimism among the Israelites. While the land was fertile and full of good things, it was heavily fortified and full of giants. "We seemed like grasshoppers . . . to them!" (Num 13:33), the spies reported.

This fear-filled report sent the people into a tailspin. They cried out and wailed the whole night, and then sought to appoint a leader to bring them back into Egypt (Num 14:1-4). They wanted an anti-exodus. In fact, the story ends with these words from Moses: "The LORD . . . will *not* be with you" (Num 14:43).[3]

So, when Joshua appoints spies to go into the land, the reader has reason to furrow her brow and look over her glasses: "Joshua, are you sure that sending spies is a good idea? Remember all the guarantees you had (Josh 1)? Why would you even need to spy out the land?"

---

[2]I'm using "Canaanites" as a shorthand for the proscribed nations, which include Hittites, Gir-gashites, Amorites, Canaanites, Perizzites, Hivites, and Jebusites.
[3]Cf. Josh 1:5: "I *will* be with you."

Perhaps Josh thought that he sent two *good* spies, like he and Caleb had been forty years previous. They were the only spies who reported faithfully that God could and had given them the land (Num 13:30).

In any case, things look even grimmer when considered geographically. The spies set out from *Shittim* (pardon my French). Shittim was the place where Israel "played the harlot" and worshiped other gods (Num 25; 25:1 ASV). Shittim is where Israel pursued the women of Moab and "yoked themselves to the Baal of Peor," so much so that "the LORD's anger burned against them" (Num 25:3). Not the fondest of Israel's memories (cf. Ps 106:28; Hos 9:10). If there was a lesson from that event, it was this: Stay away from foreign women. They'll lead you into idolatry (spiritual prostitution) and provoke Yahweh's anger.

So, Joshua sends the spies from Shittim, spiritual-fornication-land. They don't seem particularly good at spying, since the king of Jericho quickly learns about them (Josh 2:2). They don't appear to do any spying. They don't inspect the enemy's defenses. They don't map out the city. They don't sabotage Jericho's weapons or supplies. Instead, they went straight to the house of a prostitute! Their motivations are unclear, but the story is rife with provocative language. Most English translations downplay the innuendos here. They "go into" (a term that can connote sex) the house of Rahab (whose name means "open") and "lie down there."[4] The king's messengers ask Rahab to "bring out the men who entered you." Sorry guys. Not a good look.

Rahab the prostitute embodies everything that God's people were to avoid. Spiritual prostitution and sexual promiscuity were closely linked in the Israelites' minds. Marrying foreign women was a gateway to apostasy, as seen the last time Israel was at Shittim. That's why God commanded the people to tear down the sacred altars and idols of the nations *and* avoid intermarriage (Deut 7, 20). Intermarriage was like stepping into the spider's parlor, so to speak. On that basis, the people were specifically instructed to avoid making covenants with the Canaanites. "Show them no mercy" or else they would turn the hearts of the people from Yahweh.

---

[4]On this scene's innuendo, see Lissa M. Wray Beal, *Joshua*, Story of God Bible Commentary (Grand Rapids, MI: Zondervan Academic, 2019), 78.

Later Israelite history seems to bear this out. Solomon is proof positive for those beset by such fears. He married seven hundred women and brought all manner of idolatry into Israel (1 Kings 11:3-8). Likewise, King Ahab married the Phoenician Jezebel and introduced Baal worship to Israel.

Even more sinister, the name Rahab sounds eerily similar to the mythical chaos monster called *Rakhab* who threatened all that is good and right (Job 26:12; Ps 89:10; Is 30:7; 51:9)![5] Lingering with a foreign prostitute seemed like a recipe for disaster.

Yet, in an astonishing turn of events, we learn that Rahab is a model Yahweh follower! She extends hospitality to foreigners, protects them from harm through civil disobedience, extols the mighty deeds and character of Yahweh, and acknowledges his supremacy. She basically quotes from the Torah: "For the LORD your God is God in heaven above and on the earth below" (Josh 2:11; cf. Ex 15; Deut 4:39). In fact, unlike the kings of Canaan, who merely "hear" about Yahweh, Rahab knows Yahweh's deeds (Josh 2:9-10). Even more, she makes a covenant (forbidden in Deut 7:2) with the Israelite spies to preserve her entire family when Israel comes to take the land. I wonder how many undocumented "family" members Rahab eventually snuck into this covenant with Israel!

DETERMINING WHO'S IN AND OUT

Let's step back and take stock of this story about Rahab and how it helps us think about the issue of violence. First, it's safe to say that Joshua is not a straightforward tale of genocide. The book complicates that sort of reading from the outset. In fact, the book is designed to critique the ethnocentric and nationalistic assumptions on which a genocidal ideology depends.

Granted, weaving those critiques into a story that seems to include genocide seems like a strange brew, but there may be reasons. Maybe the simple conquest story was a cultural given that needed to be reexamined, and one way to do that was to retell it in a way that foregrounded the story of Rahab. Maybe the book of Joshua is itself a close *re*-telling of a popular conquest story that some Israelites had circulated. The narrative space

---

[5]Gordon H. Matties, *Joshua*, Believers Church Bible Commentary (Kitchener, ON: Herald Press, 2012), 70.

given to the Rahab story in the book's second and sixth chapters signals to us that her story is foundational for understanding the conquest. It's a window into God's surprising work among the Canaanites.[6]

And, as I'll suggest in a later section, even the warfare chapters have their own surprises.

Second, it strikes me that in Israel's very first encounter with the Canaanites they receive hospitality, protection, and a lesson in Yahweh's mighty deeds. These are the very values that Torah seeks to inculcate in Israel (Deut 10:18). Rahab embodies Torah in word and deed. The spies' experience also sounds like the experience of some missionaries who go to share Jesus and find that God is already present. Holding the spotlight on Rahab's story—of all the stories that could have been told—suggests that the author is foregrounding the stereotypical Canaanite outsider only to subvert that stereotype. The Gospel writers do the same thing. Luke shows Jesus extolling the faith of the Roman occupier, the Samaritan, women, and other "sinners." Later, Luke shows the faith and hospitality of the Greek, Roman, and "Barbarian."[7] Outsiders often prove to be the best models of faith in Scripture.

Third, this lead-off story *appears* to violate the terms of engagement with the Canaanites written in the law itself (Deut 7, 20). Israel wasn't to make oaths with Canaanites, and certainly not prostitutes! But Joshua tells a story that reflects loyal *observance* of that very law, suggesting a deeper idea of obedience to the law. This fits with how biblical scholars think law worked in the Bible. Laws were not inflexible systems meant to be rigidly applied. Instead, a law collection provided a set of wise rulings and admonitions designed to form a just and wise people. Each situation would require wisdom for that specific circumstance.[8] The end of Joshua affirms Israel's

---

[6]Cf. Deut 2:4-5, 8-9, 19-21, where we learn previously unknown details about conquests that God performed for the Edomites, Moabites, and Ammonites. These conquests also include the ousting of giants!

[7]Joshua W. Jipp, *Saved by Faith and Hospitality* (Grand Rapids, MI: Eerdmans, 2017), 32.

[8]See Raymond Westbrook, "Introduction: The Character of Ancient Near Eastern Law," in *A History of Ancient Near Eastern Law*, 2 Vols, ed. Raymond Westbrook (Leiden: Brill, 2003), 1:1-90; cf. Bernard Jackson, *Wisdom Laws: A Study of the* Mishpatim *of Exodus 21:1–22:16* (Oxford: Oxford University Press, 2006); Joshua A. Berman, *Inconsistency in the Torah: Ancient Literary Convention and the Limits of Source Criticism* (New York: Oxford University Press, 2017); David Firth, "Reading Deuteronomy after Joshua: On Reversing the Interpretive Flow," *European Journal of Theology* 21, no. 1 (2022): 6-20.

obedience during the days of Joshua: "Israel served the LORD throughout the lifetime of Joshua and of the elders who outlived him" (Josh 24:31). We're left to conclude that the story may have been written as a conscious interpretation of the law—a law that seems uncompromising when read apart from the story. The book highlights the law's capacity to accommodate the enemy within Israel's own community. Put more directly, Joshua presents the spies' oath as an act of covenant faithfulness.[9]

Fourth, the story of Rahab challenges us to reconsider the question, Who's in and who's out? Rahab the Canaanite is included in the people of God. By contrast, we read in Joshua 7 that an Israelite named Achan dies the death of a Canaanite (in accordance with Deuteronomic law) because he sought personal gain from the conquest. So Rahab's family was spared but Achan's family was destroyed. By highlighting these two specific cases, Joshua sends a signal that "not all Israel is Israel; not every Canaanite is a Canaanite" (cf. Rom 9:6). The narrative space devoted to this subject (two entire chapters) signals that the author is intentionally disturbing the boundaries dividing insider and outsider identities. The first Canaanite in Joshua upends expectations, and "the stock notion of Canaanite wickedness is ironized and radically relativized, if not demolished altogether."[10]

Rahab's story doesn't end here. She's included among the people of Israel. She's initially included outside the camp, but eventually *in Israel* (Josh 6:22-25).[11] Joshua tells us that she lives in Israel "until this day." We don't know when "this day" was, but the point seems to be that her family was an enduring part of Israel's. God grafted Rahab into Israel's family tree. She's the ancestor of Boaz and King David. She appears in Matthew's genealogy as one of four prominent Old Testament female ancestors of Jesus (Mt 1:5). She's even listed as an example of someone who lived by faith in Hebrews 11, which doesn't even mention Joshua! She's an example of

---

[9]Rachel Billings, *"Israel Served the Lord": The Book of Joshua as Paradoxical Portrait of Faithful Israel* (Notre Dame, IN: University of Notre Dame Press, 2013), 43.

[10]Ellen F. Davis, "Critical Traditioning: Seeking an Inner Biblical Hermeneutic," *Anglican Theological Review* 82, no. 4 (2000): 733.

[11]Matties, *Joshua*, 153-54 writes, "That Rahab is an insider by confession (ch. 2) has not yet resolved the question of whether there might be another way in which she is 'inside' Israel. The point here is not to juxtapose confession with geography or ethnicity, but to highlight the fact that she continues her status as *herem* (*outside the camp*) and yet has remained alive."

justification by works in James 2:25. One later Jewish tradition suggests that she even became Joshua's wife![12] It's almost as if God takes pride in drawing the marginal characters into the center of his plan, characters like Tamar the Canaanite, Ruth the Moabite, and Rahab the Canaanite.

OUTSIDERS IN

Rahab isn't the only non-Israelite to join Israel in the book. When Israel renews its covenant at Mount Ebal and Mount Gerizim, we're told twice that "All the Israelites . . . both the foreigners living among them and the native-born were there" (Josh 8:33, 35). Deuteronomy similarly insists that Israel should include the stranger and foreigner (Deut 5:14; 10:18-19; 14:21, 29; 16:11, 14; 24:14, 17, 19-21; 26:11-13; 27:19; 31:12).[13] Foreigners were even included in the covenant renewal ceremony in Deuteronomy 29:10-11 and 31:12. Covenant fidelity required it! So, Joshua's emphasis on fidelity to the Torah (Josh 1:8) ironically undermines any simplistic exclusion (or destruction) of other peoples. Joshua recognizes this complexity.

In Joshua 8:30-35, all Israel renewed the covenant with Yahweh at Mount Ebal. Notably, this covenant included foreigners and native-born Israelites. In the very next chapter, we see a living example. The Canaanite Gibeonites sneak into a covenant with Israel and end up benefiting from Israel's military protection (Josh 9). Their ruse seems to signal something larger about the surprising kind of covenant eagerness that God rewards!

We can note other non-Israelites in the mix by looking elsewhere in the book. Caleb, Joshua's spying sidekick, was the son of Jephunneh, a Kenizzite (Num 32:12; Josh 14:6, 14), and the Kenizzites were an Edomite clan (Gen 36:11, 15, 42).[14] The Edomites descended from Esau according to Genesis, and Esau had married a Canaanite woman named Adah (Gen 26:34). Though Edomites were supposed to be excluded to the third generation by law (Deut 23:7-8), God includes Caleb on the basis of his loyalty (Num 32:12). The inclusion of Caleb shows us God's love for the non-Israelite, and even his willingness to give them land (Josh 14; 15:13-19).

---

[12]Talmud b. Megillah 14b, where Rahab is also the progenitor of eight prophets, including Jeremiah.
[13]See discussion in Mark Glanville, *Adopting the Stranger as Kindred in Deuteronomy*, Ancient Israel and Its Literature 33 (Atlanta: SBL Press, 2018); Matties, *Joshua*, 205.
[14]See David G. Firth, *The Message of Joshua* (Downers Grove, IL: InterVarsity Press, 2015), 24-25.

It turns out that Caleb's daughter Aksah, who was given as a wife to Caleb's Kennezzite brother Othniel, also advocates for some of this land. So Aksah became a model of a female foreigner who exhibits exemplary boldness and receives a portion in the inheritance of Israel (Josh 15:19)! Later, Joshua grants a portion of Israel's territory to the non-Israelite Archites (Josh 16:2).[15] And the cities of refuge in Joshua 20 are for Israelites and aliens. Time and again a careful reading of Joshua suggests that there was even a place at the table for Canaanite people. They too could choose to serve Yahweh (Josh 24).

Other texts in Joshua acknowledge that Canaanites were not displaced and continued to live alongside Israelites up until the book was written (Josh 16:10; 17:12-13). This shouldn't surprise us. Other texts in the Old Testament suggest that the Canaanites were *already* woven into the genealogy of Israel. They couldn't be kept out because they were already in. Jacob's son Simeon married a Canaanite woman (Gen 46:10; Ex 6:15). King David's progenitor Judah had three children by a Canaanite woman (Gen 38:2-5) and by his daughter-in-law, who was likely a Canaanite (Gen 38:12-30). Beyond marriage, we also see that Abraham paid tithes to a Canaanite priest Melchizedek, who blesses him by their *common* God (Gen 14:17-24).

The importance of Canaanites for Israel's life continues in the book of Samuel. David bought a threshing flood from a man named Araunah the Jebusite, whose people continued to live within Israel beyond the conquest (2 Sam 24:18-24). That threshing flood became the sight of the future temple (2 Sam 24:25; cf. 2 Chr 3:1).

Panning out we see that Joshua fits within the larger trajectory of God's purposes for Israel. Israel was supposed to be a people who blessed the nations (Gen 12:1-3) and included—indeed, *loved*—the stranger and foreigner (Lev 19:34).

Recognizing these Canaanite- and foreigner-including texts doesn't undermine all other references to killing Canaanites. Those stories are still

---

[15]Brueggemann, "The God of Joshua . . . Give or Take the Land," *Interpretation* 66, no. 2 (2012): 173-74. The land claims of the daughters of Zelophehad and the Levites clearly follow Caleb's model. Each is a kind of "land grant narrative" that runs through Josh 13–21. They each ask to receive a portion of land based on Yahweh's previous promise. Richard Nelson, *Joshua*, Old Testament Library (Louisville, KY: Westminster John Knox), 177.

there. However, they at the very least *complicate* our ability to portray the conquest as a straightforward account of genocidal destruction.

CONQUEST AND OUTSIDERS IN THE GOSPELS

The Gospels wrestle with the same insider-or-outsider questions. While Judas was the quintessential insider-turned-outsider in the Gospels, I want to close this chapter with an important counterbalancing episode from Jesus' ministry. This episode deliberately recalls the book of Joshua. In fact, it's a story of a *different* Joshua who encountered a *different* Canaanite woman in the land. We read in the Gospel of Matthew that Jesus—i.e., Yeshua, or Joshua in Hebrew[16]—met a "Canaanite" woman (Mt 15:22). It's highly anachronistic for Matthew to use the term "Canaanite," since it's the only time that the term is used in the Gospels.[17] The term must be deliberate. As Jesus encounters her, she asks for *mercy*, because her daughter was oppressed by a demon.

For Jesus ("Joshua") to meet a Canaanite asking for mercy (remember: "show them no mercy," Deut 7:2, 16) sounds like a reenactment of the conquest. But rather than applying Deuteronomy 7 literally, Jesus engages in a battle of wits about who's in and who's out. *In other words, Jesus negotiates with the enemy.* Seeing the woman's "great faith," he heals her daughter. By moving toward this woman whom others wanted to dismiss so quickly (Mt 15:23), he found a Canaanite outsider with the faith of an Israelite insider (cf. Lk 4:23-27). We've seen that before.

It shouldn't surprise us, then, that Hebrews presents Jesus' high priestly lineage in Canaanite terms. He's a priest according to the order of the Canaanite Melchizedek (Heb 5–7; cf. Ps 110:4).

OUTSIDERS' OUTSIZED ROLE

Isaiah 56:1-8 is one of my all-time favorite portions of Scripture. In it, the prophet urges the people to make a place for the eunuch and foreigner in the worshiping community. Anyone who keeps the covenant could join. God gives the eunuch, excluded by some because of Deuteronomy 23:1

---

[16]The Hebrew name of Jesus is *yeshua'*, a shortened form of the biblical *yehoshua'*.
[17]Mark uses "Syrophoenician" (Mk 7:26, NRSV).

and their inability to produce children, a "memorial and a name / better than sons and daughters" (Is 56:5). The phrase "memorial and a name" (Heb. *yad vashem*) is the name of Israel's Holocaust Memorial in Jerusalem. It's a memorial for those whose names were destroyed, and who otherwise might be forgotten. God also includes the foreigner. The rhetoric is moving. They're welcome at "my holy mountain," Jerusalem (Is 56:7). Including foreigners in the holy city is an important statement. But God brings them closer. They're welcome at "my house of prayer," the temple. Here God draws them to his very home, as Solomon had prayed in 1 Kings 8:41-43. But God brings them even closer. They're welcome "at my holy altar," the place where worshipers met with God and received God's welcome, atonement, and fellowship. The inclusion of these individuals, Isaiah tells us, is part of God's larger plan to welcome entire nations at his altar (Is 56:8). Welcoming individuals provided a way for God's people to anticipate God's eschatological plans.

If read hastily, Joshua's story may seem like a far cry from this prophetic vision. But throughout the book we see signs that so-called "outsiders" play an outsized role. Rahab and the Gibeonites occupy our attention in two of the book's six conquest chapters (Josh 6–11), and shorter-but-significant episodes with the angel of Yahweh and the covenant renewal ceremony alert readers to the fact that God's broader purposes for the nations are being anticipated here. Conversely, Achan serves as a cautionary tale for any "insider" who thought that covenant "insiders" get a free pass. The book's challenge to sharp insider and outsider distinctions in its narrative section (Josh 1–11) allow us to look across the book at other ways God asks his people to take the plank out of their own eye and build a longer table for Canaanite covenant keepers.

9

MINORITY REPORT

THE BATTLE OF JERICHO is probably the best-known story in Joshua. It's a regular feature of most kids' Bibles. From an early age Jericho shapes many Christians' opinions about what the book is all about. It shapes impressions about the book's tone before most even read the entire book. The *Jesus Storybook Bible,* a top-selling children's Bible, tells one story from the book of Joshua, and it's about Jericho.[1] Another best-seller, *The Beginner's Bible,* tells two stories from the book, and they're both about Jericho.[2]

Some adults approach the problem of violence in Joshua as if kids' Bibles told the whole story. They act as if what happened in Jericho was representative of the book, as if Jericho was the beginning of a story of unrelenting destruction.

It's understandable to think this. Joshua itself seems to speak about Jericho as a battle that represented *all* battles in the book: "Then you crossed the Jordan and came to Jericho. The citizens of Jericho fought against you, as did also the Amorites, Perizzites, Canaanites, Hittites, Girgashites, Hivites and Jebusites, but I gave them into your hands" (Josh 24:11). However, that's only one side of the story.

As I suggest below, there are *two different perspectives on the conquest* in Joshua. The story of Jericho belonged to only *one* kind of storytelling in the book. It's the Majority Report, since it's the one most readers assume. It's a story of utter and complete conquest. Another existed, and it needs to

---

[1]Sally Lloyd-Jones, *Jesus Storybook Bible: Every Story Whispers His Name* (Grand Rapids, MI: Zondervan, 2012).
[2]Catherine DeVries, *The Beginner's Bible: Timeless Children's Stories* (Grand Rapids, MI: Zondervan, 2005).

be heard. That second is what we might call the Minority Report.[3] The Minority Report tells a story of incomplete and gradual conquest. This story is not just a story of failure, however. Instead, it's a story of the long and messy process by which Israel gained a foothold in the land. It's a story of God's initiative and timing. It's also a story that's less violent and more historically specific than the Majority Report.

But before looking at how this other story sits alongside the first, let's look at how earlier books set our expectations for two stories of conquest.

BEFORE THE CONQUEST

Joshua 1 states that God would give Israel the land. How? God doesn't say at first. The main point was that by giving the land, God remained faithful to promises made to Moses in the Torah. This leaves the door open since the Torah seems to envision two very different kinds of invasion. Let me take two promises from Deuteronomy as examples: "The LORD your God will *drive out* those nations before you, *little by little*. You will not be allowed to eliminate them all at once, or the wild animals will multiply around you" (Deut 7:22). This passage, and those like it, expect a slow and gradual conquest that *displaces* the Canaanites.[4] Yet only a few chapters later, Moses tells the people that the conquest would happen quickly and decisively: "But be assured today that the LORD your God is the one who goes across ahead of you like a devouring fire. He will *destroy* them; he will *subdue* them before you. And you will *drive them out and annihilate* them *quickly*, as the LORD has promised you" (Deut 9:3).[5] This version uses the language of driving out, but also envisions destruction and annihilation. Which were the people to expect? Surely slow and steady displacement *and* quick destruction are incompatible!

---

[3]A phrase from my friend Brad Jersak, drawn from the 2002 movie "Minority Report," starring Tom Cruise.

[4]Other texts emphasize the slow displacement of Canaanites (Ex 23:29-30; cf. Lev 18:24-26). For an in-depth discussion of the Canaanite displacement, see William J. Webb and Gordon K. Oeste, *Bloody, Brutal, and Barbaric?: Wrestling with Troubling War Texts* (Downers Grove, IL: InterVarsity Press, 2019), 231-62.

[5]While the word translated "quickly" seems to include the possibility of a long timespan in Deut 4:26, the context of Deut 9:3 suggests a quick sequence of actions. Moreover, the language is jarringly contrary to the claims of Deut 7:22.

Table 9.1 highlights the two perspectives on conquest. The differences are striking.

Table 9.1. Displacement vs. destruction

Displacement (Minority Report)	Destruction (Majority Report)
Promise to Gradually *Displace*: "*Little by little* I will *drive them out* before you, until you have increased enough to take possession of the land." (Ex 23:30) Texts: Exodus 23:27-30; 33:2; 34:11; Leviticus 20:23; Numbers 32:21-22; Deuteronomy 4:38; 7:1, 22; Joshua 3:10; 13:6; 23:1-5; 24:11-12	Command or Promise to *Destroy*: "You must *destroy them totally*. Make no treaty with them, and show them no mercy." (Deut 7:2) Texts: Exodus 23:23; Deuteronomy 7:2, 16; 9:3; 20:16-17; 1 Samuel 15:3
Fulfillment by Displacement: "I sent the hornet ahead of you, which *drove them out* before you—also the two Amorite kings [Sihon and Og]. You did not do it with your own sword and bow." (Josh 24:12) Texts: Joshua 24:12; Judges 6:9	*Fulfillment by* Destroying: "They *devoted* the city to the LORD and *destroyed* with the sword every living thing in it—men and women, young and old, cattle, sheep and donkeys." (Josh 6:21) Texts: Joshua 6:21; 8:24-26; 10:28, 37, 39-40; 11:11, 14, 20; cf. Deuteronomy 2:31; 3:6

We could list other examples. For instance, Joshua 10:42 (NRSV) refers to the Israelites taking lands "at one time" and then Joshua 11:18 says it took "a long time."

The Minority Report suggests that the conquest was a gradual process of Canaanite displacement. The Majority Report describes a blitzkrieg. Which one was it? I'll discuss historical questions in chapter eleven. For now, it's worth noting that we don't know for sure until Judges. Judges makes it clear that the Minority Report is the more precise story (historically speaking) of how the whole conquest went. Judges begins with the Israelites fighting more Canaanites, and God eventually tells the people that he'd stop driving them out because of their disobedience (Judg 2:20-23). There may have been isolated battles in which Canaanites groups were wiped off the map, but those weren't the norm.

Two Stories of Conquest

At this point it's worth stepping back to think about how the Majority and Minority reports work together. I want to offer a summary thesis. It helped me understand the book's complexity and communication strategy. Here's the big idea: *Joshua offers two perspectives on the conquest, one ideal and one real—the* Majority *and* Minority *reports. Each has its own purpose in the book, and each says something that couldn't be said using just one perspective.*[6]

These two stories *can* be read together. They constitute a surface tension in the book, but not a deep contradiction. If understood properly, the Majority Report comports well with the Minority Report. My purpose, however, is to take seriously the powerful language of each report—the shocking demands of the Majority Report and the realism of the Minority Report.

According to the Majority Report, God promised to comprehensively destroy the seven "-ite" (e.g., Hivite) nations singled out for destruction. These are the nations that Joel Kaminsky calls the "anti-elect."[7] God singled them out uniquely for destruction. The mode of warfare by which Israel would destroy them was called *herem* warfare in Hebrew. *Herem* warfare refers to comprehensive destruction that renders something or someone temporarily or permanently ineligible for common use.[8] In a religious context it involved destroying and dedicating all valuables to God as an offering. It operated similarly to a burnt offering that was given over to God on the altar. For instance, after destroying Jericho, Israel burned the city, took its valuables, and put them "into the treasury of the LORD's house" (Josh 6:24). According to the Majority Report, the result of the *herem* wars was total military success:

> So Joshua subdued *the whole region* (lit. land), including the hill country, the Negev, the western foothills and the mountain slopes, together with *all* their kings. He left no survivors. He totally destroyed *all* who breathed, just as the LORD, the God of Israel, had commanded. (Josh 10:40; cf. Josh 11:20, 23; 21:43-45)

---

[6] As a caveat, I refer to these as "narratives" though they're at times juxtaposed to one another within the space of two verses.

[7] Joel S. Kaminsky, *Yet Jacob I Loved: Reclaiming the Biblical Concept of Election* (Nashville: Abingdon, 2007). Kaminsky distinguishes between the elect, non-elect, and the anti-elect. Rachel Billings, *"Israel Served the Lord": The Book of Joshua as Paradoxical Portrait of Faithful Israel* (Notre Dame, IN: University of Notre Dame Press, 2013), 40, helpfully adds a fourth category, the "pro-elect," that includes people like Rahab and the Gibeonites.

[8] David G. Firth, *The Message of Joshua* (Downers Grove, IL: InterVarsity Press, 2015), 26; John H. Walton and J. Harvey Walton, *The Lost World of the Israelite Conquest: Covenant, Retribution, and the Fate of the Canaanites* (Downers Grove, IL: IVP Academic, 2017), 175-76. I discuss this term further in the next chapter.

Later, we read, "For it was the LORD himself who hardened their hearts to wage war against Israel, so that he might destroy them totally, exterminating them without mercy, as the LORD had commanded Moses" (Josh 11:20). In short, the Majority Report details a swift and complete conquest of the land, and the comprehensive destruction of Canaanite enemies.

According to the Minority Report, however, God promised to *displace* the Canaanites little by little. The mode of warfare was conventional and never comprehensive. The results were mixed. Israel settled only a fraction of the Promised Land. Canaanites still ran amok, and eventually, Israel found itself exiled from the land it failed to fully settle (Josh 23:13).

REENGAGING THE MINORITY REPORT

Before trying to make some sense of the Majority Report (the more troubling of the two), and how the two narratives work together, let's think through the book's Minority Report. According to this story of conquest, God promised the people land little by little. From a historical perspective, the Israelites had to eke out an existence and slowly gain a foothold as they tried to oust Canaanite kings who held key cities. The people initiated conventional warfare against major urban centers and displaced some but not all of their inhabitants. The purpose of these wars was likely to weaken the Canaanite city-states, which were ruled by warlords from large(-ish) cities but were also in decline during the 1200s BC. I'll discuss this further in chapter eleven.

The Minority Report provides a more nuanced picture of what might have happened when early Israel struggled with the inhabitants of Canaan. Israel *didn't* "dislodge" the Jebusites living in Jerusalem (Josh 15:63); they *didn't* "dislodge" the Canaanites in Gezer (Josh 16:10); they *didn't* "occupy" the towns in the Transjordan (Josh 17:12-13); Judah took the hill country but *didn't* "drive out" those living on the plains because of their iron chariots (Judg 1:19) . . . and so on. In short, the so-called conquest was incomplete.[9]

The Minority Report also tells us that in areas where Israel supposedly *destroyed* populations entirely (according to the Majority Report), many

---

[9]In 1 Kings 9:20-21, Solomon hires Canaanites from cities that were "totally destroyed" by Joshua.

Canaanites still remained. Though Israel had allegedly destroyed Zephath (or Hormah, Num 21:3), Hebron (Josh 10:36-37), and Debir (Josh 10:39), Joshua and Judges later indicate Canaanites still held those cities after those battles (Josh 14:6-15; 15:15; Judg 1:10–11, 17). In other cases, Israel defeated the *kings* of cities like Jerusalem, Dor, Taanach, and Megiddo (Josh 12:8-10, 21-23), but later could not even enter them because they were occupied by Canaanites (Josh 17:12; 2 Sam 5:6-8)! Clearly the defeat of *kings* involved the survival of their *subjects*, and likely the emergence of new Canaanite rulers.

One more example. In Joshua 10:33 we're told that "Horam king of Gezer had come up to help Lachish, but Joshua defeated him and his army—until no survivors were left." The "no survivors" may refer to the army that came and fought in the open, and not to the inhabitants of Gezer itself. In any case, we learn later that the Ephraimites "did not dislodge the Canaanites living in Gezer; to this day the Canaanites live among the people of Ephraim but are required to do forced labor" (Josh 16:10). The list goes on.[10]

These are but a few examples of the way that Joshua offers a complicated description of what happened during the conquest. *It was a slow, complex, and incomplete process.* Israel engaged in *occasional conventional warfare* against major Canaanite (Late Bronze Age) strongholds, were often unsuccessful, and ended up settling the less populated central highlands of a land still full of Canaanites.[11] Moreover, what Joshua reports as victories were often short-term victories over *kings* and not the annihilation of their subjects (Josh 12).[12]

If you look at figure 9.1, a map of the actual territories Israel captured during Israel's campaigns (darker shading in the north and south), you'll see how regionally limited their victories were. The areas in the darker shading were the primary areas conquered during Israel's northern and southern campaigns, according to Joshua 10–11.

---

[10]The examples from this paragraph were cited in Webb and Oeste, *Bloody*, 156-58.

[11]Similar settlement patterns obtain for the Transjordanian highlands as well. See Ann E. Killebrew, *Biblical Peoples and Ethnicity: An Archaeological Study of Egyptians, Canaanites, Philistines, and Early Israel, 1300–1100 BCE*, Archaeology and Biblical Studies 9 (Atlanta, GA: SBL, 2005), 171.

[12]Noted by Chris McKinny, personal conversation, 06/22/2021.

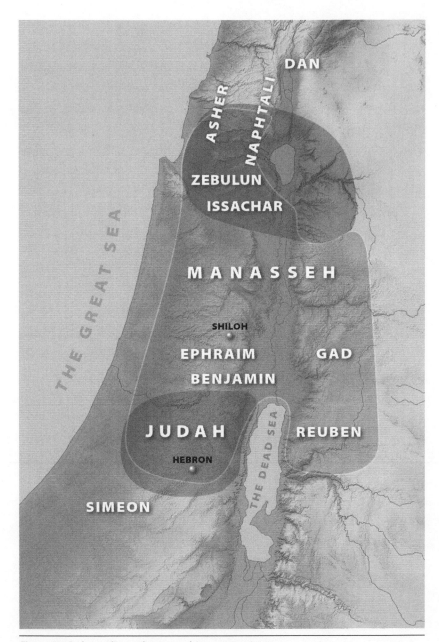

Figure 9.1. Early Israelite settlement and conquest regions

Eventually, Israel settled the areas in lighter shading, but that settlement took hundreds of years. As for Joshua's day, Joshua 13:1 sums it up well: "When Joshua had grown old, the LORD said to him, 'You are now very old, and there are still *very large areas of land* to be taken over.'"

Very large indeed!

In his farewell speech, Joshua told the people that many lands remained unclaimed. God would eventually "push back" and "drive out" the nations that remained (Josh 23:5). But remain they did. Joshua adds an *if* here. Yahweh would give them the remaining land *if* the people avoided mixing with the remaining nations through marriage or worship. Those things would lead them astray (Josh 23:7, 12). Instead, they were to cling to Yahweh and keep the teachings of Moses (Josh 23:7-8). Torah keeping would ensure their success.

If Israel didn't cling to Yahweh and keep Moses' teachings, he would let the Canaanite nations remain. They would become thorns in their sides until *Israel* was eventually driven from the land (Josh 23:12-13). Israel wasn't exempt from displacement. This is, in fact, what happened. The dis-placers became the displaced.

So is the Minority Report just telling us that Israel was *really bad* at con-quest and should've been better? Not necessarily. Joshua never condemns the people for not settling all the land. It was simply a fact. It was part of the slow process by which God was giving Israel the land. We've been told before Joshua that it would be gradual (Ex 23:27-30). The only failed battle due to sin was Ai, which Israel quickly remedied. The Minority Report states that the long and gradual process by which Israel gained a foothold in the land was part of God's plan. The ongoing presence of Canaanites posed temptations, to be sure, but those temptations were not due to sin on Israel's part. They were just part of life between promise and fulfillment, between the already (promised) and the not yet (settled).

In sum, before painting all the warfare texts in Joshua with the same broad brush, it is important to distinguish between the surface and deep perspectives on conquest, between the already and the not yet, between the Minority and Majority Reports. But we can't lose sight of the important purpose that the Majority Report serves. It calls Israel to undivided Torah devotion and uncompromising commitment to Yahweh. I'll discuss all of this in the next chapter, where we'll look at the doubly troubling *herem* (comprehensive destruction) texts. We'll then be able to ask why Joshua might weave these two reports together. (Hint: It's not just to confuse us.)

10

SHOW THEM NO MERCY

IN A 1994 ESSAY, Tremper Longman III draws an enlightening yet disturbing comparison between the extremist ideology of Osama bin Laden and that expressed in the *herem* (comprehensive destruction) texts of Deuteronomy and Joshua:

- Both believed in the idea of sacred space occupied by "infidels;" in the case of bin Laden it was the presence of Westerners in Saudi Arabia.

- Both believed that their acts were "holy war," blessed and sanctioned by God.

- Both were intent on destroying every last person, without consideration of age or status.[1]

If we were exposed to these parallels outside of Scripture, many of us would want nothing to do with the deity in question. But what do we do when the God of Scripture authorizes indiscriminate killing of all ages and stages, including babies? Moreover, what do we do when he even anticipates the inclination toward mercy, and forbids it?

Jewish and Christian interpreters have wrestled with the "show no mercy" commands for eons. The rabbis denied the straightforward sense of Joshua and imagined that a scenario like this one took place: "Joshua sent out three proclamations . . . to the Canaanites: he who wishes shall leave; he who wishes to make peace shall make peace; he who wishes to fight shall do so."[2] This line of reasoning echoes a similar belief that Noah preached

---

[1]Tremper Longman, "The Case for Spiritual Continuity," in *Show Them No Mercy: Four Views on God and the Canaanite Genocide*, ed. Stanley N. Gundry (Grand Rapids, MI: Zondervan, 1994), 159-90.
[2]*Lev. Rab.* 17.6, noted in Moshe Weinfeld, *Deuteronomy 1–11*, Anchor Bible 5 (New York: Doubleday, 1991), 384.

repentance to his contemporaries, warning them about the Great Flood to come, a detail Genesis never mentions (2 Pet 2:5).[3]

Some argue that the Canaanites were so evil that they deserved to be entirely wiped off the map. The Bible makes a point of detailing some of these evils (Deut 18:9-22). Yet the call to wipe out the Canaanites included the death of children and animals, the elderly, men and women. It is impossible to maintain an argument based on moral culpability that includes all such groups. And the idea that collective punishment was necessary to clear the land for a holy people undermines itself through an act of injustice. Further, the claim that *none* of us deserves life anyhow flies in the face of the many biblical texts that maintain belief in a God who judges justly to preserve the innocent (Gen 18:25).

It may also come as a surprise to some that the book of Joshua itself does *not* make a strong *moral* case for the conquest. In fact, as Ellen Davis points out, "[T]he only recorded sins in the Promised Land are those committed by Israelites."[4] Other texts in the Pentateuch foreground Canaanite sins, but not Joshua. Within Joshua itself, we rarely glimpse a rationale for the conquest. When one does appear, it's *religious*. Granted, their worship of other deities may have involved immoral practices, but Joshua focuses instead on the *disloyalty* their worship would foster among the Israelites (Josh 23:7-8). For Joshua, idolatry was a poisonous vine that Israel was to thoroughly root out.

A WORD ABOUT *HEREM* TALK

The word *herem* occurs throughout Deuteronomy, Joshua, and other Old Testament books to denote "comprehensive destruction." Closely related to the Hebrew word *qiddash* ("to consecrate" for divine service), *herem* frequently carried sacred implications.[5] For instance, it described property given to God that couldn't be redeemed (Lev 27:21, 28-29). Sometimes it referred to a priestly portion of an offering to God (Num 18:14). An offering might be given to God but shared by the priest as God's representative.

---

[3]*Sib. Or.* 1.171-173.
[4]Ellen F. Davis, "Critical Traditioning: Seeking an Inner Biblical Hermeneutic," *Anglican Theological Review* 82, no. 4 (2000): 733-51 [742].
[5]Daniel I. Block, *Deuteronomy*, NIV Application Commentary (Grand Rapids, MI: Zondervan Academic. 2012), 208.

In other cases, the idea of *herem*-as-vowed-gift-to-God recedes into the background. This is especially so when speaking about idols, illicit altars, or sacred items—or even Canaanites. The idea of comprehensive destruction moves into the foreground. The application of *herem* to non-Israelites emerges first in Numbers 21:1-3 in the context of a defensive war against Canaanites. After an attack on Israel where the king of Arad took Israelites captive, the people vowed to "totally destroy" (*herem*) his cities if God gave them into their hands (Num 21:2). God does so, leading the people to destroy the cities, naming that place (or region) Hormah (from the verb *haram*).

It's not until Deuteronomy that we see *herem* emerge as systematic policy regarding the entire Canaanite population. If you read straight through the Pentateuch, this policy shift is surprising. Thus far, Israel was commanded to destroy and smash idols, but not Canaanites! Numbers signals a turn toward the possibility of Israel engaging in *herem* warfare against its enemies, but on an occasional basis. Deuteronomy takes *herem* to the next level!

If we compare the "destroy" commands from Exodus and Deuteronomy, the objects of total destruction look different:

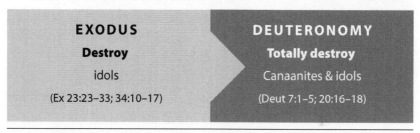

Figure 10.1. Comparison of "destroy" commands in Exodus and Deuteronomy

Exodus commands the people to "demolish" the Canaanites' gods, "break" their religious paraphernalia into pieces, "break down" their altars, and "cut down" Asherah poles. None of the commands in Exodus focus on Israel's need to destroy the Canaanites.[6] God promises that he would oust Canaanites personally, or by means of an angelic power or mysterious

---

[6]Ex 23:33 hints at the need for Israel to take part in ousting the nations: "Do not let them live in your land, or they will cause you to sin against me, because the worship of their gods will certainly be a snare to you." The Hebrew is more ambiguous here: Literally, "They must not live in your land," but without a corresponding command.

"hornet" (Ex 23:27-28; 33:2; 34:11). The people would certainly *participate in* driving out the Canaanites, but such statements aren't framed as commands (Ex 23:31, 33). The *commands* in Exodus focus Israel's destructive energies on idols and altars.[7]

In Deuteronomy, the language shifts. Now it's the Canaanites who are to be "totally destroyed" (see Deut 7:2; 20:17) along with their idols (Deut 7:26). Ousting Canaanites from the land is quite a different matter from running them through, one by one, with a sword. I'm not trying to minimize the trauma of forced expulsion.[8] My point is that the commands to enact a (slow) displacement from Exodus shifted toward a hard-lined and uncompromising command in Deuteronomy.[9]

When we turn to Joshua, several things happen. First, in some cases, it seems that the hard-lined commands of Deuteronomy were enacted. After Jericho's walls tumble, we're told that Israel "devoted the city to the LORD and destroyed (*herem*) with the sword every living thing in it—men and women, young and old, cattle, sheep and donkeys" (Josh 6:21).

Joshua reports that Achan and his family were *herem*-ed (Josh 7:15, 25) along with kings and cities in Northern and Southern Israel (Josh 10–11). It usually tacks on a phrase like "he [Joshua] left no survivors" or "he left nothing alive that breathes."

What do we do with this violent talk?

HARD WORDS

The *herem* language is supposed to shock and startle. So, a first step is to simply notice that response in ourselves. We might wonder if they *don't* disturb us.

---

[7] I should add that in Ex 22:20 Israel was to "totally destroy" (*herem*) anyone *in Israel* who worshiped an idol. Numbers offers the first explicit command for Israel to attack the Canaanites. But we should note the distinction between the command to *destroy* idols and the command to *drive out* the Canaanites (Num 33:50-56).

[8] We only need to recall the preference for suicide among some Native Americans along the Trail of Tears, and the experience of other forcibly displaced people, to recognize the folly of sugar-coating expulsion. On which, see Claudio Saunt, *Unworthy Republic: The Dispossession of Native Americans and the Road to Indian Territory* (New York: W. W. Norton, 2020).

[9] For a compelling critique of the idea that Exodus really envisioned the people "driving out" the Canaanites by "totally killing" them, see William J. Webb and Gordon K. Oeste, *Bloody, Brutal, and Barbaric?: Wrestling with Troubling War Texts* (Downers Grove, IL: InterVarsity Press, 2019), 244-49. They do observe, however, that rhetorically, the goals of "total kill" were *achieved by* expulsion according to several biblical texts.

That's part of hearing this literature on its own terms. As Daniel Block says of the *herem* command in Deuteronomy 7, this is a "rhetoric." It takes the laws of Exodus 23:20-33, where Israel was commanded to destroy idols, and ratchets up the demands. Block writes, "Exodus 23:20-33 is to Deuteronomy 7 what a text of Scripture is to a sermon: the latter draws out the significance of the former."[10] In Deuteronomy, Moses is trying to urge, warn, and startle an audience to take seriously its identity as God's people. The demands are severe. There's a zero-tolerance policy toward all things Canaanite. And according to some texts in Joshua, that's precisely what Israel did.

For Israel, the zero-tolerance "total kill" commands served as a warning to Israel that *if* they allowed even trace remnants of idols into their community, their existence would be at stake. That's why Moses warns the people that if an *Israelite* "prophet or dreamer" even suggested worshiping other gods, they should be executed for "inciting rebellion" (Deut 13:5). Such acts were considered seditious, and Deuteronomy treats the threat of idolatry like threats against the state.[11] Deuteronomy takes things a step further to reinforce the point. Addressing idolatry in the household, we read:

> If your very own brother, or your son or daughter, or the wife you love, or your closest friend secretly entices you, saying, "Let us go and worship other gods" . . . do not yield to them or listen to them. Show them no pity. Do not spare them or shield them. You must certainly put them to death. Your hand must be the first in putting them to death, and then the hands of all the people. (Deut 13:6, 8-9, NIV modified)

Moses wants the people to consider the worst-case scenario. Notice the intimate language. Your *very own* son or daughter. The one *you love*. Your *closest* friend. The policy is ruthless. Turn them in for execution. And should you recuse yourself from exacting punishment on your very daughter or closest friend? By no means! Here the commands hit hardest. Without pity, *your hand* was to take the first stone to begin the execution.

Deuteronomy 13 then talks about those who mislead a city (Deut 13:12-18). If reports emerge that "troublemakers" are leading a town into idolatry, the

---

[10]Block, *Deuteronomy*, 206.
[11]Rob Barrett, *Disloyalty and Destruction: Religion and Politics in Deuteronomy and the Modern World*, Library of Hebrew Bible/Old Testament Studies 511 (New York: T&T Clark, 2009).

people were to investigate. Should the allegation prove true, they were to "put to the sword all who live in that town. You must destroy it completely (*herem*), both its people and its livestock" (Deut 13:15, NIV modified). Then they were to burn everything and everyone "as a whole burnt offering to the LORD your God," and the town should never be rebuilt (Deut 13:16).

Nothing hits harder than these laws. Deuteronomy knows this. That's why the people had to be told to "show them no pity. Do not spare them or shield them" (Deut 13:8). For Moses, that impulse had to be overcome.

As repulsive as these laws might seem to us, they had a logic that we can at least describe. Idolatry threatened the whole community. The zero-tolerance policy was designed to protect the people from sure destruction. The commands against Canaanites in Deuteronomy 7 were preceded by threats that make this point:

> Fear the LORD your God, serve him only and take your oaths in his name. Do not follow other gods, the gods of the peoples around you; for the LORD your God, who is among you, is a jealous God and his anger (*'af*) will burn against you, and he will destroy you from the face of the land. (Deut 6:13-15)

The threat of Israel's own destruction loomed behind the commands to destroy others. In each case where Deuteronomy mentions God's anger (*'af*), it's due to Israel provoking God by turning to other gods or idols.[12] By enacting executions within their community, Yahweh turns from "fierce anger" and shows compassion (Deut 13:17).

After surveying language of threat and destruction in Deuteronomy, Rob Barrett concludes that "[w]hile general disobedience to YHWH's commands is sometimes cited as the trigger [for God's threat's to destroy] (e.g., Deut 28:15), the overwhelming concern in the text is Israel's rejection of the first commandment."[13] The *herem* commands were the "*negative counterpart*" to the positive command to love and worship Yahweh alone (Deut 6:4-9).[14]

My point here is that the anti-Canaanite commands in Deuteronomy are just one piece of a larger complex of commands in Deuteronomy designed

---

[12]Barrett, *Disloyalty and Destruction*, 55.

[13]Barrett, *Disloyalty and Destruction*, 57.

[14]Rachel Billings, *"Israel Served the Lord": The Book of Joshua as Paradoxical Portrait of Faithful Israel* (Notre Dame, IN: University of Notre Dame Press, 2013), 66.

to eliminate the threat of idolatry and foster undivided commitment to Yahweh.

By rhetorical design, such commands speak in black-and-white terms.

The *goal* of this uncompromising rhetoric is to remind Israel that their loyalties lie with Yahweh alone. To *love* Yahweh, according to Deuteronomy, involved displaying an allegiance that abolished all threats of idolatry.[15] The mere mention of other gods was not to be tolerated (Deut 18:20).

Before rushing to think about how to "resolve" or mitigate the ethical problems these laws create, it's important to let them have their say. They're meant to move, stir, and disturb. But ultimately, they're designed to foster devotion to Yahweh.

Having heard that word, what then?

ALIGNING THE RHETORIC

First, it's important to align Deuteronomy's *herem* rhetoric with the Majority Report in Joshua. Deuteronomy's vision of destroying Canaanites is partially enacted in Joshua. Cities like Jericho, Ai, Hazor, Makkedah, and Laish were *herem*-ed by the Israelites. These stories illustrate the enactment of Deuteronomy's vision of total loyalty to Yahweh's demands, and the eradication of threats to idolatry. Relatedly, Exodus's vision of destroying worship sites and displacing Canaanites is partially enacted in Joshua's Minority Report.

MINORITY REPORT	MAJORITY REPORT
Destroy idols / Canaanites **displaced**	**Totally destroy** Canaanites & idols
(Ex 23:23–33; 34:10–17)	(Deut 7:1–5; 20:16–18)
(Josh 23:7, 16; 24:2, 14–16, 20, 23–24)	(Josh 7:1, 11–15; 10:28, 37; 11:11)

Figure 10.2. Comparison of reports

The Exodus (and Deuteronomic) commands to destroy *idols* finds surprising fulfillment in Joshua. Throughout the book, the only idols to be

---

[15]William L. Moran, "The Ancient Near Eastern Background of the Love of God in Deuteronomy," *Catholic Biblical Quarterly* 25 (1963): 77-87.

discarded and removed were among the Israelites! It was *Israel* who had to choose whether to follow the gods of their ancestors or Yahweh (Josh 24:2, 15). It was *Israel* who had to remove the gods among them (Josh 24:11, 23). Joshua never mentions a single Canaanite altar or idol. The named threats were on the inside!

The Deuteronomic command to destroy Canaanites also finds surprising fulfillment. In addition to many Canaanites, the Israelite Achan is destroyed (Josh 7). Moreover, the threat of destruction hung over Israel toward the end of the book when Reuben, Gad, and the half-tribe of Manasseh built an unauthorized altar on the far side of the Jordan (Josh 22:11). Though the episode turned out to be a misunderstanding (the altar was a witness or monument, not designed for sacrifice), the event warned Israel that they could face the same *herem* fate as Achan (Josh 22:18, 20).

As I said in the previous chapter, the two reports—Majority and Minority—are both important. The Majority Report enacts Israel's undivided Torah devotion and uncompromising commitment to Yahweh—as Deuteronomy envisioned. The Minority Report shows a more nuanced enactment of the Exodus commands to eliminate idols but focuses on Israelite idols. It also shows the *beginning* of Yahweh's promise that he would displace the Canaanites. These two stories run side-by-side and interweave at points. How can they do so?

OVER THE TOP

Did Deuteronomy envision the literal application of its laws? Answering this question involves two issues. One relates to *rhetoric*, and one relates to *readers*. Let's start with rhetoric.

It's important to look at this "total kill" language in its ancient context. Ancient war reports often included exaggerated trash-talking. When King Mesha of Moab brags about destroying the Israelite city of Nebo (on a monument), he says: "I went by night and fought against it from the break of dawn until noon, taking it and slaying all, seven thousand men, boys, women, girls, and maidservants, for I had devoted them to destruction (*herem*) for (the god) Ashtar-Chemosh."[16] While it's possible that Mesha

---

[16]*ANET*, 320, col. 2, lns. 14-17.

did kill *everyone* in Nebo, the context of his claim that he *herem*-ed Israel suggests otherwise. Just a few lines earlier, Mesha claimed, "I have triumphed over him [Ahab] and over his house, while Israel hath perished forever!"[17] This boast sounds like the one made several hundred years earlier by Pharaoh Merneptah: "Israel is no more, his seed is not."[18]

But Israel wasn't gone "forever."

These claims reflect ancient warfare rhetoric. When kings claimed that they destroyed someone "forever" or left "nothing alive that breathes," it was like saying, "We won, suckers!" It's the kind of trash-talking that was common and known in the ancient world, and one that wouldn't have conveyed genocidal actions. Notice Joshua 10:20: "Joshua and the Israelites finished dealing them a stunning blow until they were finished off. *Some survivors among them escaped* into the fortified cities" (Josh 10:20, CEB). Joshua doesn't hide the fact that these "finished off" groups had survivors. As William Webb and Gordon Oeste point out, ancient Near Eastern war reports often exaggerated the severity, extent, and speed of their victories.[19]

There are additional reasons to think the *herem* commands were hyperbolic. As noted earlier, Israel was to practice *herem* against anyone *in their community* who led them into idolatry. If someone led a town into idolatry, Israel was to destroy it completely (*herem*)—including all human and animal inhabitants—as a "ruin forever, never to be rebuilt" (Deut 13:16). By that standard, Jerusalem and virtually every city in Israel should've been destroyed at some point in Israel's history! As Rachel Poteet puts it, "If this commandment were carried out with any regularity there would not be a city standing in Israel."[20]

Right after the command to totally destroy the Canaanites (Deut 7:2) Moses tells the people that "the LORD your God will drive out those nations before you, little by little" (Deut 7:22). In other words, the actual

---

[17]*ANET*, 320, col. 2, ln. 10.

[18]*ANET*, 378.

[19]Webb and Oeste, *Bloody*, 136-50; K. Lawson Younger, "The Rhetorical Structuring of the Joshua Conquest Narratives," in *Critical Issues in Early Israelite History*, ed. Richard S. Hess, Gerald A. Klingbeil, and Paul J. Ray, Jr., Bulletin for Biblical Research Supplements 3 (Winona Lake, IN: Eisenbrauns, 2008), 3-32.

[20]Rachel Poteet, personal correspondence with the author, September 22, 2021.

process would be slow and steady. This creates a tension between Deuteronomy 7:2 and 7:22, unless verse 2 was means to be read hyperbolically.[21]

A COMPLEX LAW

When we return to Deuteronomy 7, we see evidence of a *tension* within the *herem* law. Let's look closely.

Table 10.1. Deuteronomy 7:1-5

DEUTERONOMY 7:1-5
Totally Destroy
When the LORD your God brings you into the land you are entering to possess and drives out before you many nations . . . and when the LORD your God has delivered them [the Canaanites] over to you and you have defeated them, then you must *destroy them totally* (Heb. *herem*). Make no treaty with them, and show them no mercy. (vv. 1-2)
Separate
Do not intermarry with them. Do not give your daughters to their sons or take their daughters for your sons, for they will turn your children away from following me to serve other gods, and the LORD's anger will burn against you and will quickly destroy you. *This* is what you are to do to *them: Break down their altars, smash their sacred stones, cut down their Asherah poles and burn their idols in the fire.* (vv. 3-5, NIV modified)

In Deuteronomy 7:1-2, Moses expects the people to *totally destroy* the Canaanites. The phrase "destroy them totally" (*herem*) means treating them like a burnt offering for God. Yet, in Deuteronomy 7:3-5 we see the call to *separate*. The Israelites were not to intermarry with the Canaanites. How do you intermarry with those you've exterminated? It's difficult! As Walter Moberly puts it, "A corpse does not raise the prospect of temptation."[22]

To be fair, we might say that Deuteronomy 7:3-5 highlight the threats for failing to enact Deuteronomy 7:1-2. In other words, failing to *utterly destroy* the inhabitants of the Promised Land leaves the Canaanite temptation around. However, if *herem* is hyperbolic (as argued above), there would undoubtedly be Canaanites who remain, as Deuteronomy 7:22 suggests. In addition, verse 5 suggests that *herem* was meant to be focused on worship sites.

---

[21]Moreover, the book of Deuteronomy suggests that *even God* didn't literally apply such laws to idolatrous Israel. Israel is also called God's "son" (Ex 4:22; Deut 14:1; 32:6) and is also accused of being rebellious and unfaithful. However, Deuteronomy anticipates mercy to Israel on the far side of exile (Deut 30:1-6). God doesn't enact *herem* on his child. Perhaps Israel wasn't to do so on theirs. Caryn A. Reeder, *The Enemy in the Household: Constructive Family Violence in Deuteronomy and Beyond* (Grand Rapids, MI: Baker Academic, 2012), 17-58.

[22]R. W. L. Moberly, *Old Testament Theology* (Grand Rapids, MI: Baker, 2013), 61.

The details are important here: "*This* is what you are to do to *them*." The word *this* tells us how the Israelites were to render the Canaanites to God. The italicized word "*them*" refers to the Canaanites, not the idols. It links to the phrases "with *them*" in verse 3, and to "*their* altars," "*their* sacred stones," and "*their* Asherah poles" in verse 5. In other words, Deuteronomy 7:3-5 qualify verse 2, telling us that *the way for Israel to rid themselves of Canaanites is to tear down their places of worship.* This is religious vandalism, not the extermination of whole people groups! Or, if you prefer scholarly parlance, this is a "reform movement," not a genocidal campaign.

Moreover, the totally destroy commands (Deut 7:2) are to be enacted *after* the Canaanites are gone. Deuteronomy 7:1 makes this clear: "*When* the LORD your God *brings you into the land* you are entering to possess and *drives out before you many nations . . .*" Then they're to leave alive nothing that breathes. How can this be? How can they leave alive nothing that breathes (among the nations) *after* God has driven out those nations? Once again, the only logical object of such destructive energy is against Canaanite worship sites.[23]

The "totally destroy" and "separate" perspectives align with what we've seen already in chapter nine. The Majority Report portrayed Israel's total and decisive destruction of the Canaanites. Comprehensive destruction. Total obedience. Radical loyalty to Yahweh. The Minority Report strikes a different tone. It foregrounds Israel's slow displacement of the Canaanites who still lived alongside them. Both reports are important because of their function. One shows the *ideal* of total covenant loyalty in a land wholly devoted to God. The point of this perspective is not to glory in the ideal of total extermination of people groups, but in the ideal of total obedience to God. Another shows the *real*—trying to live a life of loyalty among the Canaanites. It shows what life is like in between promise and fulfillment, between the already and the not yet.[24]

While it's hard to erase the threat to human life from Deuteronomy 7:1-2, it stands in tension with the wording of Deuteronomy 7:3-5: (1) Verses 1-2

---

[23]Judg 2:2 reinforces this point. Deut 20:15-18 makes a purely metaphorical reading of the *herem* laws difficult, though v. 18 makes clear that Moses' primary point isn't "ethnic elimination, but ethical scrupulosity" and the destruction of religious sites (Block, *Deuteronomy*, 206).

[24]Lissa M. Wray Beal, *Joshua*, Story of God Bible Commentary (Grand Rapids, MI: Zondervan Academic, 2019), 371-72.

use extremist and hyperbolic language to get Israel's attention. (2) Verses 3-5 suggest that destroying Canaanite worship paraphernalia and avoiding intermarriage were the way to destroy the Canaanites. Put together, *herem* warfare functioned as a rallying call for total and radical separation from Canaanite worship. It was an appeal to eliminate illicit forms of worship.

Does this mean that Israel *didn't* really kill scores of Canaanites? At this point, we can at least suggest that Deuteronomy 7 doesn't anticipate a genocidal blitzkrieg. In fact, Deuteronomy 7:22 anticipates slow displacement. This is also a historical question that we'll address in chapter eleven. But for now, let's remember that the law itself directs our attention toward the destruction of idols, not image bearers.

And here's where Deuteronomy wants to take us. As it turns out, the threat of idolatry and false worship wasn't just a problem out there. It was something Israel needed to deal with "in here" (Josh 23:16; 24:2, 14-15, 23). Israel was idolatrous, according to Joshua. Yet, Joshua never commands *herem* against Israelites for that idolatry. Instead, he urges them to remove them from their midst, as Deuteronomy 7:3-5 commands.

APPLYING *HEREM* TO YOUR DAILY LIFE

Do we have any evidence that biblical authors understood Deuteronomy 7:1-5 and related Joshua texts in those terms? That we do! Recognizing this is crucial. I'll provide one example from Exodus to set the stage, and then three examples from Joshua and the rest of the Old Testament before discussing New Testament parallels.

Moses and the Canaanites in Exodus. At Sinai, God tells Israel that he'd drive the Canaanites from the land. But then he warns them to avoid making covenants with the Canaanites, as if they would remain in the land. Israel was to tear down their altars, break their pillars, and cut down their Asherah poles. If they failed to do so, they would get drawn into Canaanite forms of worship (Ex 34:11-16). The implication in this passage is that Canaanites would certainly *be there among the Israelites.* Should Israel covenant with them, they might invite Israelites to an illicit sacrificial event (Ex 34:15), for instance. Their ongoing presence was assumed. The question wasn't whether to let 'em live or die, but how to deal with their idols and religious practices that would surely accompany their ongoing presence.[25] This text suggests that driving out the Canaanites (an event that neither Joshua nor any other Old Testament book records happening) was focused on driving out Canaanite religious practices.

Joshua's farewell speech and the command to totally destroy. My grandfather on my dad's side (Poppop) was a pastor for over sixty-five years. He preached thousands of sermons over his lifetime. Whenever we'd say goodbye after a visit, his eyes would mist up and with deep love he'd say, "Stay close to Jesus." It is a wonderful distillation of the one message that ran beneath the thousands he preached. Stay close to Jesus.

Joshua offers his parting words to Israel in Joshua 23–24. Perhaps it was with a tear in his eye—and knowing the path Israel would likely take—the now-elderly leader urges the people to stay close to Yahweh (Josh 23). He reminds them that two paths diverge before them. One leads to life and blessing. The other leads to the curse of death. Joshua wanted Israel to weigh the cost of disloyalty and embrace the goodness of covenant loyalty and Torah obedience. The people of Israel, including the foreigners among them, had already heard the law in its entirety at Mount Ebal and Mount Gerizim (Josh 8:30-35). But they needed a sober reminder from the elderly Joshua of what covenant allegiance entailed:

> Be very strong; be careful to obey all that is written in the *Book of the Law of Moses*, without turning aside to the right or to the left, *so that* you do not associate with these nations that remain among you; do not invoke the names of their gods or swear by them. You must not serve them or bow down to them. But you are to hold fast to the LORD your God, as you have until now. (Josh 23:6-8, NIV modified to reflect the Hebrew)

Joshua urges the people to avoid intermarriage with foreigners and steer well clear of idolatry (Josh 23:7, 12). These admonitions are straight from Deuteronomy 7:1-5, the original *herem* command. But curiously, Joshua doesn't yell, "Finish the job! Kill every last one!" Instead, he says that Israel needs to avoid intermarriage and idolatry, or else *Yahweh* would not drive

---

[25]Ex 23:20-33 does envision the removal of Canaanites from the land but is clear that this would be *God's* doing. Israel's destructive energy was to be directed against idols, a point reinforced by Deut 12:1-3.

out the Canaanites. Not a word about killing Canaanites. This tells us two things. First, in this text Joshua interprets the *herem* command nongenocidally. Israel was to focus on loyalty to God and the removal of idols. He shifts our focus from *total destruction* of Canaanites toward *separation* from Canaanite religion, just as we saw in Deuteronomy 7:3-5. Second, the conquest is Yahweh's job. *He* would drive out the Canaanites (remember, "little by little," Ex 23:30).[26]

If avoiding idols is the negative command, the positive is covenant loyalty to Yahweh. Joshua encourages the Israelites: "You are to hold fast to the Lord your God, *as you have until now*" (Josh 23:8). Israel's loyalty *and* the ongoing presence of Canaanites in the land might seem to be at odds with one another. Wasn't Israel supposed to oust them? Is Joshua building them up, helping them live into their future? Is it like parents who tell their shy kids, "You're a brave and confident kid!" They see that future self and call it out. Even if so, he still acknowledges their loyalty. He sees it! They'd stuck with Yahweh thus far (at least according to this speech).

This is a big deal. It means that the presence of Canaanites in the land at the end of Joshua's life isn't a sign of Israel's disobedience. Their continued existence is not inherently bad. The bad thing would be Israel following those Canaanites to worship! *Herem* laws are about making sure that can't happen in the places where Israelites live. "The intent is not xenophobia but religious purity."[27] The intent is not *total destruction* of Canaanites but *separation* from Canaanite religious practices.

JOSIAH, HEZEKIAH, AND THE COMMAND TO TOTALLY DESTROY

The next example of a non-genocidal interpretation of the *herem* laws comes from the time of King Josiah, a spiritual giant among Judah's kings. According to Kings, "He did what was right in the eyes of the LORD and followed completely the ways of his father David, not turning aside to the right or to the left" (2 Kings 22:2). That's a solid résumé.

Josiah looks like Joshua. Joshua and Josiah are the only leaders in all of Joshua–Kings who lead the people in a covenant renewal ceremony

---

[26]Wray Beal, *Joshua*, 397-98.
[27]Wray Beal, *Joshua*, 398.

(Josh 8:30-35; 2 Kings 23:1-3).[28] Both leaders celebrate a great Passover celebration as well (Josh 5:10-13; 2 Kings 23:21-23). Kings makes a point that Israel hadn't celebrated such a Passover in all the days of its judges and kings (2 Kings 23:22). Implication? Josiah's was the best Passover party since Joshua's. Most importantly, Joshua and Josiah are both praised for their obedience to the law (Josh 1, 23–24; 2 Kings 22–23). You get the idea. Josiah was a new Joshua.

In Kings, we read how the High Priest during Josiah's time (Hilkiah) found the long lost "Book of the Law" in the temple. Many think it is some form of the book of Deuteronomy. When Josiah heard the book read, he tore his clothes in horror that he and the people were not in compliance.

So, Josiah went on a rampage, tearing down every known place of illicit worship. He wanted to bring Judah into compliance with the book of Deuteronomy. The narrator of Kings makes a point of the fact that Josiah carried out all the commands of Deuteronomy 7:5 (the *herem* text), *but not against Canaanite people*. Instead, he carried out *herem* against (Israelite!) places of worship. Notice how deliberately the author of Kings calls our attention back to the command from Deuteronomy:

Table 10.2. Deuteronomy 7:5 and 2 Kings 23

Deuteronomy 7:5	2 Kings 23
"break down" (Heb. *natats*) altars	DONE (Heb. *natats*; 23:7, 12, 15)
"smash" (Heb. *shabar*) the sacred stones	DONE (Heb. *shabar*; 23:14)
"cut down" (Heb. *gada'*) the Asherah poles	DONE (Heb. *karat*; 23:14)
"burn" (Heb. *saraf*) the idols	DONE (Heb. *saraf*; 23:4, 6, 11, 15)

The author of Kings shows us that Josiah carried out the *herem* command of Deuteronomy 7:1-5 *without* exterminating entire people groups. To be sure, Josiah did brutally kill some Israelite priests who succumbed to idolatry (2 Kings 23:20). This was not an entirely nonviolent episode! But that act was an enactment of the Deuteronomy 13 law against *Israelite* idolatry and not an enactment of the Deuteronomy 7 laws. With respect to

[28]Richard D. Nelson, "Josiah in the Book of Joshua," *Journal of Biblical Literature* 100, no. 4 (1981): 531-40.

the Canaanites, Josiah didn't interpret the Deuteronomic command in literal terms. He focused on the destruction of illicit places of worship (Deut 7:3-5). He didn't hunt down Hivites and Girgashites, but instead, he understood the true sense of the law by seeking radical separation from all forms of "Canaanite" religion that resided in Israel.

The book of Chronicles portrays King Hezekiah in similar terms. After a great Passover celebration (analogous to Joshua 5), the people went throughout the land to eradicate forbidden worship sites. Chronicles uses the same terminology as Deuteronomy 7:5:

Table 10.3. Deuteronomy 7:5 and 2 Chronicles 31

Deuteronomy 7:5	2 Chronicles 31
"break down" (Heb. *natats*) altars	DONE (Heb. *natats*; 31:1)
"smash" (Heb. *shabar*) the sacred stones	DONE (Heb. *shabar*; 31:1)
"cut down" (Heb. *gada'*) the Asherah poles	DONE (Heb. *gada'*; 31:1)

Could it be that this is how the *herem* texts in Joshua are meant to be applied? For Joshua, keeping the Law of Moses meant not intermarrying with the nations and not serving their gods. Here's what Deuteronomy, Joshua, and Kings suggest: Whatever earlier practices of total destruction that these texts reflect, they have been reframed in terms of separation through devotion to Yahweh. The initial command to destroy totally Canaanites was *interpreted* correctly by later biblical writers to be a command about separating from other gods and their influences.

Walter Moberly suggests why this might be:

> Although it appears that there was once an actual practice of herem on the battlefield, both in ancient Israel and among its near neighbors, Deuteronomy uses and indeed privileges the notion of herem only because it was seen to lend itself to a particular metaphorical usage for practices appropriate to enabling Israel's everyday allegiance to YHWH within a world of conflicting allegiances.[29]

He notes correctly that during the time when most scholars think Deuteronomy was edited (during the reign of Hezekiah or Josiah), extermination

---

[29]Moberly, *Old Testament Theology*, 68.

of Canaanites was not even feasible.[30] Hivites, Jebusites, and so on were no longer around. Yet Deuteronomy preserved the extreme language of this shocking practice to emphasize unrelenting and totalizing *separation* from pagan practices and *allegiance* to Yahweh. The *function* of *herem* language is to inspire total allegiance to Yahweh.

In the next chapter, I'll expand this point. While Joshua focuses on the removal of idols *within Israel*, the prime objects of destruction among the Canaanites are *imperial*—weapons, walled cities, kings, and wealth.

EZRA AND THE COMMAND TO SEPARATE
FROM THE PEOPLE OF THE LAND

Another nonviolent interpretation of the *herem* laws appears in Ezra 9. This is a difficult passage for another reason (it seems to promote divorce and expulsion of children), but it reinforces the point that generations of Israelites did *not* interpret Deuteronomy 7:1-2 literally, but in terms of the ideals of religious separation described in Deuteronomy 7:3-5. By this point in the story, Israel had returned from Babylonian Exile to a small portion of their former land. The province of Yehud in which they now lived constituted a fraction of the old tribal territory of Judah. Their numbers were greatly reduced. They lacked adequate defenses, a standing military, and a king. The rebuilt temple paled in comparison to its Solomonic predecessor (Ezra 3:12). This was a stripped back version of Josiah's Judah. Most pointedly, they were now slaves to Persia in their own land (Ezra 9:9; Neh 9:36).

The people of God wrestled with the question of how to rebuild life in such difficult times. With eyes fixed on the Mosaic law, some Judeans recognized the danger of mixed marriages. Throughout the law, and especially Deuteronomy 7:1-5, God warned the people to avoid intermarriage with the Canaanites so that their hearts wouldn't go astray.

One significant person who already betrayed this law in Israel's history was Solomon, serving as a witness to the consequences of dismissing Deuteronomy's command. Solomon married scores of foreign women, who "turned his heart after other gods" (1 Kings 11:4). Solomon's failure to

---

[30]That Deuteronomy was edited during the time of Hezekiah, Josiah, or later, doesn't mean that the laws contained in it are all later.

remain separate from these women, and specifically their gods, led to the destruction of the unified Israelite kingdom (1 Kings 11:11-13). And later, King Ahab married the Phoenician Jezebel, who introduced Baal worship into the Northern Kingdom (1 Kings 16:31).[31]

With such warnings in their ears, a group of officials approach Ezra, a leader of the postexilic community. They bemoan the people's careless marriage practices:

> After these things had been done, the leaders came to me and said, "The people of Israel, including the priests and the Levites, have not kept themselves separate from the neighboring peoples with their detestable practices, like those of the Canaanites, Hittites, Perizzites, Jebusites, Ammonites, Moabites, Egyptians and Amorites." (Ezra 9:1)

A striking detail from this verse might slip our attention. Most of the nations mentioned no longer existed. This list is anachronistic, with some obvious exceptions (e.g., Egyptians).[32]

So why include them? It includes these long-gone nations to show the people's attempt to carry out the demands of Deuteronomy. Deuteronomy 20:17 commands Israel to comprehensively destroy the "Hittites, Amorites, Canaanites, Perizzites, Hivites and Jebusites." Similarly, Moses had promised that God would drive out the "Hittites, Girgashites, Amorites, Canaanites, Perizzites, Hivites and Jebusites" before commanding Israel to destroy them (Deut 7:1-2).

According to Ezra, the land to which Israel returned after the exile lay defiled. The nations defiled it through idolatry (Ezra 9:11-12, 14). So, these officials proposed a radical solution to the threats posed by "Canaanite" marriages (Ezra 10:3). The people should divorce their non-Israelite wives. By separating from foreign wives, Ezra's officials thought the people would remove the defilement of the nations.

We might certainly raise questions about the injustice of the officials' proposal. Wasn't it unjust to divorce these women because they *might* lead

---

[31]From the perspective of the narrator. The historical circumstances of Israel's relationship to the Canaanite Baal were far more complicated.

[32]Some names may have retained their geographical distinctiveness, though the stereotyped framing of these nations suggests that the people are harkening back to an earlier time to make a polemical point about the general problem of religious assimilation.

the people into idolatry? Wasn't Ruth the Moabitess David's great-grand-mother? Didn't the prophet Isaiah say that foreigners should *not* be separated from the people of God, but that those who keep covenant should be brought near instead (Is 56:1-8)?

Yes!

For our purposes, however, it is notable that the officials discerned a way to observe the Deuteronomy 7 and 20 laws *without* killing. Faithfulness, for this group, didn't require a literal application of the *herem* commands to people. From these examples, it seems that from Joshua through Ezra, most Israelites interpreted the *herem* commands (Deut 7:1-5; 20:16-18) nonviolently, even if the divorce measures they took were extreme. While we also see literal application in Joshua (Josh 6–7, 9–11) and a few other places in the Old Testament (1 Sam 15), it is likely that these stories are meant to be applied to the lives of Joshua's first readers by rooting out idolatry *within* Israel.

ALTERNATIVE *HEREM*

In addition to nonliteral application, Joshua suggests that there were additional nonviolent ways of carrying out the *herem* against the Canaanites. If *herem* involved some form of "setting aside by destroying," were there ways of setting aside by *not* destroying? In some Majority Report texts, *herem* clearly happens violently. But other texts reach in a different direction.

When Israel welcomed the Canaanite Rahab into the fold, they first placed her and her family "outside the camp" (Josh 6:23). That's a curious detail. The phrase "outside the camp" held several meanings in the Old Testament. It could designate a *clean* place for depositing sin offerings (Ex 29:14), but it could also designate a place for the unclean (Lev 10:4; 13:46; 14:3; Num 5:3-4; 12:14-15; 31:19; Deut 23:11-13) or a place for punishment (Lev 24:14). The description in Joshua fits closely with texts where someone unclean was placed temporarily outside the camp *until they became clean*. Israel placed Rahab and her family outside the camp for a time, but then incorporated them into the people of Israel. Just two verses after locating them "outside the camp" Joshua tells us that "she lives among the Israelites to this day" (Josh 6:25). It seems that Israel had other ways of addressing the "uncleanness" of the Canaanites that also provided for their eventual inclusion. Rahab and her family were set aside temporarily so that they would not be destroyed, but they would eventually be brought inside.

Another dimension of *herem* is its sacred quality. Israel put aside the precious metals of Jericho "into the treasury of the LORD's house" (Josh 6:24). The Canaanites and their possessions (at least in Jericho) belonged to God. When the Gibeonites duped Israel, we read at first that they were cursed as "woodcutters and water carriers" for the whole Israelite assembly (Josh 9:21). But just a few verses later Joshua tells us that they became "woodcutters and water carriers *for the house of my God*" (Josh 9:23). The narrator reports that they ended up providing for the needs of "the altar of the LORD at the place the LORD would choose" (Josh 9:27). As David Firth notes, even though the story doesn't mention *herem*, the *herem* concept of devoting something wholly and exclusively to God is certainly at play here. The Gibeonites do end up devoted to Yahweh!

It might be for their loyalty that God chooses Gibeon as the place to dwell before taking up residence in Jerusalem. It was there that God appeared to Solomon (1 Kings 3:4).[33] Later, Nehemiah tells us that the Gibeonites stood side-by-side with Israel in rebuilding Jerusalem's walls after the exile. Their faithful response to Yahweh enabled their inclusion within Israel.[34]

READERS

None of this eliminates the violence of *herem* texts in Joshua 6–7 or 10–11. However, one more question needs our attention.

For whom is Joshua written?

Ask two scholars a question and you get three opinions, so the saying goes. We simply don't know when Joshua was finalized. Some early

---

[33]Discussed in David G. Firth, *The Message of Joshua* (Downers Grove, IL: InterVarsity Press, 2015), 187.

[34]David G. Firth, *Including the Stranger* (Downers Grove, IL: InterVarsity Press, 2019), 32. These texts affirm what we've already known about Israel's relationship to outsiders. They could be incorporated into Israel, Canaanite or not, based on their willingness to relate to the God of Israel. Already in the law we've seen that non-Israelites could be circumcised and then participate fully in Israel's feasts (Ex 12:48; Num 9:14; 15:15-16).

interpreters thought Joshua wrote most of the book except his death (Josh 24:29-33).[35] However, clues in the book suggest a later date.

"To this day" statements in Joshua place the book at the earliest during the time of the monarchy. For instance, Joshua 15:63 states that the Jebusites live among the Judeans in Jerusalem "to this day." Since Judeans didn't occupy Jerusalem until the time of David, the book dates to that point at the earliest.

The city lists in Joshua 15:21-62 and 18:21-28 fit squarely in the monarchic period, perhaps in the ninth century BC.[36] While some of these cities (only about 40 percent) were occupied in the Late Bronze Age, when Israel emerged in the land, 100 percent were occupied in the Iron II (Monarchic) period.

The book of Joshua is part of a larger macronarrative that reaches from Joshua 1 until the end of Kings. There's good evidence that these books were edited and stitched together at the end of that process.[37]

In short, it seems likely that the book initially took shape during the monarchy, and then received its final shape during the exile or shortly after.[38] That doesn't mean the book doesn't include earlier stories. It undoubtedly does! However, it does mean that *the book was likely composed for a time when the literal destruction of Canaanites was not possible or pursued.* This is important to bear in mind when considering how the book is meant to be received and applied. The stories of *herem* were read in a time when threats abounded, to be sure. Idolatry constantly threatened God's people. Joshua's *herem* texts portrays its ruthless elimination.

IMPLICATIONS

Here are several implications of our brief look at the "show them no mercy" total destruction texts.

---

[35]*Baba Bathra* 15a.

[36]Chris McKinny, personal correspondence with the author, Jan 14, 2022.

[37]While I don't adopt all the particulars, Richard Nelson's article is useful for understanding this process: "The Double Redaction of the Deuteronomistic History: The Case is Still Compelling," *Journal for the Study of the Old Testament* 29, no. 3 (2005): 319-37; Wray Beal, *Joshua*, 22.

[38]On the complicated question of Joshua's date, see discussion in Firth, *Joshua*, 2-5 and David M. Howard Jr., *Joshua*, New American Commentary (Nashville: Broadman & Holman, 1998), 29-30, who both date the book to the time of David. Most other scholars date the book to the exile or beyond (e.g., Wray Beal, *Joshua*, 19-21).

First, Deuteronomy reframes the focus of "totally destroy" (*herem*) commands in terms of a summons to remain loyal to Yahweh and destroy all "Canaanite" religious influences. Joshua itself includes this summons as its rallying cry in Joshua 23–24, when Joshua twice asks the people of *Israel* (!) to rid themselves of their idols (Josh 24:14, 23). What were they doing with idols? Joshua suggests that they've had them for a long time (Josh 24:14-15). Canaanite qualities like idolatry characterized the people of Israel long before they even entered the land. We saw this at the beginning of the book as well, where the people are in the land but not yet circumcised. The problems to be rooted out were "out there" and "in here." In other words, *Deuteronomy, Joshua, Kings, and Ezra refocus the call to genocidal war (Deut 7:1-2) in terms of a call for radical separation from external and internal idolatry.*

Second, we must ask about stories like the destruction of Jericho, Ai, and other cities where it seems that Israel did apply the *herem* commands to actual Canaanites. What do we do with those passages? To begin, it is very likely that the stories are filled with exaggeration concerning the destruction involved.[39] As Webb and Oeste point out, total kill language is used of cities where we later learn that many Canaanites remained.[40] They couldn't have all died. The *herem* language exaggerates the extent and severity of killing, as was common in ancient warfare.

Given the kind of reframing that the laws of Deuteronomy permits, it is reasonable to ask whether the stories of Jericho and Ai are meant to be read similarly. Jericho and Ai (and the other *herem* warfare texts) seem to use the extremist *total destruction* language of Deuteronomy 7:1-2 to commend the religious *separation* practices of Deuteronomy 7:3-5 for readers who lived at much later times.

Third, Joshua is part of a literary collection that includes Joshua–Kings, which extends at least into the exile. While the traditions contained in the book come from before the exile, the earliest hearers of the book as we see it today would've likely been the exiles or those who returned from exile to

---

[39]For a thorough study on the way that Joshua employs standard ancient Near Eastern rhetorical hyperbole in its conquest accounts, see K. Lawson Younger Jr.'s *Ancient Conquest Accounts: A Study in Ancient Near Eastern and Biblical History Writing* (Sheffield: JSOT Press, 1990).

[40]Webb and Oeste, *Bloody*, 155-58.

a small version of their former land. At that point Israel's concerns no longer related to ousting the Canaanites. Instead, they related entirely to how they might avoid the threats of idolatry and, as we'll see later, imperialism. They also related to questions of identity among people with mixed heritage. The book helps address those urgent threats to Israel's covenant relationship with God that pertained across the ages.

I don't think we can completely escape the violent reality of *herem* texts, or the idea that God called Israel to participate in battles for the land either as judgment on the Canaanites, and especially to weaken the already-declining Egyptian grip on Canaan via Canaanite city-states (on which, see chapter eleven). The exact shape of those battles needs significant historical and rhetorical nuance. However, reading along the grain of the *herem* texts directs subsequent generations of Israel toward religious fidelity, and not toward the destruction of human life.[41]

Jesus and Radical Discipleship

I've argued that the first instance of the *herem* law in Deuteronomy (7:1-5) already takes the totalizing idea of destructive warfare and reframes it in religious terms. This brings Deuteronomy closer to the original concerns regarding the destruction of idols in Exodus. The zeal associated with killing enemies on the battlefield was transferred to zeal for the laws about avoiding idolatry and intermarriage. Joshua and other Old Testament passages reframe the concept of extermination in terms of separation.

Using extremist language to portray spiritual loyalty sounds . . . extreme. But lest we assume that we escape such language by fleeing from Joshua to Yeshua, bear in mind his extreme demands.

Consider the radically violent language that Jesus uses: "If your right eye causes you to stumble, gouge it out and throw it away. . . . If your right hand causes you to stumble, cut it off and throw it away" (Mt 5:29-30).[42] YEOUCH! If we're going to take Jesus' words seriously, and take Scripture

---

[41]Any attempt to extend a literal application of *herem* to Canaanites is put to rest by the note in Judges that God purposefully left the Canaanites in the land to test Israel (Judg 2:20-22). It's important to note, however, that the *problem* in Judg 2 is not Israel's failure to exterminate the Canaanites, but their covenant disloyalty via embrace of Canaanite deities.

[42]Moberly, *Old Testament Theology*, 73.

seriously, are we required to self-mutilate for the Kingdom? Jesus didn't stop to say, "Now I'm speaking metaphorically here, FYI."

But we don't need that qualification. His audience didn't, and neither do we (I hope!). And the force of Jesus' summons depended on him *not* stopping to qualify it. Jesus also told his followers that they couldn't follow him unless they "hate father and mother, wife and children, brothers and sisters—yes, even their own life" (Lk 14:26, NIV modified)! Again, this isn't meant to be taken literally. But it *is* meant to be taken seriously. Following Jesus meant forsaking *all* and taking up the cross.

The apostolic community of the first century worked hard at discerning which biblical laws continued to be valid for Jesus' followers. As the book of Acts reports, Gentile followers came to be welcomed into the fellowship (Acts 11:1-18) and were required to observe a limited range of laws (Acts 15:19-20). Of particular interest to the Rahab story (and later to that of Achan in Josh 7) is the encouragement "to abstain only from things polluted by idols" (Acts 15:20, NRSV; cf. Col 3:5).[43] The early church took up the ethic of Joshua. It took the story seriously but didn't apply it literally.

This is how I'm suggesting we read the *herem* commands to totally destroy. Like the radical and shocking call of Jesus upon his followers, the enduring challenge of Joshua is to forsake all competing loyalties, in fact, to destroy idols and altars, to show *them* no mercy!

So, we see that the Majority and Minority reports have an important place in the book of Joshua. The Majority highlights the need for radical and uncompromising obedience and loyalty. The Minority helps us think through life *between* promise and fulfillment and gives us a more complex picture of Israel's beginnings. These two stories of origin (in Canaan) help shape our understanding of life with Yahweh, in the land, among idols and threats, and within the surprising plan of God.

---

[43]Gordon H. Matties, *Joshua*, Believers Church Bible Commentary (Kitchener, ON: Herald Press, 2012), 79-80.

11

COMPLETING THE EXODUS
IN CANAAN

I WAS ONCE PERUSING a used bookstore in Denver. I picked up a book called *The Art of Biblical Narrative* by Robert Alter.[1] The glue holding its pages in place had weakened, with pages falling out. But the title piqued my interest. I've learned that when a book calls, you answer. Plus, I saw that little National Jewish Book Award medallion on the cover. I'm partial to those, so I bought it.

I had no idea that the book I picked up would revolutionize how I read the Bible. Alter's premise is that the biblical writers were sophisticated artists who crafted their stories with care and creativity. Prior to Alter's groundbreaking little book, many scholars and popular writers thought that the biblical writers were literary hacks who didn't know how to tell a good story. They might've told tales around the campfire, but what we find in the Bible—so they thought—is a loose collection of stories that lacked the kind of sophisticated artistry on display in the grand Greek epics. Alter showed that Hebrew writers wrote *differently*, but with no less artistry than the Greeks.

This included the way that they wrote history.

I mention that story here to highlight a crucial historical point. Biblical historians don't just give us the facts. They paint a historical picture. My friend and former supervisor Phil Long calls this "verbal representational art."[2] With representational art, Long notes, "the subject matter does not

---

[1] Robert Alter, *The Art of Biblical Narrative* (New York: Basic Books, 1981).
[2] V. Philips Long, *The Art of Biblical History*, Foundations of Contemporary Interpretation 5 (Grand Rapids, MI: Zondervan, 1994), 70.

just present itself to the artist as a painting waiting to be painted." The artist must make choices about what to paint, how to paint it, which visual perspective to adopt, the medium of painting, and so on.[3] Moreover, different artistic genres will relate to history in different ways.

I sometimes use the example of Monet's water lilies in class. Monet's paintings are constrained by their subject matter, the "facts on the ground," if you will. For instance, the water lilies don't have eyeballs and don't float in the sky. But they aren't photographs by any stretch. If you set a picture of Monet's water lilies alongside a photograph of the same lilies, you'd notice major differences. But proceeding to ask, *Which picture is true?* is misguided. True about what? The two art mediums are doing different things. The photograph captures a similar-to-life visual representation of the lilies. The impressionist painting conveys the *experience* of movement into nature (during a time of rapid industrialization) and the experience of encountering water lilies. What might seem like visual distortion—vague brushstrokes and the like—are key to conveying a real historical experience.

We might think about Joshua in similar terms.

If you had a time-lapse video camera on a drone flying around Canaan in the Late Bronze and Early Iron Ages, you'd observe a bewildering network of comings and goings, of skirmishes and battles, of migration and movement, and of various groups forming and clustering into a loose network of people that eventually called themselves Israel. At the same time, you'd notice the Sea Peoples moving into the coastal regions of Canaan, upsetting the power balance that Egypt sought to maintain. That *experience* was convulsive, especially when viewed through the lens of history. The Canaanite ground was shifting, and with it, Canaanite walls trembled. A new thing was happening in a world undergoing seismic shifts.[4]

The book of Joshua doesn't give us the drone footage, at least in the conquest stories of Joshua 1–12. Instead, it weaves together different

[3]Long, *Art of Biblical History*, 70.
[4]Ann E. Killebrew, "The Emergence of Ancient Israel: The Social Boundaries of a 'Mixed Multitude' in Canaan," in *"I Will Speak the Riddle of Ancient Times": Archaeological and Historical Studies in Honor of Amihai Mazar on the Occasion of His Sixtieth Birthday*, vol. 1, eds. A. M. Maeir and P. de Miroschedji (Winona Lake, IN: Eisenbrauns, 2006), 555-72.

artistic forms to tell the story of Israel in Canaan. The closest thing to drone footage that Joshua offers is in Joshua 13–21, which describes Israel's *settlement*, a process that occurred over a period of time that continued well after the death of Joshua. To get a handle on the conquest portion of the story (Josh 1–12), we must keep three things in mind. We'll discuss them in this chapter as we consider how history helps us think about the book's violence.

1. Joshua gives us an artistic rendering of the past.

2. Joshua is set in a time of earth-shifting historical events.

3. Joshua was edited and updated long after its original composition.

We'll touch on these points throughout this chapter but will focus most of our attention on how the book's setting affects how we read its violence.

HISTORICAL ART IN JOSHUA

The book of Joshua doesn't use the same art style from beginning to end. Sometimes it paints events with broad brushstrokes, and in other cases, with remarkable historical detail. We can compare it to a mix of caricature and realism. Caricature is a form of cartoon that exaggerates features and under-represents others. In his book *Understanding Comics*, Scott McCloud says that "when we abstract an image through cartooning, we're not so much eliminating details as we are focusing on specific details. By stripping down an image to its essential 'meaning' an artist can amplify that meaning in a way that realistic art can't."[5] It might zero in on the bright eyes or large muscles of a character to make a specific point. It might also use a single event to represent a range of experiences and events. McCloud points out that the "intensity of a simple story or visual style . . . toward a purpose can be an effective tool for storytelling in any medium." Through this intensity cartoons (and caricature-style storytelling) "focus our attention on an idea."[6]

McCloud's observations about comics fit the way Joshua tells the Majority Report (see chapter nine). The Majority Report seizes on the

---

[5]Scott McCloud, *Understanding Comics: The Invisible Art* (New York: William Morrow, 2003), 30.
[6]McCloud, *Understanding Comics*, 31.

embattled elements of early Israel to intensify the ideas that (a) God fought for Israel in faithfulness to his promises and (b) loyalty to Yahweh was to be uncompromising. Sharply defined and highly intensified art forms like caricature are especially effective for highlighting those ideas.[7] A relationship to history still exists, but it doesn't come from the drone's camera. Recognizing this doesn't make the book of Joshua less inspired or God-breathed. As Hebrews reminds us, in the past God spoke "at many times and in various ways" (Heb 1:1). God speaks through parables, history, prayers, of all varieties and stripes to convey his word to his people throughout the ages.

Joshua uses a more *realist* style to write the Minority Report. Realism portrays the world, warts and all, and seeks a "faithful representation of reality."[8] It rejects the *idealism* of other art forms. As you may recall, the Minority Report recognizes that Israel's conquest was a slow process. It was incomplete. It faltered and at times derailed. And while this report is still not the complete picture, it offers less idealism than the Majority Report. But realism still has its agenda. It emphasizes the ordinary. It foregrounds the humanity of its subjects. It reacts to idealism with its naturalism.[9]

As a historical genre, realism is no less *artistic*. It also uses light, shadow, perspective, story, and subject simplification, and so on. It is not just a copy of reality. Long tells the story of his art teacher who would challenge critics who called realism less "artistic" to inspect a two-inch square of his paintings at very close range: "[W]hat they would find would not be nature, or even an exact copy of the appearance of nature, but a tiny abstract painting."[10] Long notes that on the one hand, his teacher's paintings were *fictional* and not *literal* renderings of reality. But on the other hand, "his paintings were very much representations of reality, imparting to receptive viewers a truer sense and appreciation of the scene."[11] Recognizing this helps us see that

---

[7]McCloud, *Understanding Comics*, 31, talks about the role of intensification.

[8]"Realism (arts)," Wikipedia, last edited June 9, 2022, https://en.wikipedia.org/wiki/Realism_(arts).

[9]Though it should be noted that some realist painters who eventually formed a splinter "naturalist" movement suggested an idealism of its own. They claimed that realists should only paint the *beautiful*.

[10]Long, *Art of Biblical History*, 64.

[11]Long, *Art of Biblical History*, 64.

even the Minority Report is a partial view of the past. Inspecting its close details often reveals another zone of caricature-like art.

On the other hand, Joshua wants us to see complexity. The story of Israel's beginnings in the land was complicated. The book doesn't hide the fact that Israel failed in some major ways. The conquest remained unfinished. Canaanites remained in the land (and in Israel's own community). And many Canaanites besides Rahab and the Gibeonites were part of the Israelite community (Josh 8:30-35). Interweaving these two art forms allows the book of Joshua to say two things at once. Ellen Davis summarizes the contribution of these two art forms. One "affirm(s) the total reliability of YHWH's word to Israel." The other recognizes that much remained to be realized. It maintains that *"YHWH is faithful, yet Israel is slack, and therefore much that YHWH wishes to do for the people remains unrealized."*[12] To make these points, caricature and realism served Joshua well.

Recognizing the artfulness of history-telling can help us navigate (but not solve!) some of the historical and moral complexities in the book. It can help us wrestle through the historicity of some of the book's most graphically violent episodes, like the story of Jericho. But in addition to literary sensitivities, we also benefit from some specific historical and archaeological examples.

THE ART OF JOSHUA'S HISTORY

I was standing at the edge of Jericho's crumbled remains. It was 1999, and it was dusty, hot, sunny, and . . . hot. Jericho sits at 846 feet below sea level, at the bottom of the Rift Valley that extends from Africa, through the land of Israel, and into Turkey. It's 3,300 feet lower than Jerusalem, and though only 15 miles away, it's a completely different climate because the moisture off the Mediterranean hardly ever reaches there. Temperatures can soar well above 110 degrees Fahrenheit. It astonished me that humans have lived *there* since at least 6,500 BC (with a few gaps). It didn't strike me as a "Most Livable City in the World" candidate.

---

[12]Ellen F. Davis, *Opening Israel's Scriptures* (New York: Oxford University Press, 2019), 133, emphasis original.

I remember my Christian professor describing Kathleen Kenyon's pioneering archaeological excavation of Jericho in the 1950s. Kenyon disputed the findings of John Garstang, who claimed that he found the crumbled walls of Jericho from Joshua's time. She dated the city's destruction and crumbled walls to 1550 BC, long *before* Israel would've entered the land. The city was occupied in the Late Bronze/Early Iron periods, when Israel likely settled in the land. But there's hardly any evidence of destruction from the two time periods when biblical scholars date the exodus (the 1400s BC and 1200–1100s BC).[13]

Still, if you Google popular blogs and articles on Jericho's walls, you'll find countless claims that Joshua's destroyed walls *have* been found, that they did fall down due to an Israelite conquest. However, almost all such claims have been soundly refuted by radiocarbon dating and material evidence.[14]

After that first trip to Jericho, I recall journaling about this uncertain chapter in biblical history. I sat in my dorm room in Jerusalem's Beit Bernstein burning an oil lamp while writing. I was trying to get in (biblical) character, but my goodness, oil lamps are really smoky! I wrote something like, *For some reason, the uncertainty about Jericho's history doesn't rock my faith.* It was probably a relief. If the destruction of Jericho didn't happen exactly as Joshua reported—with men, women, children, animals destroyed—then perhaps the entire conquest wasn't so straightforwardly genocidal. My confidence in the Old Testament as Scripture didn't come a-tumblin' down if one event didn't happen as straightforwardly as reported.

I later revisited the question of Jericho in light of Phil Long's distinction between the truth *value* of a text and its truth *claims*.[15] Truth value depends on the truth claims. If the Gospels *claim* that Herod the Great ruled when Jesus was born (Mt 2:1), and it didn't happen, then the truth *value* of that

---

[13]Lorenzo Nigro, "The Italian-Palestinian Expedition to Tell es-Sultan, Ancient Jericho (1997–2015): Archaeology and Valorisation of Material and Immaterial Heritage," in *Digging Up Jericho: Past, Present, and Future*, ed. Rachel Thyrza Sparks et al. (Oxford: Archaeopress Archaeology, 2020), 175-214; Lorenzo Nigro, "Jericho and the Dead Sea. Life and Resilience," in *Life at the Dead Sea: Proceedings of the International Conference held at the State Museum of Archaeology Chemnitz (SMAC), February 21-24, 2018, Chemnitz*, ed. Martin Peilstöcker and Sabine Wolfram, Ägypten und Altes Testament 96 (Münster: Zaphon, 2019), 139-58; Poitr Bienkowski, *Jericho in the Late Bronze Age* (Warminster: Aris and Phillips, 1986).

[14]Rachael Thyrza Sparks et al., *Digging Up Jericho*.

[15]Long, *Art of Biblical History*, 29-30.

text would be in question. But if a parable, for instance, makes no *truth claims* about real historical events, then the *value* of that portion of Scripture isn't bound to its historicity. It isn't claiming to be history.

So far so good. Yet accessing the truth claims about Jericho's destruction, or for that matter, the entire conquest, isn't so easy. What historical truth claims does the text make? And what is the nature of those claims? Answering those questions requires sensitivity to the way ancient people wrote history in the first place, and how the Bible came together. It requires genre and literary sensitivities. But it also requires historical awareness. We need to know the world out of which these stories came, including the history of early Israel.

And we're going to get much of that wrong.

We're simply too far removed from the world of ancient Israel to line up all the details correctly. But that doesn't mean we know nothing. In this section, we revisit Jericho and the "conquest" with our literary and historical antennae up. What can the archaeology, history, and literature of Joshua tell us about the book's violence? What do we do with all the details we can't work out?

ISRAEL'S BEGINNINGS

Scholars who talk about Israel's origins in the land of Canaan usually use words like "emergence" or "appearance" to describe such times. Israel's earliest days in the land likely resulted from a combination of groups arriving from outside and some forming together from inside. Most scholars favor the idea that most Israelites *emerged* from within Canaan. Certain groups of Canaanites gradually differentiated themselves from the local populations to become Israelites. To be sure, a minority of scholars maintain that most Israelites came from outside and did so violently.

Israel's beginnings in the land likely involved a mix of indigenous Canaanites and groups migrating from outside, including some Hebrews who traced their ancestry back to the twelve sons of Jacob. I'd maintain that a group of Hebrews came from Egypt into the land and joined with other migrating groups. That group from outside was already a "mixed multitude" of Hebrews and others (Ex 12:38). Indigenous Canaanites probably joined outsider groups who migrated and battled their way toward settlement. These groups eventually coalesced around a common "Israelite" national identity. The prophet Ezekiel hints at this complexity when tracing the spiritual ancestry of Jerusalem, "Your ancestry and birth were in the land of the Canaanites; your father was an Amorite and your mother a Hittite" (Ezek 16:3; cf. 16:45).[16]

This process of coalescing probably took several hundred years. And even those groups arriving from outside Canaan weren't all outsiders. We know from Egyptian works like the *Instruction of Merikere*, *The Prophecy of Nefertiti*, and other documents that neighboring groups ended up in Egypt as slaves, POWs, and migrants.[17] Historically speaking, it is plausible that they wanted to return home and took any opportunity to do so. Exodus affirms the ethnically complex nature of the people who left Egypt (Ex 12:38, 48). Moreover, Leviticus 24:22, Numbers 9:14 and 15:14-16, and Deuteronomy 10:18-19 each assume that the community of Israel included resident foreigners, some of whom would have assimilated into Israel.

I hope you're getting the picture. Our understanding of Israel's beginnings involves educated guesses. That means that we must hold loosely our ability to say precisely how the biblical account relates to history. Thankfully, its truth *value* doesn't depend on tying up all the loose ends. If it did, Joshua wouldn't help! Joshua gives us at least three main angles on Israel's

---

[16]To be sure, as Block notes, "Ezekiel is not giving a lecture in ethnography. His intention is rhetorical and sharply polemical. . . . In this context 'Canaanites' and 'Hittites' and 'Amorites' represent human depravity at its worst." Daniel I. Block, *Ezekiel 1–24*, The New International Commentary on the Old Testament (Grand Rapids, MI: Eerdmans, 1997), 475. But it should also be noted that Israel had deep connections to the Hittites in Genesis and elsewhere. Hebron was part of Hittite territory (Gen 23), and Abraham's wife Sarah was buried there. In fact, the reference to "your mother was a Hittite" here in Ezekiel may refer to Sarah as Israel's mother (Is 51:2). Hebron was also Israel's first capital (2 Sam 2:11; 5:3-4), and Hittites Ahimelek and Uriah served among Israel (1 Sam 26:6; 2 Sam 23:39). Hittites (via Hebron) and Amorites are connected to Jerusalem in Josh 10:5. Bustenay Oded notes that Hatti replaces Amurru in Neo-Assyrian and Neo-Babylonian texts as a designation for lands west of the Euphrates. See Bustenay Oded, "'Your Father Is an Amorite and Your Mother a Hittite' Ezekiel 16:3," in *Marbeh Ḥokmah: Studies in the Bible and the Ancient Near East in Loving Memory of Victor Avigdor Hurowitz*, ed. S. Yona et al. (Winona Lake, IN: Eisenbrauns, 2015), 389-99. It's those ancestral associations that bolster Ezekiel's rhetorical point.

[17]Discussed in James K. Hoffmeier, *Israel in Egypt: The Evidence for the Authenticity of the Exodus Tradition* (Oxford: Oxford University Press, 1999), 52-76; Ann E. Killebrew, *Biblical Peoples and Ethnicity: An Archaeological Study of Egyptians, Canaanites, Philistines, and Early Israel, 1300–1100 BCE*, Archaeology and Biblical Studies 9 (Atlanta, GA: SBL, 2005), 151-52.

beginnings: (1) quick conquest; (2) slow displacement of Canaanite peoples; (3) inclusion of Canaanite groups within Israel (see Josh 9). The book is doing more than painting a simple picture of what happened.

Archaeological and historical analysis help round out our picture of what may have led to the eventual establishment of Israel in the land of Canaan. We can observe the broad contours of Israel's early settlement patterns, for instance. A mixed group of insiders and outsiders first settled east of the Jordan and then slowly migrated west, settling in the central highlands of the tribal area designated for Manasseh and then over the western slopes.[18] While it seems that this migration happened *slowly*, the pattern fits the general geographical picture in Joshua, but not its timeline. For instance, the summary of northern and southern campaigns in Joshua 10–11 probably occurred over several hundred years.[19] The book of Joshua likely "telescoped" events that took place over several centuries—fitting them into the time frame of Joshua's life as part of the book's caricature.

JERICHO IN HISTORY AND CARICATURE

History is complicated. But if we want to move toward the truth of the matter, we sometimes must look at truth's multifaceted and messy complexity. Jericho is an unusually complicated site for archaeological study. It suffered serious erosion. It's really old. It's still being excavated and re-examined.[20] And full and detailed excavation reports are slow in coming.

What do we know about Jericho? First, archaeologists found no occupation or destruction *layer* from the Late Bronze Age, when Israel is said to have conquered the land. There are some *remains* from that time. Kenyon and later excavators confirmed this. That agrees with Joshua's claim that there were Canaanites at the site during the time of the conquest but guarantees nothing about their destruction or defeat. Some suggest that there was a small Late Bronze settlement, but that it was unwalled. Others

---

[18] Adam Zertal, *The Manasseh Hill Country Survey*, 6 vols., Culture and History of the Ancient Near East 21 (Leiden: Brill, 2004–2021).

[19] The text of Joshua 10–11 and its relationship to the rest of Joshua is admittedly complex. After saying that Joshua took the whole land (Josh 11:23), we read in Joshua 13:1 (NRSV) that "much of the land still remains to be possessed."

[20] A joint Palestinian-Italian team has been re-examining and excavating the site since 1997. See www.lasapienzatojericho.it/History.php.

conjecture that a fortress tower of some sort once stood there but has since worn away. The mud bricks of Jericho eroded heavily, and some portions of the site completely crumbled due to site erosion. We'll never know about those portions of the city.

Lacking a destruction layer doesn't necessarily mean that a defeat of some kind didn't happen. It's just harder to square with the biblical account. As an analogy, the prominent Late Bronze Age city of Megiddo (in the northern portion of Israel) also lacks a destruction layer, despite Pharaoh Thutmose III's claim that he destroyed it.[21] Joshua claims that Israel conquered Megiddo's king, and archaeology confirms a destruction layer from the 1100s BC, when Israel was probably beginning to flourish in the land. However, to keep us on our toes, Judges states that the city of Megiddo *wasn't* captured by the Israelites (Judg 1:27). This could be because Joshua only claimed that Israel captured Megiddo's *king* (Josh 12:21), and not the king's *subjects*. However, the opening summary of Joshua's victories telescopes these events to give the impression that they happened at once: "Here is a list of the kings of the land that Joshua and the Israelites conquered on the west side of the Jordan. . . . Joshua gave their lands as an inheritance to the tribes of Israel according to their tribal divisions" (Josh 12:7). In reality, the gap between conquering the *kings* and actually occupying their *lands* was fairly large according to Scripture and archaeology. Perhaps we shouldn't be surprised that getting a clean take on events from 3,300 years ago is tricky.

Back to Jericho. Given the uncertainties about the nature of its Canaanite occupation during the time Joshua claims, we might need to adjust our perceptions of the city's size. If we imagine a massive city with imposing architecture and sky-scraping defensive towers, we've got the wrong picture. The Jericho that Israel encountered appears to have been a smaller settlement atop an older and larger Middle Bronze city (2000–1500 BC).[22]

Jericho is called a "city" (*'ir* in Hebrew), but that doesn't mean it was a bustling metropolis with four lane highways. The word *'ir* covers everything

---

[21]Richard S. Hess, "The Jericho and Ai of the Book of Joshua," in *Critical Issues in Early Israelite History*, eds. Richard S. Hess, Gerald A. Klingbeil, and Paul J. Ray, Bulletin for Biblical Research Supplements 3 (Winona Lake, IN: Eisenbrauns, 2008), 38.

[22]Nigro, "Jericho and the Dead Sea," 149; Nigro, "The Italian-Palestinian Expedition,"196.

from large cities to small towns and administrative centers.[23] The author of Joshua doesn't emphasize its size. By contrast, the author of Joshua calls Gibeon a "large city" and Hazor "the head of [the] kingdoms" (Josh 10:2; 11:10).[24] Jericho was likely a smallish but well-fortified citadel positioned to guard one major entrance into the land from the east. It might've been a "meh!" city by ancient standards, at least in terms of its sparse population. We don't even know if many women and children lived there. Perhaps Rahab and her children were among the few women and children, brought there for Rahab to "service" the soldiers posted in the city. That might even explain her eagerness to get out! This reconstruction is hypothetical, but it bears consideration, given the slim archaeological evidence and the size of the entire site itself (just a few acres).

Just as the city was likely small, its "king" was no geopolitical mover and shaker. His domain was relatively small but strategic. Hess suggests that this king would've been responsible for securing or preventing access to key routes between Jordan and Canaan and was likely answerable to a superior in the hill country (and ultimately, to Egypt).[25] Ancient letters recovered from the Egyptian city Amarna (from about 1352–1336 BC) indicate that this type of king was likely responsible for a few hundred troops. One of those letters is from the regional Canaanite "king" of the coastal city Byblos to the Egyptian king. It gives us a window into life on the ground: "Send ships to fetch the Lady's property and me. [Sen]d 50-100 men and 50-100 m[en fro]m [Meluh]ha, 50 chariots, [to g]uard [the city] for you. Se[nd] archers and bring peace to the land."[26] The same king later asks for just forty soldiers to defend Byblos against its enemy. In another letter, the king

---

[23] An example would be the "city of Amalek," which is likely a nomadic encampment (1 Sam 15:5).

[24] NRSV. Noted by Hess, "Jericho and Ai of the Book of Joshua," 33-46.

[25] Hess, "Jericho and Ai of the Book of Joshua," 41. Yet see Charlie Trimm, *The Destruction of the Canaanites: God, Genocide, and Biblical Interpretation* (Grand Rapids, MI: Eerdmans, 2022), 74, who criticizes the possibility of such organized control of outposts like Jericho and contends that civilians would've been present if Jericho was a military base.

[26] EA 132.53-59. Hess, "Jericho and Ai of the Book of Joshua," 42, citing William L. Moran, ed. and trans., *The Amarna Letters* (Baltimore: Johns Hopkins, 1992), 214. While no Amarna Letters mention Jericho (*Ruha* in Egyptian), an administrative tablet from 1300s BC Jericho was found. It reflects the existence of a palace and some sort of city. See Nigro, "Italian-Palestinian Expedition," 202; Wayne Horowitz, Takayoshi Oshima, and Seth L. Sanders, *Cuneiform in Canaan, Cuneiform Sources from the Land of Israel in Ancient Times* (Jerusalem: Israel Exploration Society, 2006), 96-97, 231.

of Jerusalem named Abdi-Heba asks for fifty men to defend his city.[27] In yet
another example from the Amarna Letters, a king from Megiddo, a city far
larger than Jericho, asks for one hundred soldiers to defend his city! "It
would not seem preposterous," Hess reasons, "if the number of men de-
fending Jericho was about 100 or fewer."[28] While Hess may overstate the
case, given the existence of a palace of some sort during this period, the city
may have been a minor military base needed to protect against marauders
and invaders from the east and to guard access to Jericho's springs.[29]

What this means for violence in Joshua. How does this historical
picture of Jericho impact our reading of the violent story portrayed in
Joshua? Joshua reports that Israel "devoted the city (*herem*) to the LORD
and destroyed with the sword every living thing in it—men and women,
young and old, cattle, sheep and donkeys" (Josh 6:21). At face value, this
could sound like the genocide of a major urban population. But as noted
in chapter ten, *herem* suggests comprehensive destruction, and not necessarily the killing of every single person of all categories.[30] On this reading,
Joshua 6:21 isn't trying to specify the types of individuals killed. If Rahab
and her family were preserved, and this was a smallish military town, the
"everyone" killed was likely a group of soldiers. While still extremely violent and troubling, it changes our picture of the events. It's a caricature
of an event that was probably a smallish battle that an author used to
emblemize the total commitment to Yahweh required for Israel's life in
the land.

The historical realities surrounding Jericho's demise were likely more
complicated. Joshua even suggests as much. Joshua 24 reports that the
people of Jericho came out and fought Israel when they crossed the Jordan
and arrived at Jericho (Josh 24:11). We never hear of such hostility from
the inhabitants of Jericho in Joshua 6.[31] Joshua 6 suggests that Israel

---

[27]EA 289.37-44.
[28]EA 244.32-36. Hess, "Jericho and Ai of the Book of Joshua," 42.
[29]Lawson Stone, "Early Israel and its Appearance in Canaan," in *Ancient Israel's History: An Introduction to Issues and Sources*, ed. Bill T. Arnold and Richard S. Hess (Grand Rapids, MI: Baker Academic, 2014), 144.
[30]Hess, "Jericho and Ai of the Book of Joshua," 39; David G. Firth, *The Message of Joshua* (Downers Grove, IL: InterVarsity Press, 2015), 137.
[31]Josh 24:11-13 also introduces the idea that Yahweh sent a hornet ahead of the people (cf. Ex 23:28).

assaulted an otherwise besieged people. The idea of a hostile response to Israel's arrival fits with other battle accounts in the book (see below). But the account in Joshua 6 is probably designed to do more than just report history. Even if Joshua 24:11 is a summary of all campaigns in Josh 6–11, it only highlights the symbolic weight attached to Jericho, and the fact that it represented more than itself in Israel's memory. Somehow, all future battles were contained in Jericho.

So, while the Battle of Jericho might've been small, and the "city" not much to write home about, it held symbolic and strategic importance for the people of Israel and the author of Joshua. As a negative analogy, we might consider the death of the firstborn at Herod's hands in Matthew 2:16. While Bethlehem was a small city and likely no more than ten to thirty boys were killed (still a tragedy!), the story holds a very significant place in the gospel story.[32] For the bloodthirsty and brutal Herod, the slaughter is hardly a standout. But for Matthew, the story embodies the suffering of God's people at the hand of oppressive rulers and the ongoing experience of exile (Mt 2:18).

Jericho was the first test of Israel's loyalty, and the first military engagement in the land. To highlight the symbolic significance of this event, Joshua's author lingers over this story, tracing its outlines in vivid form. For instance, the word "all" appears twelve times in the story to emphasize Israel's total victory. He also lets the camera focus on the priests and ark as they circle the city seven times. The author also foregrounds other non-military details, like the protection of Rahab's family and her inclusion in Israel.

Caricatures highlight and exaggerate certain features and mute or diminish others. They don't do so to mislead or distort, but to capture the essence of a person, or to highlight their memorable features. The story of Jericho highlights the successes (God fighting and giving the land) and failures (Israel taking forbidden "fruits" of the land)[33] of Israel's beginnings. On this score, our children's Bibles get this story right!

---

[32]Matthew Wilkins, "Matthew," in *Zondervan Illustrated Bible Backgrounds Commentary: Matthew, Mark, and Luke*, ed. Clinton E. Arnold (Grand Rapids, MI: Zondervan, 2011), 74.
[33]By Achan in Josh 7.

In short, the case of Jericho cautions us against assuming too readily that the literary portrait of Jericho's destruction is a mirror image of past events—and against letting our imaginations about the city's size and power run wild. Understanding the historical context of Jericho cautions us to avoid reading the text's story of slaughter against the backdrop of the massive walled city so often portrayed in artistic renderings of this story. But the literary portrait challenges us to take seriously the power of Yahweh and his call for total commitment. We're to take the story "seriously without taking it woodenly."[34]

Let's look further at what a historical perspective on Joshua can teach us, and how that perspective shapes our understanding of the "conquest."

RETHINKING THE "CONQUEST"

The word *conquest* probably conjures up images of an outside power subjugating and taking control of a place. We might think of the Norman conquest of England, or Alexander the Great's conquest of Persia. Those with superior weapons or tactical skills win, and often quickly.

But Israel's beginnings in Canaan aren't so simple.

To gain perspective, we must look at several powerful forces at work in the Late Bronze (1550–1200 BC) and Early Iron (1200–1000 BC) ages in the eastern Mediterranean and far beyond.[35] Toward the end of the Late Bronze Age and into the Early Iron Age, the entire Mediterranean world suffered an unprecedented collapse of urban culture. From Greece to Canaan and into Syria, cities burned and fell, trade routes broke down, entire kingdoms went into decline, and entire populations shifted. We don't know exactly why, but food shortages and famine seem to be key factors. Earthquakes and refugee crises didn't help. People were on the move, and kingdoms crumbled. As Eric Cline puts it in his book *1177 BC*, "it was as if civilization itself had been wiped away in much of this region [Greece, Egypt, and the Near East]."[36]

---

[34]R. W. L. Moberly, *Old Testament Theology* (Grand Rapids, MI: Baker, 2013), 59, speaking about the seven nations in Deut 7:1-5.
[35]See Eric H. Cline, *1177 BC: The Year Civilization Collapsed*, rev. ed. (Princeton: Princeton University Press, 2021); Amihai Mazar, *Archaeology of the Land of the Bible 10,000–586 BCE*, Anchor Bible Reference Library (New York: Doubleday, 1990); Stone, "Early Israel." The precise end dates of the Late Bronze Age cannot be fixed, as lingering Canaanite control lasted well into the twelfth century BC.
[36]Cline, *1177 BC*, 9.

The Late Bronze Age collapse of urban culture helps us understand another feature of this time. During the Late Bronze Age, when the Old Testament portrays Israel's entrance into the land, Egypt controlled most of Canaan. Or at least, it *tried* to control Canaan through a system of old-school local kings who ruled over city-states in Canaan. These cities were located at key junctures throughout the land of what eventually became Israel. Egypt dominated most of Canaan starting about 1470 BC, when it defeated a coalition of nations that had been giving it headaches for some time. Among these defeated peoples was a group known as the Hyksos, who probably originated in Canaan, or just to the north. They had swept down into Egypt and controlled Egypt for about 170 years (ca. 1720–1550 BC).

Egypt eventually expelled them. They chased the Hyksos home and even took over their land (Canaan) to make sure they wouldn't raise hell again.[37] They collected tribute and ruled Canaan through a network of city-states. But Egypt's problems with the local people of Canaan continued.[38]

The Amarna Letters (mid-1300s BC) found in Egypt describe the Egyptians' numerous run-ins with disruptive groups in Canaan—groups they were trying to keep at bay. Egypt had trouble controlling Canaan and was losing its grip. The Canaanite kings constantly appealed to the motherland for help managing various troubles on the ground. Groups like the *Habiru* (outlaw and mercenary bands) and *Shasu* (semi-nomadic groups) eroded Egyptian resources and patience in Canaan. Egypt maintained some measure of control of Canaan well into the 1100s BC in lowland regions like Beth Shan, when Israel was probably arriving and emerging in the land. Egypt eventually lost control of coastal regions to the invading "Sea Peoples" (including the Philistines).[39]

---

[37]Jonathan N. Tubb, *Canaanites*, Peoples of the Past, Vol. 2 (Norman: University of Oklahoma Press, 1998); Killebrew, *Biblical Peoples and Ethnicity*.

[38]Mary Ellen Buck, *The Canaanites: Their History and Culture from Texts and Artifacts* (Eugene, OR: Wipf & Stock, 2019), 30-55.

[39]Meindert Dijkstra, "Canaan in the Transition from the Late Bronze to the Early Iron Age from an Egyptian Perspective," in *The Land of Canaan in the Late Bronze Age*, ed. Lester L. Grabbe (London: Bloomsbury Academic, 2017), 72; Mazar, *Archaeology*, 288-91. The Sea Peoples invaded long before the reign of Ramesses VI. We may note Israel's ongoing difficulties with Canaanites in the Jezreel Valley and Beth Shan (Josh 17:16, Judg 1:27), where Egypt maintained ongoing control well into the 1100s BC. For an intriguing, though not entirely convincing, argument that

Though most agree that Israel gained its foothold in Canaan slightly after the time of the Amarna Letters—sometime in the 1200s BC—the world those letters describe was alive and well. In other words, early Israel likely confronted Egypt-controlled Canaanite kings who didn't want to let go of power in a changing world.[40]

Judges 6:9 equates the Egyptian oppressors with the Canaanites that God drove out of the land: "I rescued you from the hand of the *Egyptians*. And I delivered you from the hand of *all your oppressors*; I drove them out before you and gave you their land." The implication here is that the people that God drove out of Canaan were Israel's oppressors, akin to the Egyptians. The parallelism between "the Egyptians" and "your oppressors" in Judges 6:9 may even betray an explicit recognition that the Canaanites in the land *were* Egyptian oppressors whom God expelled. And it was for their *kings* that Joshua reserves its greatest critique.

DEFEATING EGYPTIAN-BACKED KINGS

Now our story of the "conquest" takes a most interesting turn. Lawson Stone observes that the war stories in Joshua 9–11 emphasize the capture and killing of Canaanite *kings* at regional urban centers at major Canaanite crossroads. These were *kings* of cities, and not elders of peasant villages.[41] We read a summary of thirty-one defeated kings in Joshua 12. That list caps off the conquest segment of Joshua (Josh 1–11) before the settlement allocations in Joshua 13–21. Killing these thirty-one kings, Stone notes, "would have disrupted Egypt's system of command and control and drawn the attention of the pharaoh."[42] Though likely over a

---

Judg 10:11 actually refers to this ongoing Egyptian control, see S. Cameron Coyle and Steven M. Ortiz, "Judges 10:11: A Memory of Merneptah's Campaign in Transjordan," in *An Excellent Fortress for His Armies, A Refuge for The People: Egyptological, Archaeological, and Biblical Studies in Honor of James K. Hoffmeier*, eds. Richard E. Averbeck and K. Lawson Younger Jr. (Winona Lake, IN: Eisenbrauns, 2020).

[40]The last evidence of Egyptian-backed control in Canaan comes from the time of Pharaoh Ramesses VI (1141–1134 BC); Elizabeth Bloch-Smith and Beth Alpert Nakhai, "A Landscape Comes to Life," *Near Eastern Archaeology* 62, no. 2 (1999): 63. However, their influence in Canaan persisted.

[41]For a study of Joshua's focus on the defeat of Canaanite kings, see Thomas B. Dozeman, *Joshua 1–12*, Anchor Yale Bible 6B (New Haven: Yale University Press, 2015), 65-77.

[42]Stone, "Early Israel," 160.

long period of time, it seemed that the defeat and overthrow of these thirty-one kings eventually brought Pharaoh himself into the land of Canaan in 1209 BC.[43]

Pharaoh Merneptah (Ramesses II's co-regent and successor) launched a campaign to punish the local populations of Canaan. In a victory monument that marked his campaign he bragged about subduing multiple Canaanite territories and decimating Israel: "Israel is no more, his seed is not."[44] While Merneptah didn't actually eradicate Israel (it's a caricature!), the report is instructive. It tells us that Israel was enough of a pest in the region to warrant Merneptah's attention. It also tells us that Israel wasn't yet territorially defined. The name "Israel" in the Merneptah monument uses the designation for a "people" rather than a "territory." It's likely that they were still gaining a foothold in the central highlands and causing trouble for Egypt's hold on Canaan.

A run-in with Merneptah probably reduced and splintered whatever gains Israel had made, reflecting the kind of regional conflict and warlordism that we see in the book of Judges.[45] But the Merneptah monument also tells us that the people of Israel were identifiable *as a people* already in the 1200s BC. They were only a people, not yet a network of city-states or a group with a clearly defined geographical boundary. God had promised the land, but the people had not yet settled it.[46]

The book of Joshua describes two main military "campaigns" that follow the destruction of Jericho and Ai: one toward the south (Josh 9:3–10:43), into what became Judah; another toward the north (Josh 11:1-15).[47] Oddly, as Stone points out, Joshua speaks hardly a word of battles in "the very region that saw the earliest and heaviest Israelite settlement."[48] Based on archaeological records, it seems like the earliest Israelites settled primarily *between* the two regions where most battles reportedly happened (the center of the lightly shaded area in figure 11.1).

---

[43]See *COS* II.40-41.
[44]*ANET*, 378.
[45]Stone, "Early Israel," 161.
[46]Iain Provan, V. Philips Long, and Tremper Longman III, *A Biblical History of Israel*, 2nd ed. (Louisville, KY: Westminster John Knox, 2015), 222.
[47]Summarized in Josh 11:12-15.
[48]Stone, "Early Israel," 162.

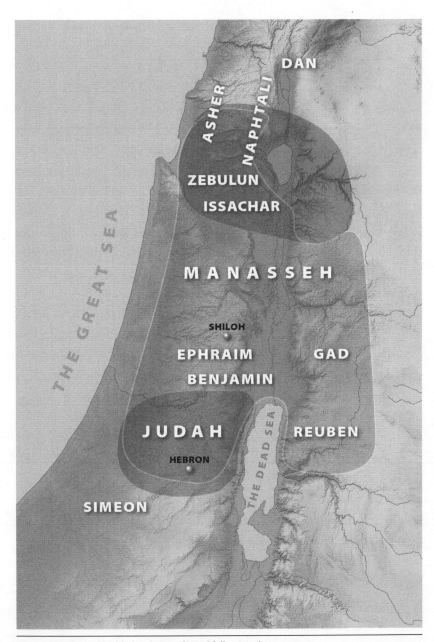

Figure 11.1. Second highlighted map of Israel following the conquest

By weakening the network of royal city-states in its northern and southern campaigns, Israel would have created two buffers at the northern and southern regions within which it *settled*.[49] In other words, the aims of the campaigns were likely to demilitarize the royal strongholds to the north and south of regions where Israel peaceably settled. This focus on disrupting the city-state strongholds finds vivid expression in Joshua 11, where Yahweh commands to hamstring the horses and burn with fire the chariots of the northern kings (Josh 11:9). This is basically the ancient equivalent of dismantling weapons of mass destruction. And in this invasion, the WMDs actually existed![50]

In this way, Joshua portrays Israel engaging in a series of battles against Egyptian-controlled cities in the north and south. It also portrays them settling the region of Manasseh in the Transjordan and in the central highlands. In this rendering, Israel ended up with a "ring of fire" to protect their settlements.[51] In addition, the geography of the highlands provided protection from other local forces that would've threatened Israel, such as Transjordanian raiders, the Sea Peoples, and other local populations.

Some of the existing Canaanite population who lived in rural villages and settlements dotted around the highlands were probably sympathetic to the dismantling of Egyptian control. The Canaanite city-state kings sustained their power through systemic "exploitation of village communities," and by stripping the land of its resources.[52] The Canaanite city-states were strongholds of Egyptian colonization, set up to drain all local resources.[53] Many locals likely said, "Good riddance!" to the Canaanite kings. Whether or not they would've welcomed Israel's presence with open arms is another matter, though many who joined Israel likely originated from local Canaanite populations. It is notable that the book of Joshua doesn't feature attacks on these unwalled villages or settlements and does show the willingness of some to join with Israel (Rahab, Gibeonites).

---

[49]Stone, "Early Israel," 163.

[50]See www.intelligence.senate.gov/sites/default/files/publications/110345.pdf, accessed July 8, 2022.

[51]Stone, "Early Israel," 163; Lawson G. Stone, "'I'm Gonna Make You Famous': Joshua 6:23-27," *The Asbury Journal* 72, no. 2 (2017): 125.

[52]Killebrew, *Biblical Peoples*, 33.

[53]It should be noted that the Canaanite cities were semi-independent but ultimately subservient to Egypt.

In sum, Israel's emergence in the land of Canaan corresponds with the decline of Egyptian power in the region. The broad outlines of the book of Joshua depict Israel settling outside the orbit of Egyptian-backed Canaanite power. The military battles described in the book likely took place over a long period of time and reflect the actions of a people trying to carve out space for life in less populated and less accessible highland regions. Joshua's account of these events likely condenses events into the lifetime of Joshua and focus on Israel's ability to overcome the militarily superior forces of Canaan.

COMPLETING THE EXODUS

What happens when we combine literary insights with the historical picture just sketched? Here's the quick take: Joshua tells the story of Israel's conquest in ways that evoke the story of Egypt. The conquest of Canaanite kings and cities forms the final chapter in Israel's exodus from Egyptian control.

Here are some of the many ways that the conquest account in Joshua recalls the exodus.

First, an example from the book's beginnings. When the Israelites enter the land, God splits the Jordan River and Israel walks through on "dry ground," a clear echo of the Reedy Sea crossing (Ex 15:19; Josh 3:17).[54] The Reedy Sea and Jordan River crossings were part of one great work of God.[55]

Second, just as Moses was saved by the deception of the Hebrew midwives, so Rahab deceived the officials in Jericho to save the Israelites.

Third, the people circumcise themselves and celebrate the Passover as they prepare to enter the land. The Passover was instituted at the beginning of Israel's exodus from Egypt (Ex 12), and the requirement for participation? Circumcision (Ex 12:48).

Fourth, the author presents Joshua like Moses. Joshua takes off his sandals when he meets the angel of the LORD (Josh 5:13-15) just as Moses

---

[54]Popularly associated with the Red Sea, though the Hebrew *yam suf* means "Sea of Reeds."

[55]For three recent studies on exodus themes in Scripture, see R. Michael Fox, ed. *Reverberations of the Exodus in Scripture* (Eugene, OR: Wipf and Stock, 2014); Alastair J. Roberts and Andrew Wilson, *Echoes of Exodus: Tracing Themes of Redemption Through Scripture* (Wheaton, IL: Crossway, 2018); Bryan D. Estelle, *Echoes of Exodus: Tracing a Biblical Motif* (Downers Grove, IL: InterVarsity Press, 2018).

did at the burning bush (Ex 3:5). Both lead the people against formidable opponents, give concluding speeches, and are called "servant of the LORD" (Deut 34:5; Josh 24:29).[56]

Fifth, the judgment inflicted on Egypt and Canaan comes primarily by the hand of Yahweh. Granted, in Joshua the people participate in that judgment, but the emphasis is still on Yahweh's actions. Jericho's walls fall by Yahweh's power. The sun stands still for Joshua. Yahweh rains down hail-stones. And so on.

Finally, failure marks the moment of success. No sooner was Israel liberated from Egypt than they worshiped the golden calf (Ex 32–34). No sooner had Israel defeated Jericho than Achan stole the golden vessels from the Canaanites (Josh 7:1).

Other aspects of Joshua complete elements from the exodus story. For instance, the manna stops just as the people enter the land (Josh 5:12).[57] Hélène Dallaire and Denise Morris show how the literary structure of Exodus–Joshua links the departure from Egypt to the entrance into Canaan:[58]

A Israel in Egypt (Ex 1–10)
  B Passover and the Crossing (Ex 11:1–15:21)
    C Journey in the Wilderness (Ex 15:22–18:27)
      X. Sinai (Ex 19:1–Num 10:10)
    C′ Journey in the Wilderness (Num 10:11–Deut)
  B′ Crossing and Passover (Josh 1–5)
A′ Israel in Canaan (Josh 6–24)

The emphasis on completion is clear from this comparison. We could list numerous other examples of how Joshua echoes Moses and the exodus story and brings it to completion. As Dallaire and Morris point out, "The book of Joshua is structured in such a way that the exodus is remembered, paralleled, alluded to, or mentioned in nearly every chapter. It is impossible

---

[56]Roberts and Wilson, *Echoes of Exodus*, 55. All 20 occurrences of the phrase *'eved YHWH* ("servant of the LORD/YAHWEH") in the Old Testament apply to Moses or Joshua.
[57]Roberts and Wilson, *Echoes of Exodus*, 54. Roberts and Wilson also trace significant differences.
[58]Hélène Dallaire and Denise Morris, "Joshua and Israel's Exodus from the Desert Wilderness," in *Reverberations of the Exodus*, 18-34. Their proposed chiasm follows the work of Walter Vogels, "D'Égypte À Canaan: Un rite de passage," *Science et Esprit* 52, no. 1 (2000): 22.

to escape its influence in the book."[59] What we might miss, were it not for these parallels, is that *the events in Joshua are of one piece with the exodus, bound together by great acts of divine deliverance.*

When Israel sang about these events, they treated them as a unified event:

> You stretched out your right hand [over the Reedy Sea],
> the earth swallowed them. . . . You brought them in [to Canaan] and planted them on the mountain of your own possession. (Ex 15:12, 17, NRSV)

> He turned the (Reedy) sea into dry land; they passed through the (Jordan) river on foot. (Ps 66:6, NRSV modified)

> The (Reedy) sea looked and fled, the Jordan turned back. (Ps 114:3)

If we think purely in terms of liberation (exodus) versus aggression (conquest), we miss how the story is told, and the historical context of Israel's appearance in Canaan. Joshua wants us to see the conquest as the final stage of Israel's escape from Egypt's political and spiritual domination.

Joshua also reports that few Canaanite cities made peace with Israel "for it was the LORD himself who hardened their hearts" (Josh 11:20). While this may sound unduly harsh, it is worth bearing in mind that hardening hearts is always a form of judgment in the Old Testament. God wasn't in the business of taking otherwise nice people and hardening them into objects of his wrath. As with Pharaoh (Ex 4:21), God hardens as an act of judgment for injustice. In Pharaoh's case, he's hardened because he failed to recognize Yahweh and killed the Hebrew boys. The reasons for that hardening judgment aren't explicit in Joshua, but visible in other texts (e.g., Gen 15:13-14; Deut 12:29-31).

Further, just as judgment on Pharaoh was linked to his *ignorance* of Yahweh (Ex 5:2)—expressed in his injustice—so the Canaanite kings are judged based on how they respond to the news of Yahweh's power. The Canaanites typically respond with violence, with some notable exceptions. Clearly the account of Sihon and Og plays a crucial background role, so I've included that incident in table 11.1.

---

[59]Dallaire and Morris, "Joshua and Israel's Exodus from the Desert Wilderness," 33.

Table 11.1. Report vs. Canaanite response

Report/Incident	Canaanites' Response
Numbers 21:21-35 Israel seeks safe passage through Amorite territory	Sihon and Og gather to battle Israel (Num 21:23, 33) = *hostility*
Joshua 2:9-11 Jericho hears of the Reedy Sea crossing and defeat of Sihon and Og	Rahab confesses Yahweh's superiority (Josh 2:11) = *affiliation* King and rest of Jericho melt in fear, lack courage, fight Israel (Josh 2:9, 11; 24:11) = *hostility*
Joshua 5:1 Yahweh dried up the Jordan	Amorite and Canaanite kings melt in fear, lack courage (Josh 5:1) = *hostility (delayed)*
Joshua 9:1-2 Victories at Jericho and Ai	Canaanite kings mobilize to fight Israel (Josh 9:1-2) = *hostility*
Joshua 9:3, 9-10 Victories at Jericho and Ai Defeat of Egypt, Sihon, and Og	Gibeonites concede that God gave the land, pursue a covenant (Josh 9:6, 11) = *affiliation*
Joshua 10:1 Victories at Jericho and Ai Gibeon made a treaty with Israel	King Adoni-Zedek of Jerusalem is alarmed, gathers a (southern) coalition to fight Gibeon (Josh 10:2-5) = *hostility*
Joshua 11:1 Unspecified	King Jabin of Hazor gathers a (northern) coalition to fight Israel (Josh 11:1-5) = *hostility*

Canaanite *kings* lead the hostile opposition to Israel. They were *responding* to the news of Yahweh's mighty acts with violence. By contrast, Rahab (a civilian) and the inhabitants of Gibeon (not their king) affiliate with Israel. According to Joshua 24:11, even the "lords of Jericho" (my translation) initiate hostility toward Israel.

The primary aim of the exodus was so that Israel, Egypt, and the nations would "know that I am Yahweh" (see Ex 6:7; 7:5, 17; 8:10, 22; 9:14, 29, 30; 10:2; 11:7; 14:4, 18; 15:14-16.). The ten plagues and Reedy Sea crossing were choreographed to make Yahweh's name resound throughout the earth. The exodus was all about the revelation of Yahweh's power through his actions for Israel. How the nations in the wilderness and Canaan responded to this defining revelation determined their fate. Stone summarizes:

> Israel's presence in Canaan presents Egypt's nominal representatives—the Canaanite kings—with the action of Yahweh, and likewise demands a response. . . . The conquest narratives are therefore structured so as to depict

the Canaanites not as morally decadent, but as increasingly resistant to the action of Yahweh. The Israelites are depicted not as a savage, unstoppable war machine blazing over Canaan, but as reacting to the Canaanite kings' [violent] opposition to Yahweh.[60]

When we consider that these kings are remnants of Egyptian control of Canaan, the story comes into sharp relief. *Joshua portrays the conquest as a continuation of Israel's liberation from Egypt's power.* For this reason, the book continually asks its readers to connect the dots between the events of the conquest and the events in Exodus. Moreover, the focus of Israel's destructive energies was directed against the four symbols of imperial power present in Canaan:

- *Warlords*: Joshua consistently emphasizes the defeat of the Egyptian-backed warlord kings, as the summary report in Joshua 12 makes abundantly clear. Psalm 136 remembers the conquest as the time when Yahweh struck down Canaanite *mighty kings* (Ps 136:17-22).[61]

- *Walled cities*: Throughout the conquest, battles feature the destruction of *'arim* (walled cities), not unwalled villages or settlements.[62]

- *Weapons of war*: In addition to downplaying the significance of human weapons and foregrounding divine military power in Jericho and at Gibeon, in Joshua 11 Israel decommissioned Canaanite horses and chariots, preeminent weapons of war.[63]

- *Wealth*: Achan "covets" and takes clothing, silver, and gold of Babylon (Josh 7:21). As Wray Beal points out, this covenant offense is used elsewhere in the Bible to describe "coveting" the gold and silver of idols, which were to be burned (Deut 7:25-26).[64] The emphasis on

---

[60]Lawson G. Stone, "Ethical and Apologetic Tendencies in the Redaction of the Book of Joshua," *CBQ* 53.1 (1991):25-36 [34].

[61]Notably, Israel had no king at this time, and the Deuteronomic vision of kingship in Deut 17:14-20 is contrary to ideals prevalent in the ancient Near East (e.g., limits on wealth, major weaponry, and wives).

[62]The NIV unhelpfully translates Joshua 10:37 and 10:39 with the phrase "and its [i.e., the city's] villages," when the Hebrew has "and its cities," which likely refers to the walled cities connected to Hebron and Debir.

[63]Discussed in Walter Brueggemann, *Divine Presence Amidst Violence: Contextualizing the Book of Joshua* (Eugene, OR: Cascade Books, 2009), 55-60.

[64]Wray Beal, *Joshua*, 163.

imperial wealth is notable here. Somehow, Achan had become "as wealthy as Job" (see Josh 7:24; cf. Job 1:2-5).[65] By "seeing" that this wealth was "good," "coveting" and "taking" for himself Achan falls prey to the primal corrupting desire that puts the self in the place of God.

Why remove these symbols of power entirely, instead of installing its own network of kings, taking over walled cities, and using Canaanite weapons and wealth to support the war effort? David Firth hits the nail on the head: "Israel was not to secure its future along the Canaanite pattern—nor indeed on the standard patterns of the ancient Near East [i.e., by securing kings]."[66] Instead, God called Israel into a way of "conquest" that trusted in his power and forsook the Egyptian-backed Canaanite way.

Furthermore, countless texts in Joshua and throughout the Pentateuch want us to envision Israel as a militarily weak people confronting far superior forces that they overcome with the power of God (Deut 7:1, 17; 9:1, 14; 11:23; Josh 9:1-2; 10:5; 11:1-5; 12:1-24).[67] Joshua calls us to identify with a people who are militarily and numerically inferior to powerful Egyptian-backed Canaanite kings.

Rethinking the conquest in these terms doesn't erase its violent qualities. But our picture of what happened in Canaan, and how it parallels the exodus, changes the moral calculus. The violence in which Israel participated as it gained a foothold in Canaan was aimed at weakening an ages-old colonial power that held the land in a vice grip. Recognizing Israel's relative weakness before Egyptian-backed militarily superior forces casts the stories of Joshua in terms of a David versus Goliath contest.[68] But even those battles were *defensive* responses to Canaanite aggression, just as the ten plagues were divine responses to Egyptian oppression. Ethicists have typically distinguished between defensive wars and wars of aggression. The battles in Joshua 9–12 were all defensive in origin, and if we include Jericho in the mix (given Josh 24), Ai is the single outlier.[69]

---

[65]Walter Brueggemann, *Money and Possessions*, Interpretation (Louisville, KY: Westminster John Knox, 2016), 59.

[66]Firth, *Joshua*, 212.

[67]Moberly discusses this in his *Old Testament Theology*, 59-60.

[68]Noted by Moberly, *Old Testament Theology*, 60.

[69]And Ai is notable for its initial success against Israel.

READING JOSHUA WITH LATER EMPIRES

The book of Joshua wasn't completed during the time of Egyptian control. It was probably finalized centuries later, during the times of Assyrian, Babylonian, or even Persian control. While Joshua bears the imprint of those later kingdoms, it wants us to "think Egypt" when talking about Canaanite kings, even if it was edited with later powers like Assyria, Babylon, or Persia as new manifestations of Egypt.[70]

I'll talk about Persia in the next chapter, but I want to consider a much later empire. The Roman Empire. According to Revelation, the Christian life also involves conquering enemy-controlled strongholds. Ellen Davis points this out. Revelation promises great reward to "the one who conquers" and puts emphasis on this theme (Rev 2–3; 11; 17; 21). By contrast, those who fail to conquer succumb to idolatry, murder, and disregard for the law (Rev 21:8).[71] Davis notes, "Facing off against the world-conquering power of Rome, this Jewish seer . . . reframes the notion of conquest to denote the power of total fidelity to the God known through Israel's Scriptures and Jesus Christ."[72] The final reward of a new heaven and new earth for the faithful comes into focus toward the end of Revelation: "Those who *conquer* will *inherit* all this, and I will be their God and they will be my children" (Rev 21:7, NIV modified). Davis notes the striking similarity to the language of Joshua, where Yahweh assures Joshua that he would "lead these people to *inherit* the land I swore to their ancestors to give them" (Josh 1:6, NIV modified). And just as Joshua assured the people that God had already conquered the land for them (Josh 18:1), so too Jesus. Here's John again: "In the world you have trouble and suffering, but take courage— I have *conquered* the world" (Jn 16:33, NET).

CONCLUSION

I've argued in this chapter that the conquest was really a completion of the exodus. Rather than exodus versus conquest, perhaps we should think of Joshua as the final scene in the exodus. Egypt had dominated Canaan

---

[70]Dozeman, *Joshua 1–12*, 5-32.
[71]Davis, *Opening Israel's Scriptures*, 140.
[72]Davis, *Opening Israel's Scriptures*, 140.

around the same time that Israel appeared in the land. Disrupting the network of Egyptian-controlled Canaanite city-states helped Israel establish itself as a fledgling people in the central highlands. I also suggested that Israel's beginnings were complex. They comprised groups of former slaves from Egypt but also indigenous Canaanites.

Recognizing that Joshua's Majority Report is a caricature of messy historical realities changes our picture of the conquest. Its stories paint with broad brush strokes, condense complexities, and telescope events that took place over a very long period of time. While that Majority Report is important for tracing the book's theological aims, it cannot suffice for mapping a history of early Israel and its complex beginnings. The Majority Report also doesn't spell out all the political reasons for why Israel might've engaged in the particular battles it portrays. For that we need the full array of biblical and extrabiblical historical data. History helps us see that the "conquest" was not simplistically an unprovoked attack on simple village folk in the Canaanite highlands. While ethical challenges remain, it's clear that the book portrays a series of primarily defensive battles against militarily superior kings. Joshua depicts Israel dislodging these forces and forsaking the imperial values they represent—warlord kings, walled cities, weapons of war, and wealth. These battles helped Israel and their Canaanite compatriots erode Egyptian control in Canaan, gain a foothold in the land, and build the beginnings of a different kind of kingdom. They helped Israel complete the exodus.

12

GIANTS WILL FALL

ONE OF MY FIRST TEACHING EXPERIENCES took place in the basement of a small church in Fraser, Colorado. I'd gone to Fraser from Pennsylvania to help my friend Doug with his church for the summer, and to teach through the book of Deuteronomy. For one evening session, we constructed a thirteen-foot giant named Og, inspired by the book of Deuteronomy: "Og king of Bashan was the last of the Rephaites. His bed was decorated with iron and was more than nine cubits long [fourteen feet] and four cubits wide [six feet]" (Deut 3:11). We figured that a bed fourteen feet long must have supported a thirteen-foot Og. We used a stuffed elf body, with two long-rolled carpets as legs to give him the needed length. It was quite a scene around which to gather for Bible study!

Moses describes Og's bed to make the point that if God defeated giants of that size in the Transjordan (the east side of the Jordan River), he'd do it in the land as well. And that he did. Joshua tells us about it.

These giants like Og are larger than life. They might be real, but they don't tend to loiter long enough on the Old Testament's pages to permit photographs. Most literary snapshots end up "grainy." They seem happier unnoticed in the shadows of Israelite tradition. Goliath is the sole exception. He played a lead role, only to fall face down, a stone lodged in his head (1 Sam 17:49).

In this chapter we focus on that world of biblical giants—or, at least, what we can know of them. The little snippets and vignettes in Scripture provide only fragmentary pictures. But looking out of the corner of our eyes at these giants might just give us another angle on the problem of violence in Joshua. This chapter suggests that *the book of Joshua engages in a spiritual interpretation of the enemies Israel faced.* The giants of Canaan, descended from fallen "sons of God" (Gen 6:1-4), represented one of the primary opponents Israel faced. They also symbolized the ostensibly superior machismo of ancient demigod kings that Israel came to dislodge.

We'll look at four key features of these giants before considering how they help us with the challenge of violence in Joshua.

BACKGROUND

Before the Great Flood in Genesis, we read in passing that the divine beings (called the "sons of God") desired and took human women for themselves (Gen 6:1-4). Their violence and rape of human women resulted in a class of warrior rulers that dominated the ancient world.[1] Genesis then tells us that a group called the Nephilim were on the earth at that time. The writer shrouds the Nephilim in mystery but wants us to make the mental association between the warrior rulers born to the raped women and the Nephilim (Gen 6:4). Nephilim means "fallen ones." The similarities between these oppressive divine beings and the "fallen" Nephilim make sense. Like the "sons of God," they were spiritual beings. And like them, they acted like kings who took women at will. At various points in the biblical story, they pose spiritual and military threats to God's purposes.

Genesis links them to the Great Flood *and* they appear during the conquest, connecting the two events discussed in this book. The gods' rape of humans is one in a series of boundary transgressions that result in creation's collapse. Humans had "become like God" (or "the gods"), "knowing good and evil" (Gen 3:5, 22), humans submitted to the word of a creature that God had made (Gen 3:1-6), the man exercised dominion over the woman (Gen 3:16), and Cain spills Abel's blood on the ground that he was supposed to cultivate, an act that culminates in the earth's filling with the blood of violence (Gen 4:10-12; 6:11). Later, humans build a tower "that reaches to the heavens." Just as humans pursued a corrupt godlikeness, corrupted their relationship to the earth and each other, so too the gods violated the divine-human distinction.[2]

---

[1]Discussed in chap. 4.
[2]On the Nephilim and the flood, see Ronald Hendel, "Of Demigods and the Deluge: Toward an Interpretation of Genesis 6:1-4," *Journal of Biblical Literature* 106 (1987): 13-26.

After the flood, the Nephilim resurface. Israelite spies sent into Canaan report that the Nephilim giants live in the land of Canaan (Num 13:33). Moses wanted to get the measure of Canaan's inhabitants, land, cities, and wealth (Num 13:17-20). It transpired that giant Anakites lived in Hebron, in the central highlands (Num 13:21-29). Anakites descended from the Nephilim. That's the last we hear of the Nephilim. From here on, the Anakites and some other giant races like the Emim and Rephaim appear more regularly in the Bible.[3]

So, what are we to make of these giant descendants of the Nephilim? For some, the Anakites are to be taken literally. They're there, after all.

That these demigods existed is just *assumed*. The point of this story is not to establish the reality of demigod giants. Instead, the story picks up the frayed ends of various threads that weave their way through the Old Testament and in ancient stories. The Rephaim belong to an earlier era of giant kings that was now in decline, with Og as its last representative. Moreover, they constitute some of the *spiritual* realities that animated the enemies that God opposed.

The features of giants. Four features of these giants deserve attention.

First, the giants represent long-standing enemies that God was in the business of dispossessing. Deuteronomy tells us that various descendants of these Nephilim giants occupied the lands of Moab, Ammon, and Edom but God had defeated those giants before settling those other nations in their lands (Deut 2:19-23). According to Moses, a giant Rephaim race known as the Zamzummim (Deut 2:20) had previously occupied the entire Transjordanian region.[4] In other words, God had been ousting these demigod giants from other lands and was about to do it again for Israel. To this extent, God's battles were not *just* against flesh and blood, but against principalities and powers that animated forces in and around the land of Canaan.

---

[3] As if to confuse us, Deuteronomy reports that the Anakites and another giant race called the Emim are also categorized as Rephaim (Deut 2:10-11)! Just to keep things straight, the divine sons who raped women are *somehow related* to the Nephilim, from whom the Rephaim come, and the Anakites and Emim either descend from, or are categorized as, Rephaim (Deut 2:10-11; 3:11).

[4] God limits the expansion of the Transjordanian tribes to the kingdom of Og, the last of the Rephaim occupants in that region.

Israel polishes off Og, the last of these Transjordanian giants before entering the land, giving them further confidence that God could do so *in* the land as well (Deut 3:10-11).

Within the Promised Land, Anakites lived as three main clans: Ahiman, Sheshai, and Talmai (Num 13:22). These clans seem to have been headquartered in Hebron but were sprinkled around other cities as well (Num 13:22; Josh 11:21; 15:13-14). Among those other cities were Gath, Gaza, and Ashdod.[5] Goliath and his giant brothers came from Gath and seem to be associated with the Rephaim (2 Sam 21:20).[6]

Second, these giant demigod creatures reflect ancient royal ideals of supreme power and stature. According to texts in the Old Testament, these kings derived their power from dark forces. Ancient people depicted exceptionally tall kings to emphasize their power, importance, and divinity. Pictures of Egyptian pharaohs, for instance, portrayed them towering over their opponents. The point is not only their gigantic *size*, but their gigantic *status*. These were demigod kings, after all.[7]

Figure 12.1. Pharaoh Rameses II and opponents in the Battle of Kadesh

[5]Numbers associates the coastal regions and Jordanian valley with the Canaanites, and the hill country with the Hittites, Jebusites, and Amorites (Num 13:27-29).

[6]2 Sam 21:15-21 describes four Gittite warriors who are descendants of Raphah, which is probably linked to the Rephaim (Gen 14:5; 15:20; Deut 2:10-11; 3:11). Cf. the warrior hero Dan'il in the Ugaritic *Aqhat* Epic, who is a "man of Rp'i" (KTU 1.17 I 2, 17, 18, 35, 36, 37, 42, et al). Discussed in Daniel D. Pioske, *Memory in a Time of Prose: Studies in Epistemology, Hebrew Scribalism, and the Biblical Past* (Oxford: Oxford University Press, 2018), 96.

[7]Thomas B. Dozeman, *Joshua 1–12*, Anchor Yale Bible 6B (New Haven: Yale University Press, 2015), 498, following Matthew J. Suriano, *The Politics of Dead Kings: Dynastic Ancestors in the Book of Kings and Ancient Israel*, Forschungen zum Alten Testament II/48 (Tübingen: Mohr Siebeck, 2010), 158.

Figure 12.2. A relief of Ramses II from Memphis showing him capturing enemies: a Nubian, a Libyan, and a Syrian, circa 1250 BC, Cairo Museum

Figure 12.3. Victory Stele of Naram-Sin of Akkad (ca. 2230 BC), which depicts him slaying the Lullibi and their king

The Egyptian Pharaoh and Mesopotamian kings were truly larger than life! Powerfully divine and superior in strength, they definitely gave off a "Who do you think you are?" vibe.

Descriptions of giants in the Old Testament reflect these images of royal giantism. Maria Lindquist points out that King Og's fourteen-foot bed (Deut 3:11) was about the same size as the Babylonian deity Marduk's bed.[8] The parallel highlights the king's surpassing power and virility.[9]

Third, these kings weren't only big and powerful, ancient people thought they were supernatural. Og's supernatural status is hinted at in several ancient sources. One Phoenician inscription from Byblos refers to Og as a spirit of the dead or underworld deity.[10] An old Ugaritic text from around 1200 BC talks about embodied spirits of the dead called Rephaim who inhabited the earth. Their chief, named Rapiu, dwelled in Edrei and Athtarat. These are the same exact cities where Rephaim lived according to Joshua (Josh 12:4; 13:12), and where Og-of-giant-bed-fame lived (Deut 1:4)![11] The reference to Mount Hermon within Og's territory (Josh 12:4-5) connects Og with a place often considered to be a divine residence in the ancient world.[12] As Dozeman argues, "The defeat of Sihon and Og represents both political and cosmological battles against kings and royal cities."[13]

In later times, Israel—like its neighbors—believed that these giant kings from the days of Joshua (and before) now resided in the underworld, where they ruled.[14] This is further testimony to their semi-divine stature. For instance, in Isaiah, "Rephaim" rise to greet the dead king of Babylon who descends to Sheol (Is 14:9). Isaiah also says that Yahweh made the

---

[8]Brian R. Doak, "The Giant in a Thousand Years: Tracing Narratives of Gigantism in the Hebrew Bible and Beyond," *Ancient Tales of Giants from Qumran and Turfan: Contexts, Traditions, and Influences*, eds., Matthew Goff, Loren T. Stuckenbruck, and Enrico Morano (Tübingen: Mohr Siebeck, 2016), 20.

[9]Maria Lindquist, "King Og's Iron Bed," *Catholic Biblical Quarterly* 73 (2011): 477-93, noted in Laura Quick, "Og, King of Bashan: Underworld Ruler or Ancient Giant?" TheTorah.com, 2020, www.thetorah.com/article/og-king-of-bashan-underworld-ruler-or-ancient-giant.

[10]See Wolfgang Rölling in "Eine neue phoenizische Inschrift aus Byblos" in *Neue Ephemeris für Semitische Epigraphik*, vol 2 (Boston: Walter de Gruyter, 1903–1907), 1-15 and plate 1. It dates to about 500 BC.

[11]Doak, "Giant," 19-20.

[12]Dozeman, *Joshua 1–12*, 498.

[13]Dozeman, *Joshua 1–12*, 498.

[14]E.g., KAI 13:8 and 14:8; See Dozeman, *Joshua 1–12*, 498; H. Rouillard, "Rephaim," in *Dictionary of Deities and Demons in the Bible*, eds. Karel van der Toorn, Bob Becking, and Pieter W. van der Horst, 2nd ed. (Grand Rapids, MI: Eerdmans, 1999), esp. 695-96; Quick, "Og, King of Bashan."

nations' rulers fall to the pit, where they ruled as Rephaim, never to rise again (Is 26:14, 19).[15]

Using slightly different terminology to Nephilim—also giants—Ezekiel talks about ancient kings as "Nophalim" from a bygone era. They "went down to the realm of the dead with their weapons of war—their swords placed under their heads and their shields resting on their bones—though these warriors also had terrorized the land of the living" (Ezek 32:27). Later kings of the nations couldn't attain to their power and would suffer a worse fate according to Ezekiel (Ezek 32:28).

In sum, the Rephaim, Nephilim, and other ancient rulers exhibit their "divine" power in the realm of the dead. For biblical writers, that's not a compliment.

Fourth, the giants threatened Israel's faith. These giants garnered the spies' attention when they first scoped out the land—too much attention.

They report that Canaan's inhabitants were incredibly strong, with fortified cities (Num 13:28). It's important to note the *urban* emphasis here. The mighty Anakites seem to live in the cities, an observation that Moses also makes in Deuteronomy 1:28 (NRSV), where he notes that their cities were fortified "to heaven."[16] These mighty fortresses likely reflect the gigantic Middle Bronze cities still occupied in the Late Bronze Age, cities like Hazor, Lachish, and Megiddo, as well as the cities like Hebron that reached their peak around the time that Israel appeared in the land. These giants held large tracts of what would become the Judean and Israelite highlands, and that they ruled from large-ish cities (Num 13:28-29). Their three main southern cities in the Hebron hills (Hebron, Anab, and Debir) are also the only three large Late Bronze settlements found in that otherwise sparsely populated region.[17] They'd be tough to dislodge!

The spies' picture is both true and distorted. These Nephilim descendants posed a powerful threat to Israel. They were descended—according

---

[15] Is 26:19 is almost always mistranslated as the earth "giving birth to (its) dead (Heb. *Rephaim*)." However, it is clear from Is 26:14 that the Rephaim are not just the dead, in general, but the nations' rulers whose name and remembrance Yahweh had completely wiped out. Is 26:19 instead tells us that Yahweh would "bring down" the Rephaim.

[16] The same phrase characterizes the city and tower of Babel in Gen 11.

[17] M. Kochavi, "Khirbet Rabud=Debir," *Tel Aviv* 1, no. 1 (1974): 2-33.

to the biblical story—from the demigod warriors of old. They held well-fortified cities. But the spies also had things wrong. Notice that they referred to *all* the people in the land as giants "of great size" (Num 13:32). In other words, they imagined that everyone in Canaan was a descendant of the Nephilim and of giant size.[18] This exaggerated report portrays a land teeming with powerful demigod kings and rulers.

Due to their fear of giants and doubts about God's promises, the people tried to appoint a leader to take them back to Egypt (Num 14:3-4)! They'd rather have an anti-exodus than face Canaan's giants. This fear of giants led to a failed first conquest under Moses and forty years circling in the wilderness.

After those years, Moses challenges Israel to face the giants:

> Hear, Israel: You are now about to cross the Jordan to go in and dispossess nations greater and stronger than you, with large cities that have walls up to the sky. The *people* are strong and tall—*Anakites*! You know about them and have heard it said: "Who can stand up against the *Anakites*?" (Deut 9:1-2)

For Moses, "the [Canaanite] people" are equated with "the Anakites." They emblemize the chief royal and spiritual opponents of the land Israel was about to enter.[19] One of the rationales for *herem* warfare was to oust the giant race of demigods whom Genesis associates with mighty warriors of the past (Gen 6:1-4). Moses wanted Israel to trust that they could defeat these giant races with God's help, despite the fact that these giants were militarily superior. In fact, Yahweh would take care of them himself, for he is a "devouring fire" (Deut 9:3).

These giants somehow embodied the temptation to fear. *Would Israel succumb to the fear of these royal giants, or would they trust Yahweh?*

The book of Joshua also returns to the source of Israel's fear—royal giants in the land (Num 13:33). Echoes of that earlier failure sound in the name of one city mentioned in Joshua called Anab, or "Grapetown" (Josh 11:21; 15:50), recalling the huge grapes that the twelve spies took from the land (Num 13:23). Joshua offers the people another chance to face the giants.

---

[18]See Michael S. Heiser, *The Unseen Realm: Recovering the Supernatural Worldview of the Bible* (Bellingham: Lexham Press, 2015), 148, for further discussion.

[19]On at least four occasions, Moses refers to the enemies of Israel as "greater and stronger" (Deut 1:28; 4:38; 7:1, and here in 9:1-2).

The giants' defeat. With God's help the people deal them a death blow. Joshua 10:28-43 and 11:21 tell us that Israel utterly destroyed the giants' cities. Here's the summary statement, where we learn that the Israelites had broken their power: "At that time Joshua went and destroyed the Anakites from the hill country: from Hebron, Debir and Anab, from all the hill country of Judah, and from all the hill country of Israel. Joshua totally destroyed them and their towns" (Josh 11:21).[20]

After Joshua, only a few Anakites remained in Philistine cities like Gaza, Gath, and Ashdod. David and his men polish them off later, starting with Goliath (1 Sam 17; 2 Sam 21:15-22).[21] For our purposes, it's important that the writer of Joshua summarizes the military campaigns of Joshua 1–11 by focusing on the giant enemies who were the cause for Israel's fear during their first attempt to enter the land (Num 13:33). Their defeat "provides a commentary on the conquest as a whole, and recalls the legendary power of an enemy that has been destroyed with such ease."[22]

Despite the formidable Canaanite strongholds and the mighty giants Yahweh's power was greater by an order of magnitude. We're supposed to view these Canaanite giants in superhuman terms to remind us that victory is not achieved by Israel's military power (Deut 20:4). In fact, Israel was to reject the ways of Canaan.

Things didn't work out so well when Israel tried out "giant" kings for themselves. King Saul was the son of a *gibbor hayil*, or "valiant man," and stood "a head taller than anyone else" (1 Sam 9:1-2). Though a giant himself, he failed to confront the other giant who threatened Israel (Goliath). He ended up rejected by Yahweh. As Brian Doak notes of this Israelite giant, "his height must be considered holistically as a premonition, a signal of his downfall. This signal embodies a trap, because, in the usual [ancient] assessment a tall body is a leadership body, a warrior body, and a

---

[20]Anab is unidentified archaeologically, but for Debir and Hebron see William G. Dever, *Beyond the Texts: An Archaeological Portrait of Ancient Israel and Judah* (Atlanta: SBL Press, 2017), 431. Heiser, *Unseen Realm*, 152, suggests that the giants were the *primary* target of Israel's *herem* warfare. However, the book of Joshua suggests that they were just one (albeit a major one) of their targets.

[21]Goliath may be portrayed as a king, or at least the one whom the exceptionally tall King Saul *should* have squared off against (1 Sam 17).

[22]Gordon Mitchell, *Together in the Land: A Reading of the Book of Joshua*, Journal for the Study of the Old Testament Supplements 134 (Sheffield: JSOT Press, 1993), 95.

successful body."[23] In defeating the giants of Canaan, Israel was called to reject the godlike pursuit of power that these giants signified. In reality, they were descendants of the divine "fallen ones" (Nephilim) of old (Gen 6:1-4).

These fragments in Scripture suggest that the giant kings of old had divine lineage, but not in a good way. The giants were descendants of *fallen* (not dignified) gods. Later, the prophets saw them as relics of a bygone era, nearly forgotten on earth and haunting the underworld—utterly fallen. The books of Numbers, Joshua, and Samuel (with Goliath and his brothers) recount their demise. Yahweh was bringing the old order of powerful semi-divine rulers to an end, and it would soon be pummeled into the ground. Yahweh was establishing a new kingdom.

Whether or not these giants were *really* semi-divine beings is a question we can't answer here. The Bible seems to assume their existence, but without any apparent interest in explaining how they survive the Great Flood. In any case, their appearance in the land draws our attention to the principalities and powers that animated, or were embodied in, the Canaanite kings. They focus our attention on the fear they inspired, and the question of whether the people had the needed mustard seed of faith in Yahweh's power.

REFLECTING ON VIOLENCE

How do giants help us with the challenge of violence in Joshua?

First, if we follow their biblical lineage, the Anakites seem to be supernatural creatures. The Anakites descend from the Nephilim, whom Genesis associates with the offspring of divine-human unions (Gen 6:1-4). There's a superhuman, supernatural, quality to some of these opponents Israel faces. There is some overlap with the kinds of warfare Jesus wages against demonic forces in the Gospels. When Jesus sends out seventy-two disciples "like lambs among wolves" (Lk 10:3) to heal the sick and cast out demons, Jesus exclaims that he "watched Satan fall from heaven like a flash of lightning" (Lk 10:18, NRSV). Jesus isn't reporting on some event in the distant past here: "By the way, did I ever tell you about the time . . . ?" No, through the preaching and exorcism ministry of his disciples Jesus saw— right then—the beginning of the end for the spiritual forces that held

---

[23]Brian Doak, *Heroic Bodies in Ancient Israel* (New York: Oxford University Press, 2019), 134.

God's people in bondage (cf. Is 14:13; Rev 12:7-10). As Justo González observes, "The Christian message is not just that Jesus conquers all powers of evil and oppression, but also that, as lambs sent into the world by the Lamb of God, Christians have the mission and the power to gain victory over evil and oppression."[24] Jesus' battles were not against flesh and blood.

So too Joshua portrays Israel in a battle against fallen spiritual and imperial forces that held hostage the land and its people. Indeed, as Deuteronomy's laws were applied in future generations, they were generally applied in spiritual terms, ridding the land of idols for instance,[25] or imperial terms, breaking Israel's bonds with other national powers.

Second, Joshua portrays Israel's conquest as a clash of powers. The book's battles were between Israel, whose God is king, and the Canaanite city-states, for whom kings were like gods. Battle reports in Joshua consistently focus on the defeat of *kings*.

Table 12.1. The defeat of kings

Text	King(s)	Depiction
Josh 2	King of Jericho	Duped / Fear because of defeated Amorite kings
Josh 5	Canaanite and Amorite kings	Fear because of Jordan crossing
Josh 6	Jericho's king	Defeated
Josh 8	Ai's king	Defeated (exemplary killing)
Josh 9	Southern kings	Gather for war → Defeated (Josh 10–11)
Josh 10	Southern kings	Defeated (exemplary killing of 5 Amorite kings)
Josh 11	Northern kings	Defeated (exemplary killing of royal weapons)
Josh 12	All kings	Defeated

The emphasis on kings in Joshua, and especially the summary list in Joshua 12, keeps our attention on the defeat of *kings in mighty strongholds*. Moreover, Joshua 11 summarizes Joshua's hill country campaigns in terms of wars against Anakites—godlike kings (Josh 11:21). While Joshua certainly recognizes *human* foes in Canaan, it focuses our attention here in the summary section of the conquest account on royal opponents who occupied powerful cities, and on the giants who dominated the central

---

[24]Justo L. González, *Luke* (Louisville, KY: Westminster John Knox, 2010), 136.
[25]Cf. my chap. 10.

highlands where Israel would settle. Their defeat also marked a rejection of a particular *form* of rule that celebrated brutality and godlike power.

Third, while still violent, the details about Anakites and Rephaim in Joshua reinforce the point made in chapter eleven that "Israel versus Canaanites" was a "David versus Goliath" scenario. Israel was utterly unmatched in this fight against these supernaturally powerful kings (Josh 11:4). The summary of Israel's military campaign focuses on the Anakim, as if to emphasize God's faithfulness in helping Israel overcome a vastly superior enemy—an enemy that initiated war against Israel. Yahweh was bringing an end to the era of demigod kings that once held sway over the land, and he was doing it with a vastly weaker army.

CODA: ON ISRAELITE FEAR

Apparently, the Israelites needed to keep learning how *not* to fear giants. When allotting land, the tribe of Manasseh thought they'd be too cramped. Joshua told them to go settle the land of the Rephaites and Perrizites, land they'd already been assigned. But the Manassites couldn't do so. The Rephaim (Og's people) had iron chariots and dominated the Jezreel Valley (Josh 12:1-6; 17:16-18; Judg 1:19). These were likely Egyptian functionaries who held the Jezreel region long after Israel dwelled in the land.[26] Like the Israelite generation that failed to enter the land (Num 13:31), the Manassites were *afraid*.[27] How ironic that a son of Joseph would fear living in a land occupied by Egyptian forces!

We don't find out if the Manassites ever overcame their fear. We can suspect that they didn't, since the people later struggled to overcome iron chariots in the lowlands (Judg 1:19).[28] Judges tells us that Manasseh failed to oust the Canaanites from the towns in these very regions (Judg 1:27).

---

[26] Ayelet Gilboa, "Dor and Egypt in the Early Iron Age: An Archaeological Perspective of (part of) the Wenamun Report," *Ägypten und Levante/Egypt and the Levant* 25 (2015): 247-74; S. Cameron Coyle and Steven M. Ortiz, "Judges 10:11: A Memory of Merneptah's Campaign in Transjordan," in *An Excellent Fortress for His Armies, A Refuge for The People: Egyptological, Archaeological, and Biblical Studies in Honor of James K. Hoffmeier*, ed. Richard E. Averbeck and K. Lawson Younger Jr. (Winona Lake, IN: Eisenbrauns, 2020), 298-308.

[27] As Lissa Wray Beal points out, the contrast with Caleb's resolute action is striking (cf. Josh 15:13-19). Lissa M. Wray Beal, *Joshua*, Story of God Bible Commentary (Grand Rapids, MI: Zondervan Academic, 2019), 328.

[28] Unless Josh 17 reflects the same time frame, which may be the case.

13

WORSHIP AS WARFARE

Every stroke the LORD lays on them with his punishing club
will be to the music of timbrels and harps,
as he fights them in battle with the blows of his arm.

ISAIAH 30:32

CHAPTER TWELVE OFFERED A "SPIRITUAL" reading of violence in Joshua that aligns with the book's own emphases. Recognizing the giants as spiritual forces doesn't explain all the flesh-and-blood violence in the book, but it does tell us something about what the book is trying to accentuate. Just as Joshua considers Rahab to be the most important Canaanite, worthy of sustained attention, so too it directs our gaze toward the destruction of corrupt spiritual forces that ruled Canaan. By way of analogy, the Gospels orient us toward the unclean demonic forces that animated opposition to Jesus throughout his ministry, even though he also faced flesh-and-blood opponents.

There are additional spiritual dimensions to the way Joshua portrays Israel's violence that deserve our attention. One of those is worship.

WORSHIP AND RESISTANCE

On June 11, 2019, Christians in Hong Kong took to the streets with the song "Sing Hallelujah to the Lord." This event occurred during the democracy protests known as the Umbrella Movement and Occupy Central.[1]

---

[1]I'm grateful to my friend Jonathan Lo for highlighting this event. Jonathan Lo, "From the Streets to the Scriptures: 'Liberating Exegesis' in Hong Kong," in Phillip A. Davis, Jr., Daniel Lanzinger, and

Protesters opposed new legislation that would allow mainland China to extradite Hong Kong citizens to be tried in Chinese courts. The protests eventually morphed into a broader pro-democracy movement. At that time, Hong Kong law permitted public *religious* assemblies, so gathering to sing this song was technically permitted. The song soon became "an unlikely anthem and battle cry of the protests in 2019–2020" and was even sung by non-Christian protesters. Protesters hoped that the song would "have a calming effect on police and would help diffuse tensions," and it seemed to in some circumstances. It also provided protesters with legal cover. In the face of vastly superior police forces who had already fired tear gas and rubber bullets, and had hit protesters with batons, protesters resisted with a song of worship.[2]

When I heard about these acts of worshipful resistance, my mind went to a battle described in the book of Chronicles. Chronicles tells the story of King Jehoshaphat of Judah who faced a vastly superior army, a point made three times in the story (2 Chr 20:2, 12, 15). The author is painting something larger than life to emphasize the point that Judah was in peril.

Victory through praise. The story revolves around a few central questions that appear in Jehoshaphat's desperate prayer in the temple's courtyard: "Are you not the God who is in heaven? . . . Our God, did you not drive out the inhabitants of this land before your people Israel?" Based on God's actions in Joshua, Jehoshaphat builds to his point: "Our God, will you not judge them? For we have no power to face this vast army that is attacking us" (2 Chr 20:6-12).

The storyteller emphasizes Judah's powerlessness and, most importantly, its *location*. This prayer took place at the temple, the very place where Solomon had said that Israel should come if they ever faced trouble (1 Kings 8:33-35, 38).

A Levitical temple singer then arose to prophesy: "*You will not have to fight this battle.* Take up your positions; stand firm and see the deliverance the LORD will give you, O Judah and Jerusalem" (2 Chr 20:17). The

---

Matthew R. Robinson, eds., *What Does Theology Do, Actually? Vol 2: Exegeting Exegesis* (Leipzig: Evangelische Verlagsanstalt, 2022).

[2]Quotes in this paragraph are from Lo, "From the Streets to the Scriptures." For information about the song and protests, see BBC, "Hong Kong Protests: How Hallelujah to the Lord Became an Unofficial Anthem," BBC News, June 22, 2019, www.bbc.com/news/world-asia-china-48715224.

ensuing scene is almost comical. The army marches forth . . . but only to watch. They proceed *as if* going to battle when in reality, they were spectators to a divine victory. By the time they reached them, their enemies had already killed each other.

Though the army had no role, the Levitical Priests certainly did. Their special duty was to accompany Yahweh into battle and announce his arrival. In the past, the Levites would have carried Yahweh's ark, or throne.[3]

Since the ark had already "come to rest" in the temple (a major theme in Chronicles, e.g., 1 Chr 6:31-32), the Levites went forth instead as *singers*. Their praises formed an acoustic throne for the divine king who went forth to fight on Israel's behalf.[4] As the psalmist puts it, Yahweh is "enthroned on the praises of Israel" (Ps 22:3, NRSV). Rather than the ark, the priests bore Yahweh into battle on the *praises* of Israel. Interestingly, they sing "give thanks to the LORD" (2 Chr 20:21), a refrain very similar to the refrain "sing hallelujah to the LORD" sung by the Hong Kong protesters.

At the beginning of this battle against this "vast army," the singers remained silent . . . until that crucial moment, when, with the army in position, the Levites lifted their song. The Chronicles account is moving: "*As they began to sing and praise*, the LORD set ambushes against the men of Ammon and Moab and Mount Seir who were invading Judah, and they were defeated" (2 Chr 20:22). Praise enacts something powerful here. It's as if praise is the cue for Yahweh's attack. Chronicles emphasizes the coordination between singing and Yahweh's visitation. In the previous verse, we learn that Jehoshaphat appointed the Levites to literally "praise (his) holy theophany," or dramatic visitation (2 Chr 20:21, my translation). As they sang, Yahweh came in power (cf. 2 Chr 5:13). In sum, *this postexilic story portrays God achieving victory over the enemy accompanied by the praise of the powerless.*

---

[3]Throne or standard-bearing was a common motif in ancient Near Eastern warfare. Sa-Moon Kang, *Divine War in the Old Testament and in the Ancient Near East*, Beiheft zur Zeitschrift für die Alttestamentliche Wissenschaft 177 (Berlin: Walter de Gruyter, 2011); Jeffrey J. Niehaus, *God at Sinai: Covenant and Theophany in the Bible and Ancient Near East*, Studies in Old Testament Biblical Theology (Grand Rapids, MI: Zondervan, 1995), 73-80; Thomas W. Mann, *Divine Presence and Guidance in Israelite Traditions: The Typology of Exaltation* (Eugene, OR: Wipf & Stock, 2010).

[4]I explain this in my book *Monotheism and Institutions in the Book of Chronicles*, Forschungen zum Alten Testament II/64 (Tübingen: Mohr Siebeck, 2014), 165-179.

JOSHUA AND THE LITURGY OF JERICHO

As discussed earlier, there's good reason to suggest that Joshua reached its current form during Israel's exile (587–538 BC) or shortly thereafter.[5] That doesn't mean that the whole book was written late. Editors likely touched up and expanded an earlier edition of Joshua (a "Deuteronomistic" edition, in scholarly parlance) that *already* put a strong emphasis on the Levites. Though they probably weren't the same editors, the Chronicler and the postexilic editor of Joshua share an interest in the priestly dimensions of warfare.

It's not surprising, then, that the story of Jericho is told the way it is. Elsewhere, Joshua flies through battle scenes without much specificity (Josh 10–11). But for Jericho (and Ai), the tempo slows down . . . almost . . . to . . . a . . . snail's . . . pace . . . or perhaps better, to the metronome of a priestly procession.

Joshua 3–6 advances like a liturgical procession. It takes two whole chapters for Israel to process across the Jordan. If there's a main character here, it's the ark. Mentioned some twenty-seven times in these four chapters, the ark is without doubt the narrator's focus. It was Yahweh's throne in their midst. The ark exerts a kind of mesmerizing effect as it proceeds in front of the people before they cross the Jordan. Israel couldn't approach within three thousand feet of the ark and couldn't move until it moved. Yahweh's sacred presence was so dangerous and unapproachable that the people needed to stand back, much as they related to his presence at Sinai or in the Tabernacle itself:

> "When you see the ark of the covenant of the LORD your God, and the Levitical priests carrying it, you are to move out from your positions and follow it. Then you will know which way to go, since you have never been this way before. But keep a distance of about two thousand cubits between you and the ark; do not go near it."
>
> Joshua told the people, "Consecrate yourselves, for tomorrow the LORD will do amazing things among you." (Josh 3:3-5)

The actual battle at Jericho begins and ends at Gilgal, which would become one of Israel's most significant places of worship. Along the way, Israel

---

[5] See the overview in Douglas S. Earl, *Reading Joshua as Christian Scripture* (Winona Lake, IN: Eisenbrauns, 2010), 72-88.

commemorates the worship procession with stones used for an altar of worship. Leading this seven-day ceremony are the priests, who carry the ark before the people. The seven-day pattern of walking around the city (Josh 6) recalls the seven-day Passover celebration in Joshua 5:10-11, and the distinctive six-plus-one rhythm of the Jericho liturgy recalls the six-plus-one story of creation. Ancient readers would make the connection, since on that seventh holy day, when the city was finally encircled seven times and destroyed, all of its valuables were given over (as *herem*) *to the sanctuary*, God's ultimate resting place (Josh 6:24).

Like the story from 2 Chronicles 20, the Israelites were accompanying Yahweh into the land, but were in essence standing back in worshipful reverence to watch him win a victory. And like 2 Chronicles 20, the priests and people remain *silent* until they unveil—or proclaim—their secret weapon, Yahweh in their midst. The people burst forth with shouting and trumpet blasts, but Yahweh is the only military actor in the story. Their joyful shout joins the priestly trumpet blast that announces Yahweh's arrival in the city. In sum, Yahweh achieves his victory amid the priestly procession and celebration of his people in an event that culminates in an offering for the sanctuary.

HEREM AS WORSHIP: IMPLICATIONS FOR CONSIDERING VIOLENCE IN JOSHUA

In chapter ten I explained how the books of Exodus, Deuteronomy, Joshua, and Kings reframe *total destruction* commands in terms of *religious separation*. These books reframe the story of conquest such that they avoid any essential association with genocide. Whether this was for reasons of moral discomfort we cannot be sure. But the effect is the same. The story of destruction was understood to mean, "Don't cavort with idolatrous nations but remain true to Yahweh!" Moreover, Joshua emphasizes the need to separate from the trappings of Egyptian-backed imperialism: warlords, walled cities, weapons, and wealth.

I want to *tentatively propose* another similar shift taking place within Joshua. I'm calling it a *liturgical reframing*, from *warfare* to *liturgy*. Joshua is "liturgizing" the story of conquest, with Yahweh's lone military action in the foreground and Israel's participation in worship as the accompaniment.[6] This sort of reframing would hold significance for exilic and postexilic Israelites who lacked any and all military power.

Like Chronicles, Joshua draws on its historical sources to make important theological points, albeit in the form of a caricature. Joshua's conquest rhetoric participates in standard ancient Near Eastern warfare rhetoric, where "putting to the sword everything that breathes" basically meant, "winning a victory," and everyone knew it.[7]

I'm suggesting further that Joshua is *also* participating in a broader biblical pattern of liturgizing warfare—i.e., (a) heightening the drama of divine victory, (b) downplaying or eliminating any meaningful human military contribution to the victory, and (c) heightening the importance of worship within the battle scene. This sets the stage, I suggest, for the reception of such stories in worship settings for a totally different purpose, namely, to celebrate the power of Yahweh that accompanies the praise of his people.

This "liturgizing" rendered an older story of conquest meaningful for a people whose land had been effectively taken away. The returnees from exile, who were likely some of Joshua's earliest readers, were a powerless and vulnerable people in the land. They had no standing army, no king, few defenses, and little political clout. But they did have a temple. They did have priests. So, when they looked back on their history to ask, *Where is the powerful God of the past in our day?* they answer, *He's present in our worship. Therein lies our strength.*

According to Joshua, Israel's army was never its source of strength. It was "not by your sword or by your bow" that Israel defeated its enemies, Joshua later reminds the people (Josh 24:12, NRSV). Rather, it was the God enthroned as the praise of Israel who won the victory. He was the one who

---

[6]On the use of seven-day patterns elsewhere in Scripture (1 Sam 11:3, 10-11; 13:8; 1 Kings 20:29; 2 Kings 3:9) and the ancient Near East to underscore divine power in military actions, see Daniel E. Fleming, "The Seven-Day Siege of Jericho in Holy War," in *Ki Baruch Hu: Ancient Near Eastern, Biblical, and Judaic Studies in Honor of Baruch A. Levine*, ed. R. Chazan et al. (University Park, PA: The Pennsylvania State University Press, 1999), 211-28. Fleming notes striking similarities with the Ugaritic Keret legend (*KTU* 1.14 iii 2-20) and in the Mari archives (*ARM* I 131:14-16 and 26 405:3), in which of three siege references, two are for seven days.

[7]K. Lawson Younger Jr., *Ancient Conquest Accounts: A Study in Ancient Near Eastern and Biblical History Writing* (Sheffield: JSOT Press, 1990), 190-92, 243-45, 253.

"through the praise of children and infants / . . . established a stronghold
against your enemies, / to silence the foe and the avenger" (Ps 8:2).

While Joshua could be read in such a way that *warfare is seen as a form of
worship*, I'm suggesting that the momentum of the book was in the other
direction, toward the idea that *worship was a form of warfare*. The book
permits both readings, but only one leads toward the one who later took up
the name Joshua, that is, Jesus. At the beginning of his ministry, Jesus confronted and overcame Satan by affirming that he was to *"worship the Lord
your God and serve him only"* (Lk 4:8). Toward the end of his public ministry, Jesus entered Jerusalem, and as he did so,

> the crowds that *went ahead of him and those that followed* shouted, "Hosanna
> to the Son of David!" . . . But when the chief priests and the teachers of
> the law saw the wonderful things he did and the children shouting in the
> temple courts, "Hosanna to the Son of David," they were indignant.
>
> "Do you hear what these children are saying?" they asked him.
>
> "Yes," replied Jesus, "have you never read, *'From the lips of children and
> infants you, Lord, have called forth your praise* [to silence the foe and avenger]'?"
> (Mt 21:9, 15-16)

Jesus' march into Jerusalem continues the Joshua story. To the praise of
children he achieved his victory.

The book of Revelation plays a similar tune, but in a different key. In Revelation 19, Jesus rides again, but this time on a white war horse as one who
"judges and wages war" (Rev 19:11). Readers might assume that the horse-
riding king spares no rival this time. He wears a diadem, which, with the white
horse, evokes the victorious Roman military procession.[8] But the martial
imagery turns on its head. Jesus wears a robe "dipped in blood" (Rev 19:13),
which could be his enemies', but is more likely the blood of Christian witnesses who died for their faith (Rev 14:20). He wields the sword of the Word
(Rev 19:15),[9] just as Israel was to meditate on the Torah to succeed in battle.

But it's the army of heaven that captures our attention here. The army of
the redeemed saints go forth wearing *white robes* (Rev 7:9). The martyrs
who bore witness in death proceed into battle with their king, though not

---

[8]Brian K. Blount, *Revelation: A Commentary* (Nashville: Westminster John Knox, 2013), 349.
[9]Evoking the Messianic ruler from Is 11:4.

arrayed in standard garb. As Mike Glenn notes, "That's not battle dress. That's dress for worship—for the high, holy, glorious worship in heaven."[10]

Such worship reminds us of saintly scenes across the book. Revelation 13 tells us that many on earth worship the beast and are deceived. The saints who refuse to do so are martyred but overcome such evil through their defiant worship of the one and true king (Rev 6:11; 7:13-15).

We're told that these saints "triumphed over him [the accuser] by the blood of the Lamb and *by the word of their testimony*; they did not love their lives so much as to shrink from death" (Rev 12:11).[11] Worshipful martyrdom brings about victory.

Whether it's throwing open the gates of prison as Paul and Silas sing,[12] defeating a vastly superior enemy army, razing Jericho, or accompanying Jesus in victory, praise is powerful. As the psalmist says, "Some trust in chariots and some in horses, but we *proclaim* [i.e., praise] the name of the LORD our God" (Ps 20:7, NIV modified).[13]

---

[10]Mike Glenn, "The Weapon of Worship: Rethinking the Power of Worship," *Jesus Creed* (blog), June 18, 2021, https://www.christianitytoday.com/scot-mcknight/2021/june/weapon-of -worship.html.

[11]I'm not suggesting that Revelation is wholly pacifistic, but instead that the people of God do not participate in violence in the here and now, relying instead on the power of the Lamb. It should be noted, however, that Revelation does seem to envision Christian participation in the final judgment (Rev 20). See Paul Middleton's *The Violence of the Lamb: Martyrs as Agents of Divine Judgment in the Book of Revelation*, Library of New Testament Studies 586 (London: T&T Clark, 2018).

[12]Also noted in Mike Glenn, "Weapon of Worship."

[13]The word "proclaim" is sometimes translated "trust," though the Hebrew is "bring to remembrance." In Psalms and elsewhere, this is a synonym for praise (Ps 45:17; 71:16; cf. Ps 147:11-12; Is 26:13; 62:6).

PART FOUR

THE OLD TESTAMENT AND THE CHARACTER OF GOD

I've ALWAYS ENJOYED THE CLIMBING MAGAZINE *Rock and Ice*. I love following the world of rock and mountain climbing, since I used to be active in both sports. On their Facebook page, *Rock and Ice* posts the "Weekend Whipper," a video that depicts someone taking a huge fall off the rock. The ropes always catch . . . eventually. Rock climbing ropes are extremely strong, able to handle forces of up to 5,500 pounds. The seemingly thin ten-millimeter rope can do this because it's *dynamic*, which means that it's able to absorb some of the impact by stretching up to 30 percent when taking a sudden load. By contrast, static ropes can break suddenly because they have no stretch. Static ropes can handle a heavy load when static, so they're good for things like hauling loads on cranes. But climbers need ropes that can stretch and not break. They need tensile strength. It's surprising how 175-pound climbers can sometimes take thirty, forty, and even fifty-foot falls and not break or even fray the rope (assuming it was set up properly).

Many Christians take a static rope to the problem of violence in the Bible. They take what looks like the most durable material and weave themselves a rope of protection against anything that might throw them off the wall. This might take the form of trying to rid the flood or conquest stories of all violent traces. Or it might involve trying to erase any "problem of violence" in the first place. But they weave the rope so tight that it breaks with a sudden load. That broken rope can leave our faith wrecked on the rocks below.

What we need instead is a dynamic rope.

A dynamic climbing rope uses a particular kind of twisted weave that gives it flexibility. It also uses multiple yarns in its core, so that the entire rope doesn't depend on one large strand. Flexibility and elasticity help us sustain hard impacts, and multiple yarns spread the load and risk.

I've tried to argue in this book that no single approach to the problem of violence will *solve* matters. This is especially so depending on your temperament. If you're driven by a sense of justice, you'll likely find matters related to violence in Scripture especially hard. That's okay. God gave you that concern for justice and you shouldn't cauterize your moral nerves. But relating to some of the hard texts in Scripture might prove especially difficult. They seem irredeemably unjust. Your challenge will be learning how to live with unresolved questions about violence without blunting your sense of what's just—and most importantly, without losing your trust in God's justice and goodness.

On the other hand, if you're driven by a commitment to tradition or authority, then you'll probably find it harder to relate to others' ethical concerns with the Bible. You might think, *Who are we to assume that the Bible, time-tested and true, should be the problem and not us?* Those are good questions to ask. But you might also find it hard to relate to the protests and laments within Scripture itself. Your challenge might be learning how to relate to the questioning or protest traditions in Scripture, and to the doubts of others. Jude instructs us to "have mercy on those who doubt" (Jude 22, ESV), and Romans to "accept the one whose faith is weak" (Rom 14:1), and we see ample evidence that God *invites* our justice questions, even when directed at him.

I've tried to let the Bible speak in both directions. It has real ethical issues that need consideration (if not for our own sake, for others'), but it also has challenges for us. The Bible has its hand on the pulse of a violence-ridden world and has much to teach us. For instance, the biblical writers express deep concern about the ecological impact of violence, and the ways that violence takes root in a context of male efforts to dominate. The Old Testament has more than a thing or two to teach us about our problem of violence.

But staring directly at the problem of violence too long can leave you with blurred vision, or even blinded. I've seen it happen to people. Sometimes we must step back, look elsewhere, and then return to our original question to see if it looks different.

In this last part of the book, I want to do that. This isn't a diversion strategy. It's a way of remembering what's central and what's peripheral to the Bible's claims about God. Getting perspective on the problem of violence will help us listen to Scripture's full orchestra and not just its cymbals or tuba, important as they are (I played tuba!).

We'll focus on how the Old Testament itself presents God's character, what he's really like. And we'll look at how the story of God and his people makes us look differently at the problem of violence.

14

WHAT THE OLD TESTAMENT SAYS ABOUT GOD'S CHARACTER

IF YOU HAD TO DESCRIBE THE GOD portrayed in the Old Testament, how would you do it? I hope that after reading this book you're less convinced of some popular stereotypes—God is just wrathful! God is bloodthirsty!

But maybe you're still thinking, *Okay Matt, maybe God isn't always angry and vindictive. Maybe he's a mix of anger and love. Perhaps he's 50 percent wrath and 50 percent compassion.*

If I've moved the needle toward recognizing the goodness of God, I'll consider that one success. But I hope that we can nudge the needle further along, not toward resolution, but toward trust in God's ultimate goodness.

At its heart, the problem of violence in Scripture is about the character of God. Can we trust the character of God given all the challenging portraits we encounter in Scripture?

So far, my study has revisited famous stories of violence (flood and conquest) to help us find ways to (1) avoid missing the point of these stories and drawing the wrong conclusions about God; (2) avoid losing confidence in God's character because of these Old Testament stories; (3) avoid cynicism about the God revealed in the Old Testament; (4) avoid growing paralyzed by the problem of violence in the Old Testament; and (5) avoid the need for total resolution in order to move forward in your faith.

I've also sought to show the surprising mercy and compassion of God in some of the most challenging texts. God grieves violence, protects his creation from violence, includes the stranger and outsider, challenges myopic nationalism, undermines confidence in human weaponry and power, and ultimately casts a vision of creational shalom.

For some of you, the problem of violence in Scripture may still cast a dark shadow over your faith. You've read far and wide, talked with trusted friends, listened to experts, tried your best, but you can't shake the gnawing feeling that God is immorally violent.

You're not alone. I sometimes struggle with the same feelings. I know countless others who feel the same way. What I've shared in this book has helped me. In fact, I have come to cherish the flood and conquest stories. They fascinate and amaze me. But I'm not always at ease with the way these stories portray God. To that extent the stories leave me lingering in the unresolved, in the space that requires faith to grow.

In what follows, I want to offer another way of looking at the problem of violence that has proved helpful for me: *Keep central what the Bible keeps central.* Distinguish between core and peripheral portraits of God's character, between the spine and the ribs.

WEIGHTIER MATTERS

Scripture regularly distinguishes between central and ancillary matters. When faced with the question about which is the greatest commandment, Jesus didn't just say, "They're *all* important!" Instead, he maintained that to love God and neighbor was central, and then told a parable about loving one's enemy and showing mercy (Lk 10:25-37). Jesus drew together a set of Old Testament texts (Deut 6:4; Lev 19:18, 34; Hos 6:6) to say that *these* requirements were more central than others. If you miss them, you've missed the point. All the law and prophets hung on those laws, and not the other way around (Mt 22:40).

It would be quite a different matter if he said, "You are to put them to death. Stone them! On these all the Law and the Prophets depend."

Jesus wasn't innovating when he placed love for God and neighbor at the center of the law. First-century rabbis made similar arguments.[1] That's because they were reading along the grain of the Old Testament, which *already* distinguishes core and peripheral ways of thinking about God's

---

[1]E.g., *b. Shabbat* 31a and other examples where Rabbis espoused something akin to the Golden Rule, which "sums up the Law and the Prophets" according to Jesus (Mt 7:12). Discussed in David Flusser and Steven Notley, *The Sage from Galilee: Rediscovering Jesus' Genius* (Grand Rapids, MI: Eerdmans, 2007), 59-60.

character. They didn't need to read against the Old Testament to discern core and peripheral matters.

Narrative priority. First, the story arc of Scripture orients us to everything in between. We're asked to look through the lens of Genesis 1–2 (or 1–11) to interpret the rest of Scripture. Through that lens we see that violence is an aberration in creation. It's not part of how God created things in the beginning or where God's moving things in the end (Is 65–66; Rev 21–22). The arc of all Scripture bends toward peace, as Brent Strawn puts it. He writes:

> The Old Testament's vision of the future is also marked by peace and lack of conflict and strife (Isa 11:1-9; 66:17-25; Zech 8:1-8; etc.). This arc of nonviolence indicates that something "in between" the peaceful bookends has gone terribly wrong; the "in-between" is marked by violence, but it was not originally so, neither is it to be so, again, in the end.[2]

The creation story has a foundational (and final) quality that even Joshua doesn't, despite its importance for thinking about Israel's beginnings. The beginning and end of the biblical story is shalom. Those narrative compass points help us navigate everything in between.

LOSING AND FINDING YOUR WAY

I had a friend in graduate school who, like all of us doing PhD studies in Bible, had to wade through deep pools of historical critical scholarship. I've benefited from historical critical scholarship. But when it's your main diet, it can take a toll, because it constantly asks you to leave faith matters out of the equation. If you indefinitely leave aside questions of faith, your faith eventually feels implausible. This happened to my friend. He found himself in crisis, without a sense of which bits and pieces of his prior faith he could salvage. This faith crisis caused him inner turmoil and strained his marriage.

I remember many long conversations with him about his journey. I had walked a different path. Critical scholarship didn't have the same impact on me, but I understood the tensions he described. Some time went by without real progress—until one crucial conversation with one of his professors.

---

[2]Brent A. Strawn, *Lies My Preacher Told Me: An Honest Look at the Old Testament* (Louisville, KY: Westminster John Knox, 2021), 43.

This professor challenged my friend to avoid putting everything on the same shelf. The question of whether Jesus confronted one or two Gadarene demoniacs (Mk 5:1-20 vs. Mt 8:28-34) just isn't as important as the question of Jesus' divinity. He pointed my friend back to the Apostles' Creed:

> I believe in God, the Father almighty,
> creator of heaven and earth.
> I believe in Jesus Christ, his only Son, our Lord.
> He was conceived by the power of the Holy Spirit
> and born of the Virgin Mary.
> He suffered under Pontius Pilate,
> was crucified, died, and was buried.
> He descended to the dead.
> On the third day he rose again.
> He ascended to heaven,
> and is seated at the right hand of the Father.
> He will come again to judge the living and the dead.
> I believe in the Holy Spirit,
> the holy catholic church,
> the communion of saints,
> the forgiveness of sins,
> the resurrection of the body,
> and the life everlasting. Amen.[3]

This creed lies at the center of the Christian faith. Its affirmations, distilled from Scripture's own summary claims (e.g., 1 Cor 15:3-7), have been affirmed by most Christians through time and across the world.

Roger Olson distinguishes between dogmas, doctrines, and opinions. Dogmas are those creedal statements. They're essential, and where absent, "Christianity can hardly be recognized as present," and include matters like Jesus' divinity and salvific work.[4] Doctrines, in Olson's typology, are matters

---

[3] *The Book of Common Prayer and Administration of the Sacraments and Other Rites and Ceremonies of the Church: Together with the Psalter or Psalms of David According to the Use of the Episcopal Church* (New York: Seabury Press, 1979), 96.
[4] Roger E. Olson, *Reformed and Always Reforming: The Postconservative Approach to Evangelical Theology,* Acadia Studies in Bible and Theology (Grand Rapids, MI: Baker Academic, 2007), 96.

of significance that are disputed.[5] Infant baptism, different models of justi-fication, Calvinism versus Wesleyanism, varying claims about of Scripture (its inspiration, for example), and so on. Opinions are matters where agreement isn't necessary for fellowship. End-times beliefs, seven-day versus evolutionary creation, and what not. Christian theologians have a fancy word for these debated opinions: adiaphora. Adiaphora refers to matters that are of lesser importance to the faith. Those matters might be significant, but they're not essential for salvation. As Olson notes, some conservatives tend to load more onto the dogma and doctrine shelves. In extreme forms, *everything* becomes a matter of essential importance. This is a dangerous move and is out of step with historic Christianity. Conversely, some liberals empty the dogma and doctrine categories, such that every-thing is up for grabs. This is also unmoored from historic Christianity.

While not dismissing the importance of other matters in the Christian faith, the professor reminded my friend of what's core and what's peripheral. Affirming the tenets of the Apostles' Creed keeps your eyes focused on the heart of Christian belief. Start there and let God help you gain perspective on the rest, including what to do with troubling biblical texts.

This conversation proved transformative for my friend, not because it distracted him from the concerns of historical critics, but because it brought him back to the center. Let's notice a few ways the Old Testament already distinguishes the core from the periphery.

THREE OLD TESTAMENT DOGMAS

I want to suggest that the Old Testament does the same for us when it comes to thinking about God's character. I'm not talking about theological dogmas here, but as an analogy, we might speak about the Old Testament "character dogmas" about God. The Old Testament points us to the center of God's character in at least three ways. I'm grateful for Mark Boda's book *The Heartbeat of Old Testament Theology: Three Creedal Expressions*, from which I've drawn heavily here.

---

[5]The distinction between dogmas and doctrines seems to parallel what Saint Basil the Great called "dogmas and proclamations" in *On the Holy Spirit*, trans. Stephen M. Hildebrand, Popular Patristics Series 42 (Yonkers, NY: St. Vladimir's Seminary Press, 2011), 104.

Boda observes that certain portraits of God dominate the Old Testament. They occur frequently, play a major role in the places they occur, and bring cohesion to the whole Bible. Here are these core claims in brief outline.[6]

In story: Yahweh is the God of the exodus. God is known throughout Scripture as the one who responded to the cries of the Hebrew slaves and brought Israel up out of Egypt. In the exodus, Israel first becomes a nation. God's identity as "the LORD your God, who brought you out of Egypt, out of the land of slavery" (Ex 20:2; Deut 5:6) appears at the beginning of the Ten Commandments and sets the tone for all the laws that Israel receives. The exodus also plays a major role in almost every summary of Israel's story that we find in the Old Testament (e.g., Deut 6:21-23; 26:5-9; Josh 24:2-13; Judg 2:1-3; 1 Sam 12:8; Ps 78, 105, 106, 135, 136; Ezek 20:5-29).[7] Exodus language also infuses the conquest and return from exile stories.

As discussed in chapter eleven, Joshua portrays the conquest as the continuation of the exodus. The prophets portray the return from exile as a new exodus (Is 52:11-12). We could go on! Exodus language pervades almost every corner of the Old Testament and forms the foundation for the Bible's theology of redemption.[8] The exodus story draws attention to the way that *this* story will reveal God's identity to Israel, Egypt, and the nations. Throughout the plagues we hear repeatedly that God enacts judgment on Egypt *so that they may know that I am Yahweh* (Ex 8:10, 22; 9:14, 29; 11:7). It's like God writes his own founding narrative so that contemporary and future nations will know that God is a God of justice, power, and concern for the vulnerable. Those qualities are at the heart of God's self-revealed story.

In relationship: Yahweh is bound to his people. Throughout Israel's story, there's a steady drumbeat reminding Israel that "I will walk among you and be your God, and you will be my people" (Lev 26:12).[9] The desire

---

[6]Mark J. Boda, *The Heartbeat of Old Testament Theology: Three Creedal Expressions*, Acadia Studies in Bible and Theology (Grand Rapids, MI: Baker Academic, 2017). I have modified Boda's categories slightly and presented them in a different order to highlight character elements.
[7]Boda, *Heartbeat*, 29.
[8]L. Michael Morales, *Exodus Old and New: A Biblical Theology of Redemption* (Downers Grove, IL: InterVarsity Press, 2020); David Daube, *The Exodus Pattern in the Bible* (Eugene, OR: Wipf and Stock Publishers, 2020); Bryan D. Estelle, *Echoes of Exodus: Tracing a Biblical Motif* (Downers Grove, IL: InterVarsity Press, 2018); Alastair J. Roberts and Andrew Wilson, *Echoes of Exodus: Tracing Themes of Redemption Through Scripture* (Wheaton, IL: Crossway, 2018).
[9]Boda, *Heartbeat*, 68.

for relationship and presence takes shape in God's covenants with his people, and in consistent emphasis on the fact that Yahweh and his people belong to one another. Covenant is a kind of "family substitute," where those without a natural relationship agree to a kin relationship.[10] Echoes of this idea reverberate throughout Scripture. Here are examples:

> For you are a people holy to the LORD your God. Out of all the peoples on the face of the earth, the LORD has chosen you to be his treasured possession. (Deut 14:2)

> You have established your people Israel as your very own forever, and you, LORD, have become their God. (2 Sam 7:24)

> Know that the LORD is God.
> It is he who made us, and we are his;
> we are his people, the sheep of his pasture. (Ps 100:3)

> But I gave them this command: Obey me, and I will be your God and you will be my people. Walk in obedience to all I command you, that it may go well with you. (Jer 7:23)

> You will be my people, and I will be your God. (Jer 30:22)

> "This is the covenant I will make with the people of Israel
> after that time," declares the LORD.
> "I will put my law in their minds
> and write it on their hearts.
> I will be their God,
> and they will be my people." (Jer 31:33)

> Then you will live in the land I gave your ancestors; you will be my people, and I will be your God. (Ezek 36:28)

> My dwelling place will be with them; I will be their God, and they will be my people. (Ezek 37:27)[11]

The relationship involves mutual obligations and expectations, but God's relational commitment to Israel is so strong that it eclipses other moments

---

[10]Mark S. Smith, *How Human Is God? Seven Questions About God and Humanity in the Bible* (Collegeville, MN: Liturgical Press, 2014), 48; Boda, *Heartbeat*, 70.
[11]Boda, *Heartbeat*, 69.

where that relationship strains and threatens to crumble. After recounting Israel's repeated rebellion against God, Hosea shows Yahweh's refusal to give up on the relationship:

> How can I give you up, Ephraim?
> How can I hand you over, Israel? . . .
> My heart is changed within me;
> all my compassion is aroused. (Hos 11:8)

God's relationship with Israel turns him regularly toward compassion and mercy, even in the face of sin.

In character expressions: Yahweh is a God of all-surpassing mercy. God's mercy towers over his wrath or judgment. It might sound like cherry picking to say so. However, when Scripture steps back to reflect on God's character, one thing becomes clear. God isn't fifty-fifty angry and compassionate. Violence doesn't balance out his love. Instead, *the Old Testament sets God's deliverance, mercy, and love at the center of its portrait of God's character.* Wrath and judgment have their place, to be sure, but they sit outside the center of the Old Testament's picture of God.

To see how this is so, and how this isn't just an easy bypass around the problem of violence, we need to look back at Exodus 34:6-7 to understand God's defining character qualities. Then we'll look at how the Bible uses Exodus 34:6-7 as a lens for understanding God's character. Just as the Bible wants us to look at the rest of the biblical story through the lens of Genesis 1–2, so it also wants us to use Exodus 34:6-7 to understand the essence of God's character. It's that important!

Exodus 34:6-7 is the closest to a "character creed" that the Old Testament offers:

> And he [Yahweh] passed in front of Moses, proclaiming, "The LORD, the LORD, the compassionate and gracious God, slow to anger, abounding in love and faithfulness, maintaining love to thousands, and forgiving wickedness, rebellion and sin. Yet he does not leave the guilty unpunished; he punishes the children and their children for the sin of the parents to the third and fourth generation." (Ex 34:6-7)

Notice also the heavy use of participles (-ing verbs)—"abounding . . . maintaining . . . forgiving." These verses claim that God is *consistently* like this.

This text's "core" quality derives first from its narrative location—immediately after Israel broke the first and second commands (Ex 32–34). The revelation of God's character comes in response to Moses' request to know God's *ways* and for his *presence* to remain with Israel (Ex 33:12-16, 18) despite their sin. God tells Moses that his goodness would pass before Moses (corresponding to his *ways* above) and that he would reveal his glory (Ex 33:17, 19-23) to confirm his *presence* with Israel. God's ways find expression in the adjectives of Exodus 34:6 (compassionate, gracious, etc.) and the verbs of Exodus 34:7 (maintaining love, forgiving, etc.). Divine *hesed*, or merciful love, appears in the adjectival and verbal portions of Exodus 34:6-7, unifying this portrait of Yahweh.

The prominence of this character creed also derives from its repetition throughout Scripture. It is quoted at least fourteen times in the Old Testament (Num 14:18; Ps 86:5, 15; 103:8; 111:4; 112:4; 116:5; 145:8; Joel 2:13; Jon 4:2; Nah 1:3; Neh 9:17, 31; 2 Chr 30:9; cf. Deut 4:31; Ps 78:38.), and fragments of these verses reverberate hundreds of times through both Testaments.[12] Israel continued to think with this text as it reflected on God's character.

The passage doesn't let us sit comfortably. Notice that it brings God's compassionate mercy into connection with his judgment. The two sit in uneasy tension (forgiving . . . punishing). In other words, the core confession of Yahweh's character asks us to stand in awe and wonder at the God who shows boundless mercy and who also judges the guilty. We cannot divorce these qualities from each other. Instead, we are invited to consider how they might relate. This mode of considering God's character involves more than just holding tensions. It also involves avoiding a sole focus on "positive" divine character qualities in ways that negate others. We might be tempted to say, for instance, that *God is so compassionate that he never*

---

[12]For a review of significant echoes of Ex 34:6-7 in the Old Testament, see Austin Surls, *Making Sense of the Divine Name in the Book of Exodus: From Etymology to Literary Onomastics*, Bulletin for Biblical Research Supplements 17 (Winona Lake, IN: Eisenbrauns/Penn State University Press, 2017), 162-81; Gary Edward Schnittjer, *Old Testament Use of Old Testament: A Book-by-Book Guide* (Grand Rapids, MI: Zondervan, 2021), 23-24, 877.

punishes wrong. Conversely, we might overemphasize God's "need" to punish. *God is so holy that he must always judge sin.* The "ways" of God displayed in Exodus 34:6-7 involve the coordination of forgiveness and punishment, of mercy and anger, and of loyalty to thousands and judgment to several generations.

However, Exodus 34:6-7 makes no effort to keep mercy and judgment in balance. These verses force us instead to think about the "incomprehensible excess of God's goodness."[13] While Scripture challenges us to avoid purging mercy of all notions of punishment, it also challenges us to recognize the categorically unique quality of divine mercy. This is a mercy like no other. God is the *only one* in the Old Testament who is said to forgive (Heb. *salah*) sin. It's unique to his character.[14] The prophet Micah recognizes this unique divine quality: "Who is a God like you, who *pardons sin and forgives the transgression* of the remnant of his inheritance? You do not stay angry forever but delight to show mercy" (Mic 7:18). It's easy to miss just how remarkable this claim is, and how deeply it's influenced biblical thought. Throughout the Old Testament, only God is said to forgive. God has the unique capacity to forego punishment and vengeance, and delights in doing so.

Also, the thousands of generations receiving mercy vastly outnumber the three to four judged generations. In strictly mathematical terms, God's mercy outweighs his judgment by a ratio of at least five hundred to one (taking the minimum of two thousand versus the maximum of four). In a Talmudic reflection on Psalm 7:11, which says that God "displays his wrath every day," the rabbis asked *how long* he's wrathful each day. The answer? 1/58,888th of an hour. Others said, for long as it takes to say the Hebrew word moment (*rega'*). That is, God is angry but for a moment. By contrast, God's mercy knows no bounds (*b. Berakhot* 7a). While such mathematical precision is not the point here, biblical thinking about God's character does

---

[13]Claus Westermann, *Elements of Old Testament Theology*, trans. Douglas W. Stott (Atlanta: John Knox, 1982), 139.

[14]Jeremiah Unterman, *Justice for All: How the Jewish Bible Revolutionized Ethics* (Lincoln: University of Nebraska Press, 2017), 162-65; Joshua Berman, "No Apologies, Just a Kiss," *Joshua Berman* (blog), Times of Israel: The Blogs, September 12, 2021, https://blogs.timesofisrael.com/no-apologies-just-a-kiss/.

not permit us to see mercy and judgment in equal terms. The words of Jesus' brother should help us avoid seeing an equal balance of mercy and judgment in God: "Judgment without mercy will be shown to anyone who has not been merciful. Mercy triumphs over judgment" (Jas 2:13). *God's character is clearly imbalanced!*

As I often ask my students, if we want to know what the "God of the Old Testament" was like, who better to ask than the people who lived with the "God of the Old Testament?" We see time and again that as God's people look back on their long journey with God, it's his *mercy* that embraces their past.

Let's listen to Psalm 103—a psalm recited each Sunday in the Orthodox Church, and a key part of worship services in other traditions as well. This hymn of praise begins by extolling God's blessings and benefits. According to this psalm, we're *all* on benefits (Ps 103:2). In verse 7 the psalmist reflects on Israel's past experiences with God. We're transported back to Sinai, where God reminded Israel that he's "compassionate and gracious, slow to anger, abounding in love" (Ps 103:8). The psalmist quotes from Exodus 34:6-7. Exodus says that God *also* punishes to the third and fourth generations. But instead of quoting that portion of text, the psalmist says that at the end of the day, "He does not treat us as our sins deserve / or repay us according to our iniquities" (Ps 103:10).

In the psalmist's view, God isn't even as punish-y as he claims! Where we might expect a bit of judgment, we often find that he's "removed our transgressions from us" (Ps 103:12). Listen to the tenderness of this psalm:

As a father has compassion on his children,
　so the LORD has compassion on those who fear him;
　for he knows how we are formed,
　he remembers that we are dust. (Ps 103:13-14)

Psalm 103 holds our feet to the fires of God's burning compassion and steadfast love, God's *hesed*.[15] In the end, God's *hesed*, not *herem* (comprehensive destruction), preoccupies the worshiping community of Israel.

---

[15]While it's attributed to David (Ps 103:1), it was likely written much later. The Hebrew phrase *le-david* can mean by, about, with regard to, or for David, as explained in Bruce K. Waltke and James M. Houston, *The Psalms as Christian Worship* (Grand Rapids, MI: Eerdmans, 2010), 89. In any case, it reflects Israel's several hundred years of experience with the OT God (notice the "we/us" language in the psalm).

Whereas *herem* never gets a psalmic mention, we hear of Yahweh's *hesed* no less than 128 times. And while other terms for judgment appear in Psalms, none become the character metronome like God's *hesed*. Notice the words of Psalm 136.[16]

. . . His hesed endures forever (v. 1)
. . . His hesed endures forever (v. 2)
. . . His hesed endures forever (v. 3)
. . . His hesed endures forever (v. 4)
. . . His hesed endures forever (v. 5)
. . . His hesed endures forever (v. 6)
. . . His hesed endures forever (v. 7)
. . . His hesed endures forever (v. 8)
. . . His hesed endures forever (v. 9)
. . . His hesed endures forever (v. 10)
. . . His hesed endures forever (v. 11)
. . . His hesed endures forever (v. 12)
. . . His hesed endures forever (v. 13)
. . . His hesed endures forever (v. 14)
. . . His hesed endures forever (v. 15)
. . . His hesed endures forever (v. 16)
. . . His hesed endures forever (v. 17)
. . . His hesed endures forever (v. 18)
. . . His hesed endures forever (v. 19)
. . . His hesed endures forever (v. 20)
. . . His hesed endures forever (v. 21)
. . . His hesed endures forever (v. 22)
. . . His hesed endures forever (v. 23)
. . . His hesed endures forever (v. 24)
. . . His hesed endures forever (v. 25)
. . . His hesed endures forever (v. 26)

In short, God is *omni-merciful*.[17]

---

[16]*Hesed* can take the form of judgment, though as sung in this psalm and elsewhere, it refers to judgment on Israel's oppressors (e.g., Ps 136:10, 15, 17-20).

[17]As James M. Howard Jr. notes, "Yahweh is simple in his being, so all he does can be ascribed to his lovingkindness. That he is immutable can be discerned from the fact that his lovingkindness endures forever." *Psalms Volume II: Psalms 73–150* (Bellingham, WA: Lexham Academic, 2021), 443.

CONCLUSIONS

When we step back to look at the Old Testament's own summary—even creedal—claims about Yahweh, God's redemptive, relational, and merciful qualities take center stage. The Old Testament privileges these divine qualities and asks us to do the same. We're not to brush everything else under the carpet or ignore other important aspects of God's character. But we do have to put the accent in the right place. If we don't, we "strain out a gnat but swallow a camel," to use Jesus' words (Mt 23:24). We miss the "more important matters" of the Old Testament in favor of the lesser matters (Mt 23:23).

The Old Testament shows us that God's redemptive, relational, and merciful character are the pegs on which all the rest of our thinking about God ought to hang. God's compassion and lovingkindness occupy the center of our thinking about God's character. God's love is more central to his character than his judgment because judgment responds to sin, which will not endure. Judgment and justice play a very important, though secondary, role.[18] Further, in a similar way that mercy outweighs God's judgment in the character creed, God's shalom (right-relating wholeness) overshadows God's use of violence in the narrative frame of Scripture. The beginning (creation), center (cross), and end (new creation) of Scripture is the overwhelming shalom of God, the plan and destiny for the creation that he so loves. The Old Testament helps us bring these related-yet-distinguishable aspects of God's character and plan into proper coordination so that we don't overplay one particular aspect (God's judgment or the stories of violence) or underplay another (God's mercy and concern for shalom).

---

[18]Jacob Onyumbe Wenyi, *Piles of Slain, Heaps of Corpses: Reading Prophetic Poetry and Violence in African Context* (Eugene, OR: Cascade Books, 2021), 173.

15

IRRESOLVABLE

THE PROBLEM OF VIOLENCE in the Old Testament can't be solved. There, I said it. At least, it can't be solved in a way that will garner any kind of consensus or resolve the moral tensions that the flood and conquest events create. The reason, I suggest, is that the problem of violence is akin to what social scientists call a "wicked problem." Wicked problems aren't wicked because they're *evil*, but because they're *resistant to resolution*.[1] Unlike a benign problem, like a math equation, a "wicked problem"

> is a complex issue that defies complete definition, for which there can be no final solution, since any resolution generates further issues. . . . Such problems are not morally wicked, but diabolical in that they resist all the usual attempts to resolve them.[2]

An example would be poverty. Poverty is a wicked problem because of its complex interconnection with education, and education with socio-economic opportunity and health, and those issues with local and national governmental policies, and each with race and gender, and so on. Even the term "poverty" itself lacks definitional precision, which is another feature of wicked problems. How do we know that we've correctly named the problem of poverty? Does it refer to income, wealth, opportunity, quality of life? If so, how do we know that we've arrived at poverty's "root causes," such that we can say that we've even stated the nature and scope of the

---

[1]Joseph C. Bentley and Michael A. Toth, *Exploring Wicked Problems: What They Are and Why They Are Important* (Bloomington, IN: Archway Publishing, 2020), 20. Thanks to Rob Barrett (personal conversation) for introducing me to the concept.

[2]Valerie A. Brown, Peter M. Deane, John A. Harris, and Jacqueline Y. Russel, "Towards a Just and Sustainable Future," in *Tackling Wicked Problems Through the Transdisciplinary Imagination*, eds. Valerie A. Brown, John A. Harris, and Jacqueline Y. Russell (London: Earthscan, 2010), 4.

problem in its entirety? How do spiritual realities factor in a definition of poverty?

And how does anyone know when poverty is "solved"? There's no clearly identifiable end point to resolving wicked problems. There's no moment at which we put up our feet and say, "Job done." Any solution is provisional, and we can't test solutions to say, with certitude, that they even constitute a solution![3] Yet another of its wicked features. You can see the challenge.

An additional difficulty with wicked problems is that there are also hidden costs to *working on* them. Think about the humanitarian, social, and economic consequences of the "War on Terror," the "War on Drugs," and the "War on Poverty." Each left nations, communities, and individuals in peril. Policymakers and other leaders carry enormous responsibilities for these failed wars.

Many of us don't want to carry such responsibilities, even on a smaller scale. Some work at the problem of violence in Scripture only to end up with their faith in shambles. Why lead people into such "wicked problems"?

In their classic study on wicked problems, Rittel and Webber point out that wicked problems become a *moral* snare when people "treat a wicked problem as though it were a tame one, or to tame a wicked problem prematurely."[4] Trying to tame a problem like violence in Scripture is like trying to resolve homelessness with an essential oil. The right tool is needed. But perhaps more importantly, a sober assessment of the complexity of the issue is crucial. The complexity of the issue requires a multifaceted response.

The problem of violence in Scripture will also resist resolution. The issues impinging on its resolution are too varied and complex to allow for an *easy*, or any, resolution. I hope by now that you've grown wary of easy solutions. When applied to complex problems, such "solutions" always carry hidden costs. It's like signing up for that free month's membership at the gym and then realizing two years later that you've been paying monthly fees for twenty-three months. Even worse, it's like forgetting that you'd forgotten you owned the credit card used to pay those twenty-three months,

---

[3]Horst W. J. Rittel and Melvin M. Webber, "Dilemmas in a General Theory of Planning," *Policy Sciences* 4 (1973): 162-63.
[4]Rittel and Webber, "Dilemmas," 161.

and now you have outstanding debt and accrued interest. Hidden costs compound and intersect.

As a first part of our response, then, it's important to name the problem's complexity and irresolvability, and refuse the temptation to tame the untamable.

But wicked problems aren't just problems about which we throw up our hands and say, "There's no point trying if we can't solve them!"

Here's my hope as we bring this study toward its conclusion (but not its resolution), *That we develop our capacity to work through the problem of violence in Scripture while resisting the temptation to (1) offer a reductive account of the problem itself, (2) reduce the complexity of Scripture's violent texts, or (3) tame our understanding of the God revealed in Scripture.*

In his study on wicked problems, Keith Grint points out that while tame problems often have elegant (i.e., single-mode) solutions, sometimes "clumsy answers" work better for wicked problems. He writes, "[T]o get some purchase on Wicked Problems we need to start by accepting that imperfection and making do with what is available," recognizing that single-mode answers aren't possible. Such answers often fail because they fail to "generate sufficient diversity to address the complexity of the problem."[5] How true indeed for the problem(s) of violence in Scripture!

To that end, this book has sought a terrain-responsive approach to violence that involves reading the biblical terrain carefully before attempting to solve anything. It's a posture of empathy before evaluation.[6] I've also resisted taking one "approach" and applying it across the Old Testament's challenging texts.

To accompany that journey through Scripture's complex problems of violence, I offer six *easy* (just kidding, they're not) practices to help Christians in the journey through the varied terrain of violence in Scripture. I trust that these will prove useful for the good of the church.

---

[5]Keith Grint, "Wicked Problems and Clumsy Solutions: The Role of Leadership," in *The New Public Leadership Challenge*, eds. Stephen Brookes and Keith Grint (London: Palgrave Macmillan, 2010), 176-77.

[6]As discussed in Paul Rohram's essay "Empathy and Evaluation in Medieval Church History and Pastoral Ministry: A Lutheran Reading of Pseudo-Dionysius," *Princeton Seminary Bulletin* 19, no. 2 (1998): 99-115.

CHANGE YOUR GOALS

Not every problem should have a solution as its goal, or at least, its *only* goal. Sometimes naming problems and working on them helps us rule out bad options. Knowing what won't work, or what will worsen the situation is a worthwhile outcome. Sometimes *some* improvement is worth the effort and makes a major difference for struggling Christians. We *can* alleviate the problem of poverty, even if we can't untangle all factors contributing to its existence.

Similarly, the irresolvability of the problem of violence needn't stop us at the door. Working on the problem has goals *besides* resolution that are sometimes more pressing. Like helping Christians know that others experience the same doubts or ask the same questions. Or confronting honestly the Bible we have. Or discovering that we can ask the hard questions and remain faithful. Or changing our perception of the problem itself. Or helping us realize that texts we initially despised are richer and more wonderful than we imagined!

Returning to the challenge of violence can help us see things that we couldn't otherwise see. In my experience, I've discovered that the early chapters of Genesis and books like Joshua are far more interesting than I realized. I've found fellowship with many Christians who struggle with the challenges of Scripture's violence. I've learned more about the life and ministry of Jesus. I've seen Christians learn to wrestle with hard texts and live with tension. I've understood more fully the depths of Scripture's vision for peace. Those all seem like worthwhile outcomes that were achieved without resolving the problem.

TURN THE TABLES

Sometimes returning to the challenge of violence allows us to turn the tables. What if *we're* the problem of violence. Attending to Scripture involves turning the spotlight on us, submitting ourselves to critique. Books like Genesis and Joshua have a way of asking fundamental questions about our own problems of violence. Genesis would stand aghast at the ecological violence we've inflicted on the planet, and the lives ruined by our endless wars. Joshua would want to challenge the myopic nationalism that grips so much of the (white) American church, and bleeds into other places as well. These books won't let us sit easily on the "right" side of the biblical page. It's very difficult to side, simplistically, with God's people in either book when living in and benefiting from a global superpower that outsources human, animal, and ecological exploitation to weaker nations or portions of our countries in order to maintain our way of life.[7] The recent failed war in Afghanistan cost the lives of over 241,000 Afghans and Pakistanis, a number that exceeds best estimates for the total population of Canaan during the time of Joshua by as much as four times![8] Simultaneously, the United States initiated a violent war in Iraq that resulted in 405,000 deaths between 2003–2011 alone.[9] Neither of these figures includes the massive loss of life due to war-incited malnutrition and environmental destruction.

My point is not to say that we're worse, so the Bible shines brighter. But I draw attention to Scripture's critique as a caution and a plea. One caution is against the assumption that we're far less violent than ancient Israel. Perhaps we have the luxury of living peacefully for reasons completely other than our own morality. My plea is to let Scripture challenge our tendency to divorce creation from our thinking about violence (Gen 4–6). To let Scripture challenge our sharp delineations between who's in and who's out (Joshua). To let Scripture captivate us with its fuller vision of creation-restoring and nation-including shalom when nations "will no longer learn

---

[7] On human exploitation, please note the 2018 "Walk Free Report," according to which 1 of every 130 females on the planet are in slavery, and three-fourths of all slaves are women. The report indicates that in 2016 there were over 40 million slaves worldwide. Walk Free, *Stacked Odds: How Lifelong Inequality Shapes Women and Girls' Experience of Modern Slavery* (Nedlands, WA: Mindaroo Foundation, 2000), www.walkfree.org/reports/stacked-odds/.

[8] See "Afghan Civilians," Costs of War Project, Brown University, April 2021, https://watson.brown .edu/costsofwar/costs/human/civilians/afghan. Estimates of Canaan's population at the tail end of the Late Bronze Age are difficult to nail down precisely. For good discussions of this subject, see Magen Broshi and Ram Gophna, "The Settlement and Population During the Early Bronze Age II–III," *Bulletin of the American Schools of Oriental Research* 254 (1984): 43-53; Magen Broshi, "The Population of Iron Age Palestine," in *Biblical Archaeology Today, 1990. Proceedings of the Second International Congress on Biblical Archaeology. Pre-Congress Symposium: Population, Production and Power, Jerusalem, June 1990* (Jerusalem: Israel Exploration Society, 1993), 14. Estimates of eighth-century BC Israel's population rises from the far lower populations in the thirteenth to eleventh centuries BC (the estimated period of Israel's settlement) to as much as 400,000 according to Magen Broshi and Israel Finkelstein, "The Population of Palestine in Iron Age II," *Bulletin of the American Schools of Oriental Research* 287 (1992): 47-60.

[9] Philip Bump, "15 Years After It Began the Death Toll from the Iraq War Is Still Murky," *Washington Post*, March 20, 2018, www.washingtonpost.com/news/politics/wp/2018/03/20/15-years-after -it-began-the-death-toll-from-the-iraq-war-is-still-murky/.

war" *because they learned Torah* (Is 2:4, my translation; cf. Gen 1–2; Is 65; Rev 21–22). We can ask questions of Scripture, but it has a few for us as well!

As I noted in the Introduction, the way out of the farm granary is "where the rats enter and leave; but the rat's hole is low to the floor."[10] The way toward that vision may not come by flying at the light Scripture provides, but by meeting God in the dark places and finding a hand there reaching out to lead you through.

AVOID SHORTCUTS

If you search "learn German in just . . ." several videos will appear that promise German proficiency in just twenty-five minutes, one hour, or three hours. Why on earth would you watch the three-hour video when you can learn it in twenty-five minutes?! Obviously, there's no shortcut. If you've studied another language, you know this. Learning languages to the point of *proficiency* usually requires memorization of about ten thousand words, countless hours of grammar study, and regular listening and speaking practice.

In his book *The Old Testament Is Dying*, Brent Strawn points out that navigating the complex realities of faith requires full scriptural fluency. And fluency takes more time than proficiency. Strawn doesn't mean knowing chapter and verse to address life's topics. Fluency is deeper than that. Fluency involves an internalized knowledge of Scripture that allows an in-the-field ability to respond to unforeseen challenges, discern the terrain, recognize paths, and change course.

> [Twenty-five] minutes, or even 3 hours, of Bible might help us with basic greetings or ordering food, but it won't provide us with all the necessary "raw information . . . encoded cultural knowledge . . . the ability to problem-solve by means of it, [or] . . . the capacity to communicate effectively while using it."[11]

The "approach" to violence that I've adopted in this book involves slow reading, patient listening, empathetic interpretation. Lingering with Scripture helps us understand the moves it's making, avoid oversimplifying

---

[10]See Robert Bly, "Warning to the Reader" (poem), in *Stealing Sugar from the Castle: Selected and New Poems, 1950-2013* (New York: W. W. Norton, 2013), 72, https://books.google.com/books?id=qfG wAAAAQBAJ&lpg=PP1&pg=PA72#v.

[11]Brent A. Strawn, *The Old Testament Is Dying: A Diagnosis and Recommended Treatment* (Grand Rapids, MI: Baker Academic, 2017), 76.

complex issues, and allows us to consider hidden costs of decisions we make. It also helps us avoid "solving" a problem that doesn't exist. Skimming the surface of the text might give us the impression of a problem that we then set off to solve—*Phew! That felt violent. What should I do about that?* But Scripture wasn't written for that sort of engagement.

That's why the psalmist invites us to meditate on it day and night (Ps 1:2). It's why Ezra devoted himself to studying God's law (Ezra 7:10), teaching it (Ezra 7:25; cf. Neh 8:7-8), and reading all of it to the people of God (Neh 8:1-6). Scripture recognizes its own complexity and need for a community committed to pursuing its interpretation. There aren't shortcuts.

I don't know how anyone, armed with YouTube and Google, and endless "how to deal with violence in the Bible" searches, can work their way out of a corner on this topic of violence in Scripture. God made us for communities that mediate Scripture to us through gracious and compassionate lives.

PURSUE EMBEDDED THINKING

In addition, Scripture endorses a particular kind of thinking that can help us with the challenge of violence. I've called it *embedded thinking*.[12]

Embedded thinking recognizes that violence isn't an isolated challenge. It's embedded within a network of related challenges. Violence is a subset of the problem of evil, which touches on theological themes like divine sovereignty and human free will. Violence is also related to the doctrine of Scripture, the problem of the relationship between the two Testaments, issues like the historicity of the text, and so on. Embedded thinking avoids indefinitely isolating a problem like violence without consideration for the knock-on effects in other areas of our thinking about God.

While not telling us how to resolve that tangled ball of challenges, Scripture helps us by fostering embedded thinking. It does so in several ways. For instance, it sets core claims about God in relation to counterbalancing claims. We might call these character constellations.[13] We explored a classic example in the previous chapter:

---

[12]I develop this idea in my article, "Perfection and Speech about God's Character in the Old Testament," *Crux* 57, no. 3 (2021): 13-23.

[13]Lynch, "Perfection," 15.

> And he [i.e., Yahweh] passed in front of Moses, proclaiming, "The LORD, the LORD, the compassionate and gracious God, slow to anger, abounding in love and faithfulness, maintaining love to thousands, and forgiving wickedness, rebellion and sin. *Yet* he does not leave the guilty unpunished; he punishes the children and their children for the sin of the parents to the third and fourth generation." (Ex 34:6-7)

The word translated "yet" is followed by an emphatic construction in Hebrew and should be translated "Yet he *by no means* leaves the guilty unpunished." The counterbalancing relationship between divine mercy and punishment sets up a tension that other parts of the Old Testament explore. Different texts accentuate different aspects of this richly complex portrait. Some emphasize the abundance of divine mercy (Ps 103), while others explore God's judgments of oppressors (Nah 1:2-3).

But as noted, Scripture doesn't leave us suspended between mercy and judgment, as if they were equals. Divine love extends to *thousands*, while judgment to *three or four* generations. Divine mercy is embedded within a character constellation of nonequals.

Scripture also teaches us to think about God's character through *patterned sequences*. Put another way, there's a storied context to God's character. Think about God's judgment again. It might seem biblical to insist that all of God's declarations are final. Doesn't Isaiah say that "the word of our God endures forever" (Is 40:8). Indeed! So, if we isolated a verse like Jonah 3:4, we'd think that God's judgment was the final word: "Forty more days and Nineveh will be overthrown!" This is the Word of the LORD. Who can avert such decisions?

Well, humans can, apparently.

After Nineveh repents, God averts his judgment and shows mercy, much to Jonah's chagrin (Jon 4:2-3).

In other cases, God's servants hear an announcement of judgment and appeal to God's mercy. Before enacting judgment on Sodom, God announced his plans to Abraham, who appealed the decision:

> Will you indeed sweep away the righteous with the wicked? Suppose there are fifty righteous within the city; will you then sweep away the place and not forgive it for the fifty righteous who are in it? Far be it from you to do

such a thing, to slay the righteous with the wicked, so that the righteous fare as the wicked! Far be that from you! Shall not the Judge of all the earth do what is just? (Gen 18:23-25, NRSV)

This is a bold way of speaking with God, but in context, it's precisely the sort of dialogue God expects from Abraham. Abraham begins challenging God to ensure justice for the few potential victims of injustice. *Having heard the announcement of divine judgment, Abraham asks God to limit his severity.* But this way of engaging with God is not unusual in the Old Testament. In fact, *one of the purposes of prayer in the Old Testament is to ask God to limit his severity.* For reasons unavailable to us, he has construed the divine-human relationship such that our pleadings can persuade God to set limits on his judgment. Put another way, God invites humans into the process of provoking and exercising divine mercy. Covenant partners are not passive recipients of mercy, but active agents in its implementation.

Though in the end God does bring judgment on Sodom, he rescues Lot and his family *and* preserves another small town (Gen 19:20-21) that was otherwise due for destruction.

In another story, God presents the prophet Amos with the vision of a locust swarm, coming to consume the late harvest. The locusts devoured the land's vegetation (Amos 7:1-2). But Amos pleads with God to relent, appealing to Israel's small size. So, "The LORD decided not to do this. 'It will not happen,' said the LORD." (Amos 7:3, my translation). Then God showed Amos a consuming fire, coming to ruin the land. Again, Amos pleads with God on the basis of Jacob's small and vulnerable size. Israel was too weak to withstand such judgment. So again, God changes his plans (Amos 7:6). His pity moves him.

My point here is to draw attention to the sequence that these two incidents imply, a sequence that repeats itself throughout the Old Testament. God's judgments are "penultimate, and liable to revocation" when accompanied by appeals from petitioners.[14] As Abraham Heschel notes, "No word is God's final word. Judgment, far from being absolute, is conditional. A change in [a hu]man's conduct brings about a change in God's judgment."[15]

---

[14]Lynch, "Perfection," 15.
[15]Abraham J. Heschel, *The Prophets* (New York: Perennial, 2001), 247.

The *sequence* in view here runs something like this: Humans rebel →
God threatens/enacts destruction → Human intercedes/changes behavior
→ God limits his anger.

Embedded thinking fosters a habit of holding tensions, a mental and
spiritual posture that pays dividends when wrestling with the "wicked"
problem of violence. It also helps us consider the relationship between how
we think about divine mercy and other character qualities like judgment
and wrath.

It will also foster an ability to resist easy resolutions that promise too
much. Recall the oil stain discussed in chapter one. Removing the stain also
burnt down the house, a cost that exceeded its benefit.

RETURN TO THE CENTER

When I was thirty-three, I had back surgery. I was playing soccer in Cheltenham, England, and I simply kicked hard with my left foot. Something
very bad happened in my lower back (miraculously, I also scored). I ended
up with a severely ruptured L5/S1 disk. After several failed attempts at
physio and steroid injections, I eventually had a microdiscectomy and
started a long road to recovery.

But soccer didn't injure my back. That soccer kick was the "straw" that
broke my back. Problems started years earlier. One contributing factor was
my profession. I'm an academic, and like many other academics, I'd
probably sat far too long in a chair. I failed to maintain core muscle strength,
rendering my back susceptible to that injury on the soccer field. Academics
(especially white men) often forget that they have bodies and focus dispro-
portionately on developing their minds. The results are costly. (I know one
guy who blew out a disc in his back because he sneezed while turning the
steering wheel in a car).

It's also easy to throw out our faith by failing to develop core strength.
Neglecting to practice the central aspects of our faith leave us vulnerable to
injury. Building that core strength involves investing in those activities and
affirmations that build up the center.

The communion table orients our gathering as the body of Christ.

Public (i.e., communal) reading and study of all Scripture keeps us attuned to God's voice.

Reciting the Lord's Prayer and Creeds teaches us and reminds us of our core relationship and beliefs.

Praying and worshipping with the Psalms keep God's covenant loyalty at the center.

Acts of mercy define our common cause.

Christians who wrestle with Old Testament or biblical violence often find it difficult to leave the problem unresolved. They scoff at those who grasp at simple answers like, "God can do whatever he wants!" or "We all deserve to die!" or "The cross shows us that God is never violent!" But the alternative to simple answers leaves us without a clear resolution.

What I'm suggesting here is that remembering what's at the core of our faith can help put issues of violence in perspective. It won't make them go away, but it can help us remember that violence isn't the beginning and end of the story, and that the heart of God's character isn't judgment. Building up our "core strength" will enable us to extend ourselves to engage troubling topics without fear that we'll end up injured. Practicing what's core to the Christian faith can sometimes enable us to look back at the problem of violence with renewed strength for a hard task.

PURSUE MYSTERY

In the first chapter, I emphasized the need to orient ourselves toward mystery as we began our examination of the problem of violence. I want to conclude our study by returning to this theme.

My "read it slow" approach to violent texts needs a heavy dose of humility. In his letter to the Corinthians, Paul reminds his readers of the huge gap between what we know now, and what we will know at the consummation of all things (1 Cor 13:12). But more than the "what" of what we don't know now, he zeroes in on the "who." "For now we see only a reflection as in a mirror; then we shall see face to face. Now I know in part; then I shall know fully, even as I am fully known" (1 Cor 13:12). Notice that the focus on knowing is personal. Our knowledge gap doesn't derive from an insufficient hermeneutical grid, interpretive framework, or whatever. Instead, it stems from our partial knowledge of God. God

- dwell[s] in a dark cloud (1 Kings 8:12)
- alone is immortal and . . . lives in unapproachable light (1 Tim 6:16).

God's

- understanding has no limit (Ps 147:5)
- understanding no one can fathom (Is 40:28)
- paths [are] beyond tracing out (Rom 11:33).

And in God

- are hidden all the treasures of wisdom and knowledge (Col 2:3).[16]

Read in isolation, these statements could suggest that God is utterly unknowable. Utterly hidden. But here it's important to distinguish between God's utterly mysterious *otherness* and God's utter *hiddenness*. Theological affirmations of God's mystery protect the categorical uniqueness of God. "God differs differently" than the way that one person is different from another and God remains mysterious to them.[17]

Yet Paul also makes clear that we know "in part" (1 Cor 13:12). God isn't utterly unknowable. The mystery of God doesn't leave us without any accurate sense of who God is. We have a *sufficient* but partial grasp of God and God's ways. It's sufficient to foster trust and love for God and others, but not enough to unravel the wicked problem of violence in the Old Testament. Instead, God is found "in order to be sought."[18] My prayer is that the mystery of God's ways in Scripture—expressed in the particular mystery of violence—will drive us toward the ongoing pursuit of the mysterious God who encounters us in Scripture. Though that encounter occurs shrouded in darkness, I hope that we continue to wrestle with irresolvable challenges with the hope of a blessing.

---

[16]Most of these references are from Steven D. Boyer and Christopher A. Hall, *The Mystery of God: Theology for Knowing the Unknowable* (Grand Rapids, MI: Baker Academic, 2012), 29.

[17]Kathryn Tanner, *Jesus, Humanity, and the Trinity: A Brief Systematic Theology* (Minneapolis: Fortress Press, 2001), 12, quoting Henk Schoot, *Christ the 'Name' of God: Thomas Aquinas on Naming Christ* (Leuven: Peeters, 1993), 144-45.

[18]Augustine, *On the Trinity*, 15.2, in Stephen McKenna trans., *On the Trinity: Books 8-15*, CTHP, ed. Gareth B. Matthews (Cambridge: Cambridge University Press, 2002), 168.

FIGURE CREDITS

3.1. Assurbanipal hunting the lion, from the North Palace in Nineveh (ca. 645–635 BC), photograph by Osama Shukir Muhammed Amin, FRCP(Glasg), CC BY-SA 4.0, Wikimedia Commons, https://commons.wikimedia.org/w/index.php?curid=61613294, fair use.

7.1. Late Bronze sickle sword from Aphek, photograph by Chris McKinny, *Photo Companion to the Bible: Joshua* by Chris McKinny, Kris Udd, and Todd Bolen (Bibleplaces.com: 2020), DVD, used with permission.

9.1. Adapted from Israel relief location map, by Eric Gaba—Wikimedia Commons user: Sting, Wikimedia Commons, https://commons.wikimedia.org/wiki/File:Israel_relief_location_map-blank.jpg#metadata

11.1. Adapted from Israel relief location map, by Eric Gaba—Wikimedia Commons user: Sting, Wikimedia Commons, https://commons.wikimedia.org/wiki/File:Israel_relief_location_map-blank.jpg#metadata

12.1. Ramses II besieging the Cheta people in Dapur, by unknown, German lithography published in 1879, public domain, Wikimedia Commons, https://commons.wikimedia.org/w/index.php?curid=91195125, fair use.

12.2. Ramses II and his prisoners, photograph by Speedster, own work, CC BY-SA 4.0, Wikimedia Commons, https://commons.wikimedia.org/w/index.php?curid=38220820, fair use.

12.3. Victory Stele of Naram-Sin, photographed by Jastrow (2005), public domain, Wikimedia Commons, https://commons.wikimedia.org/w/index.php?curid=373954, fair use. Discussed in Brian R. Doak, *Heroic Bodies in Ancient Israel* (Oxford: Oxford University Press, 2019), 97-124.

GENERAL INDEX

SCRIPTURE INDEX